# The Russians

DATE DUE

# The Peoples of Europe

## General Editors
### James Campbell and Barry Cunliffe

This series is about the European tribes and peoples from their origins in prehistory to the present day. Drawing upon a wide range of archaeological and historical evidence, each volume presents a fresh and absorbing account of a group's culture, society and usually turbulent history.

### Already published

The Etruscans
*Graeme Barker*
*and Tom Rasmussen*

The Bretons
*Patrick Galliou*
*and Michael Jones*

The Lombards
*Neil Christie*

The Russians
*Robin Milner-Gulland*

The Basques
*Roger Collins*

The Mongols
*David Morgan*

The English
*Geoffrey Elton*

The Armenians
*A. E. Redgate*

The Gypsies
*Angus Fraser*

The Huns
*E. A. Thompson*

The Goths
*Peter Heather*

The Early Germans
*Malcolm Todd*

The Franks*
*Edward James*

The Illyrians
*John Wilkes*

### In preparation

The Sicilians
*David Abulafia*

The Spanish
*Roger Collins*

The Irish
*Francis John Byrne*
*and Michael Herity*

The Norsemen in the
Viking Age
*Eric Christiansen*

The Byzantines
*Averil Cameron*

The Romans
*Timothy Cornell*

The First English
*Sonia Chadwick Hawkes*

The Scots
*Colin Kidd*

The Normans
*Marjorie Chibnall*

The Picts
*Charles Thomas*

The Serbs
*Sima Cirkovic*

* Denotes title now
out of print

# The Russians

## Robin Milner-Gulland

BLACKWELL
*Publishers*

First published 1997

First published in paperback 1999
2 4 6 8 10 9 7 5 3 1

Blackwell Publishers Ltd
108 Cowley Road
Oxford OX4 1JF
UK

Blackwell Publishers Inc
350 Main Street
Malden, MA 02148
USA

*British Library Cataloguing in Publication Data*

A CIP catalogue record for this book is available from the British Library.

*Library of Congress Cataloging-in-Publication Data*

Milner-Gulland, R. R.
   The Russians/Robin Milner-Gulland.
   p. cm. (Peoples of Europe)
   Includes bibliographical references and index.
   ISBN 0-631-18805-3 (alk. paper)
   ISBN 0-631-21849-1 (pbk: alk. paper)
   1. Russia–Civilization. 2. Russia–History–To 1533.
   3. Russia–History–1533–1613. 4. Russia–History–
   1613–1689. 5. National characteristics, Russian.
   I. Title. II. Series.
DK32.M626 1997
947–dc21
                                    96 – 51542
                                    CIP
Typeset in 10 on 12pt Sabon by
Words & Graphics Ltd, Anstey, Leicester
Printed in Great Britain by TJ International Ltd, Padstow, Cornwall

This book is printed on acid-free paper

# Contents

# Plates

*Plates*

# Figures

# Acknowledgements

The author and publishers gratefully acknowledge Oxford University Press for permission to reproduce copyright material from Russell Zguta *Russian Minstrels* (1978), p. 91; and Aurora Publishers for permission to reproduce four illustrations from A. Sytova (ed.) *The Lubok* (1984).

The following copyright holders were also contacted: Paul Elek Publishers and Intercultura, c/o Lutterworth Press. The publishers apologize for any errors or omissions in the above list and would be grateful to be notified of any corrections that should be incorporated in the next edition or reprint of this book.

# Introduction: Aims and Methods of the Book

Several volumes, published or promised, in The Peoples Of Europe series concentrate on prehistoric, Roman or early medieval archaeology. They deal with peoples who either have vanished from the map or whose status has changed utterly in modern times (Illyrians and Franks are examples of the first category, Mongols and Bretons of the second). The Russians, I believe, call for a different approach. It is not that material archaeological remains on the land we now call Russia are insignificant or uninformative; from time to time indeed they will be mentioned in these pages. But what I shall be trying to achieve is something rather different: an 'archaeology of the mind', or cultural history. The Russians after all are a people whose historical destiny, after nearly 1200 years, has not yet run its course, who remain one of the most numerous and powerful people on earth. Their still evolving culture is distinctive, multifaceted and deep-rooted. It seems a worthwhile enterprise to trace it from its varied origins onwards and to investigate the dynamics of its evolution. Such an evolution will take us into the distant past, and most of the text will deal with the pre-1700 period that is conventionally called 'Old Russian'. Yet it is by no means my intention totally to ignore more modern events, and several enduring cultural-historical themes will be traced through to recent times.

Various factors encourage my feeling that such an endeavour is timely and worthwhile. Such a historical punctuation-mark as the end of the Soviet Union does not merely provide an opportune moment for reassessment but imposes on all our minds a restructuring of the past and its significances: Russians have been forced (as at several points in their history) into reappraising what 'Russianness' means in a most personal as well as general way; educated Russians tend anyhow to have a lively (sometimes agonized) awareness of their past and history. Kievan Russia (before the Tatar invasion of *c.*1240) is alive in the Russian conscious- ness in a way that the Anglo-Saxon period – to take a rough equivalent – hardly is for the English; any educated Russian will recognize many quotations from the Old Russian chronicles. Westerners who want (however approximately) to view Russian culture as if through Russian eyes must try to match these long perspectives. Unfortunately Russian history, insofar as it is studied at all in Western schools and universities, is often tacitly assumed to have begun with Peter the Great, or with the emancipation of the serfs in 1861, or the Revolution in 1917. Journalists and followers of things Russian are often led into bafflement or solecism as a result – a situation emphasized by the great and often bewildered interest in Russia that began to grow in the West with *perestroika*, and has been mightily fuelled by the end of the Soviet Union and concomitant events. In this volume we shall avoid treating over 1000 years of recorded Russian cultural history as a somewhat puzzling, maybe irritating prelude to the twentieth century but try to look at it for its own sake and as part of a great continuing cultural-historical process.

As Mikhail Lermontov pointed out in *A Hero of our Time*, a preface is both 'the first and the last thing in a book'; so from its author's point of view it would now seem a good moment to look back at this volume, and summarize what it has set out to achieve.

'Cultural history' is a notoriously unbounded subject: to adapt Terence's Latin tag, 'nothing human is alien to it'. Since one cannot cover everything, each person dabbling in the field must try to establish some priorities. I see cultural history's most interesting aspects as how people have modelled their world, made sense of their surroundings, teased their history into a coherent narrative, established institutions and given their culture a 'public face' through the arts, at whatever level of sophistication. Looking back, I am all too aware of what has had to be compressed or left out – far more than went in – and realize that all I have been able to do is take a series of stabs at the topic. These have dealt successively with the material culture, the political culture, the culture of belief, the verbal and visual (also conceptual) culture of what was termed Rus and became Russia. I see Russian cultural consciousness as aiming at a rather shadowy concept of wholeness or integrity (*tselnost*), and therefore necessarily to be treated in global terms. Hence I have for a long time been interested in all its ramifications, and have attempted to put this interest to work here. I am all too aware however that nobody can be a specialist in everything (most of the research I have published, for what it is worth, has been in the fields of modern poetry and art history), and I am happy to state my debts to others' work: the cultural historians who have done most to determine my own outlook have been Mikhail Bakhtin, Isaiah Berlin, Mikhail Cherniavsky, Dmitriy Likhachov, Yuri Lotman, Dimitri Obolensky, Richard Pipes, Mark Raeff and Boris Uspensky, to whom I am endlessly grateful, though I have certainly not agreed with all of them all of the time (nor would they all agree with each other). I have many more debts of gratitude to people I have consulted on specific points, and in particular members of my family (Alison, Tom and Lucy) who have advised on points of presentation and on illustrations, as well as producing a good typescript and helpful comments. I must mention that approximately one third of Chapter 4 has appeared in different format in N. Cornwell (ed.) *Reference Guide to Russian Literature*, while earlier versions of the sections 'Icons and the "Modern Movement"' and 'Symbolic Landscapes' in Chapter 5 appeared, respectively, as articles in S. Smythe and S. Kingston (eds) *Icons 88* (Dublin, 1988) and in R. Reid et al. (eds.) *Structure and Tradition in Russian Society*, a Festschrift for Yuri Lotman (Helsinki, 1993).

This book is not a straightforward narrative history, but is thematically organized, and the reader will soon see that various topics are covered more than once in different contexts. It does not attempt to discuss, or always to mention all events of historical significance; in some ways it is a complement to my *Cultural Atlas of Russia* (Phaidon/Facts on File 1989) which gives a fuller and more sequential treatment of political history. I have tried to write in a jargon-free way which nevertheless is not simplistic, and that also may give the specialist something in the way of new data, insights and interpretations. I have (for ease of reading) avoided excessive footnoting, and wherever possible have referred to English-language sources – fortunately much historical literature has been translated in recent years (translations from primary sources are by me unless otherwise specified). But knowing that many readers will have some Russian, I have often provided the Russian words for key culturally specific terms. I have done my best to let this most distinctive cultural history speak for itself, and have avoided generalizations about the 'Russian soul' or whatever, which are best left to Russians. Not being one (though I have known the country for some forty years), I feel diffident at having touched on things that Russians understandably feel to be very much their own, beyond the reach of non-Russians. For doing so I can only plead the authority of one of the greatest cultural theorists, Mikhail Bakhtin: 'There exists a very strong, but one-sided and thus untrustworthy, idea that in order better to understand a foreign culture, one must enter into it, forgetting one's

own, and view the world through the eyes of this foreign culture . . .
Creative understanding does not renounce itself, its own place in time, its
own culture; and it forgets nothing. In order to understand, it is
immensely important for the person who understands to be located
outside the object of his or her creative understanding – in time, in space,
in culture . . . outsideness is a most powerful factor in understanding. It
is only in the eyes of another culture that foreign culture reveals itself
fully and profoundly . . . We raise new questions in a foreign culture.'[1]
In this connection I should say that even when I discuss medieval
matters, I am implicitly bearing in mind the modern world, and in
writing about Russia I am hoping to encourage the reader into making
the same sort of comparisons with other societies that I tacitly make
myself – not to praise or condemn, but to see things more clearly.
Scholarship in Russian studies has attracted more than its fair share of
uncritical enthusiasts for, and (perhaps more oddly) fierce denigrators of,
all things Russian: there is room for a balanced and not unsympathetic
assessment.

It remains to mention the practical matter of the rendering of Russian
names and other terms in the text. Unfortunately there is no one agreed
system of transliteration from Cyrillic into English, partly because of the
vagaries of English spelling and pronunciation, partly because of the
varied purposes transliteration has to serve. I have chosen to use the
popular and accessible system set out, for example, in the three volumes
of the *Cambridge Companion to Russian Studies* (which has been found
in practice to give a good idea of how Russian words should be
pronounced) with one significant modification: omission of the so-called
'soft sign' (that palatalizes the preceding consonant, mostly at the end of
words). In a few cases a well-established conventional English form has
been used instead of the correct transliteration: eg. Dnieper (instead of
Dnepr), Crimea (Krym), Moscow (Moskva), St Petersburg (Sankt-
Peterburg), Tchaikovsky (Chaykovsky), Eisenstein (Eyzenshteyn). 'Alek-
sandr' has been rendered 'Alexander'; the names of rulers from Peter the
Great onwards have been rendered by their English equivalents. Place
and personal names relating to Rus generally have slightly different
forms in modern Russian, Ukrainian and Belorussian, all of which derive
from the East Slavonic language of early Rus. For simplicity and
consistency I have used the Russian forms in transliteration, while
recognizing that the others have an equal validity (e.g. I use 'Chernigov'
rather than 'Chernihiv', 'Vladimir' rather than 'Volodymyr' – even

---

[1]  M. Bakhtin *Speech Genres and Other Late Essays* trans. V. McGee (Austin,
1986) pp. 6–7.

though neither is identical with the Old Russian form!). Finally, readers may be reminded that Russian personal names have three components: first (Christian) name; patronymic (from one's father's first name, with added -ovich, -evich, -ych or -ich for men, -ovna, -evna, -ishna for women); surname (although these were uncommon – and often really 'nicknames' – till the seventeenth century; attempts were made to limit them to the aristocracy). Surnames of Great-Russian origin normally end in -ov, -ev, -yn, -in, -sky (masculine), -ova, -eva, -yna, -ina, -skaya (feminine).

As for dates: Old Russians, following Byzantine usage, counted years from the supposed date of the Creation (5508 BC). By Peter the Great's time the Western system had become normal; but until 1918 (and, in Church use, to the present) Russia adhered to the Julian calendar (eleven days behind the Gregorian calendar in the eighteenth century, twelve days behind in the nineteenth century, thirteen days behind in the twentieth). Note that the Byzantines reckoned the New Year to start on 1 September (whereas early Russians usually reckoned it from 1 March), which leads frequently to imprecision when dates are modernized. Occasionally it has been necessary in this book to specify 'Old Style' ('OS', or Julian), or 'New Style' ('NS', or Gregorian).

# 1

## Rus As Land And People

### Rus and Rossiya

The Russian language has two words for 'Russia'. The modern state that (even after the dissolution of the Soviet Union) remains the biggest in the world is known – and has been known for some 300 years – as *Rossiya*. A pseudo-classical coinage that is first noted in the sixteenth century, this word came gradually into circulation in the seventeenth, and was the term employed to designate his new empire by Peter the Great in the early eighteenth century. As an essentially bookish form, promulgated by a government keen to draw attention to new political realities, it resembles 'Great Britain', which was adopted as the title of the new United Kingdom after 1707.

Rossiya thus superseded the ancient term from which it apparently (though dubiously) derived, *Rus*,[1] which had been in use since at any rate the mid-ninth century. We shall have more to say on this term's origins, but from the point of view of an investigation into Russian cultural history the most interesting thing is that *Rossiya* did not supersede *Rus* entirely. Since

[1] *Rossiya* was probably perceived as a Latinate form by the early eighteenth century (when things Roman carried prestige); however it originated as a transcription of Greek *Rhōsia*, which in turn derives from the indeclinable word *Rhōs* that Greeks used from an early stage for the people of Rus. It has been convincingly shown that the escatologically minded Byzantines equated the Rus (whom they first encountered as raiders) with 'Rhōs' (Hebrew Rosh), a supposed leader of barbarous people cited in the prophecy of Ezekiel, as a result of a misreading by Greek translators of the Septuagint (see F. Dvornik *The Making of Central and Eastern Europe*, London, 1949, pp. 305–14); hence the otherwise unexplained vowel change from 'u' to 'o'. It is thus apparent that *Rossiya* does not derive directly from *Rus*. On the word Rossiya and its early appearances, see the entry in M. Vasmer *Russisches Etymologisches Wörterbuch*, II, (Heidelberg, 1953).

the eighteenth century the two words have lived parallel, scarcely overlapping existences in the Russian language and consciousness. The political realm of meaning has been occupied by Rossiya: it is the formal title of the Russian state. *Rus*, by contrast, is the essential Russia, the Russia that for better or worse lives in its people's hearts, irrespective of the great moments of change that have punctuated its historical destiny. Many poets have written about *Rus* – few about *Rossiya*. The perceived distinction carries interesting implications, that hardly need spelling out, for the theory or anyhow popular psychology of nationalism. It is worth nothing additionally that, although there exist two (rather clumsy sounding) words formed from *Rossiya* for 'Russian' and 'a Russian citizen' (*rossiysky, rossiyanin*), the normal adjective for 'Russian', standing in also for 'a Russian', remains of course *russky*, derived from Rus.

But *Rus* in the pre-modern period meant more than just 'Russia' – it was also a collective designation for people who inhabited the country (and it is not incontrovertibly certain which meaning preceded the other). It also implies the state that these people established, in modern terms a society or a culture that (as we shall see later) arose in the ninth century and was perceived by medieval Russians themselves as a new entity on the global scene. The processes by which modern nations came into being, developed self-awareness and coped with changing historical circumstances has obviously been a matter of huge interest to historians since the rise of modern nationalism in the last 200 or so years, and has had powerful political reverberations up to the present. The origins of the term *Rus*, its early and subsequent uses, the questions of continuity and discontinuities in the 1200 years of what we conventionally call Russian history is in fact a particularly interesting case-study in these processes – if only because of the exceptionally long time-span involved. But we should not imagine that only modern historians have tried to step back and gain an overview of what 'Russianness' means. On the contrary, thinking Russians themselves grappled with the task from quite early in the Middle Ages. In particular, incomparably the greatest source for old Russian history, the work usually known as the 'Primary Chronicle'[2] – which in its present form was compiled

---

[2]   The classic English edition is *The Russian Primary Chronicle: Laurentian Text*, trans. and ed. S. H. Cross and O. F. Sherbowitz-Wetzor, (Cambridge, Mass 1953): the new Harvard version by H. G. Lunt (based on the Hypatian text) is not yet available, save for a few exerpts, at the time of writing. In this volume all translations from the Primary Chronicle are my own (unlike most translators, I have attempted where possible to follow the chronicler's paratactic sentence structure). The standard Russian edition, with very full commentary, is by D. S. Likhachov (Moscow-Leningrad 1950). Note that Lunt prefers a textual emendation whereby the first sentence of the Primary Chronicle reads, in his version, 'Here is the tale of the seasons and the years . . . '. In their book *The Emergence of Rus 750–1200*, S. Franklin and J. Shepard prefer the phrase 'Tale of the years of time', but this is unconvincing.

c.1111–13 – was explicitly motivated by a quest for the origins and destiny of Rus. In its first sentence the chronicler sets out his intentions in a famous formulation: 'These are the narratives of bygone years regarding the origin of the land of Rus, who first began to rule in Kiev, and from what source the land of Rus had its beginning' (the whole work is consequently often referred to as the '*Tale of Bygone Years*'). We shall return many times to the Primary Chronicle, its world-view, the information it gives us and what it ignores, and the problems of interpretation that it sets us. Meanwhile, the modern investigator into the origins of 'Russianness' can scarcely do better than follow the lead indicated by the chronicler's first sentence.

In examining the triple-stranded thread of Rus as land, as people and as state we may begin with its location, and with the geographical determinants that have conditioned its people's way of life. Russia's geography is no mere 'background' to Russian culture and history – it is a constituent and necessary element within them, without which they would have been unimaginably different.

At this point a note on terminology is necessary. When the word 'Russia' is used here, it means the European part of the modern Russian Federation (which of course beyond 'Russia' includes Siberia, some offshore islands and a fragment of former East Prussia – not to mention the defined territories of many non-Slav peoples, e.g. Tatars and Chuvash). 'Rus', by contrast, is less susceptible to precise geographical definition: not only did its borders fluctuate, they were often ill-defined as well, and as we have seen the term applies to a people as well as a place. It implies topographically the heartland of early Russia, the area comprising its first principalities within, but not as extensive as modern Russia, and very importantly also, it includes much of the territory of modern independent Ukraine and Belorussia (or Belarus), both of which rightly lay equal claim to Rus as their historical progenitor. 'Kievan Rus' (or 'Kievan Russia' – a modern term) is applied to Rus from 882 (when Kiev was intentionally established as a capital and, so the chronicler tells us, 'mother of the Russian cities') till 1240 (when Kiev was sacked by the Tatars) – though Kiev itself was by no means an effective federal capital for all this period. 'Muscovite Rus/Russia' (or 'Muscovy', a Western term) implies Rus from c.1480 when Moscow established independence and unchallenged dominance, till Peter the Great's inauguration (1721) of the 'Russian Empire' that lasted till 1917, reaching its greatest extent in the nineteenth century. 'Old Russia' implies Rus at all periods up to Peter the Great. Finally, I use 'Russian' as an adjective from both 'Russia' and 'Rus', avoiding the artificial formation 'Rusian' favoured by a few modern writers.

## Rus as Land: Its Characteristics

Russia in Europe is a vast territory, roughly equal in area to all the rest of Europe (though with less than a quarter of the total European population). Ancient Rus, though smaller, was nevertheless from the time of its formation the largest European and probably world state in area: it would be exceeded only by short-lived empires of conquest, and of course expanded hugely from the mid-sixteenth century onwards. This matter of size, and concommitant sparseness of population, can hardly be overemphasized – today's visitor to Russia, flying in from the West, can perfectly well appreciate it even from a height of 30,000 feet. Individual provinces of Russia can be bigger than many European countries. To take one example: from the capital of Vologda province (by no means Russia's biggest) to its second city (Ustyug) is a day and a night by train or an hour and a half by jet plane, yet the whole province, part of the heartland of Muscovite Russia, has little over a million inhabitants. Spaciousness has seemed a Russian birthright.

Russia is a plain: a much broader continuation of the plains of north central Europe. Old Russians knew of mountain ranges, but only as delimiting their furthest horizons: the territory of Rus just touched upon the Carpathians to the south-west, the Urals to the north-east, and at times the Crimea and Caucasus to the south. There is no word in Russian for 'mountain' as distinct from that for 'hill' (*gora*), which may indicate a scarcely perceptible rise in the landscape. Similarly, Old Russia touched upon sea coasts, without ever controlling substantial amounts of coastline; but here the impingement of the outer limits of Rus was far more significant, opening up new horizons rather than closing them off: more than a thousand years ago the merchants of Rus were familiar with the Baltic (Gulf of Finland), the White and Black Seas, the Caspian and the Sea of Azov. Nevertheless neither mountain ranges nor seas, which unequivocally mark so many European frontiers, form any large part of the boundaries of Rus, which may thus seem a curiously formless mass on the map, lacking obvious natural demarcations until well into the Imperial period.

Though Russia is a great plain, it is far from being undifferentiated, let alone totally monotonous. For a start, it is by no means wholly flat (unlike, for example, the West Siberian plain immediately beyond the Urals) The largest extent of glaciation in the last (so-called Wurm) Ice Age reached somewhat south of the latitude of Moscow. To the north of its irregular boundary the landscape is marked by moraine ridges and scoured-out depressions, filled subsequently with marshes or lakes, among which rivers wander somewhat haphazardly: much of is undulating, sometimes picturesquely so. Southwards the absence of

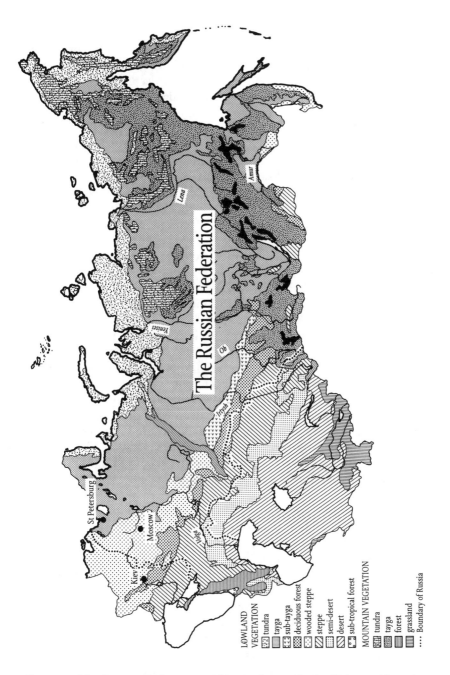

The map legend reads:

LOWLAND
VEGETATION
tundra
tayga
sub-tayga
deciduous forest
wooded steppe
steppe
semi-desert
desert
sub-tropical forest

MOUNTAIN VEGETATION
tundra
tayga
forest
grassland
.... Boundary of Russia

The Russian Federation

St Petersburg
Kiev
Moscow
Volga
Irtysh
Ob
Yenisei
Lena
Amur

*Figure 1   The Russian Federation within the former Soviet Union, with major rivers and vegetation-zones.*

glaciation is apparent in the level and regular elevation of much of the land, partly a result of the windblown loess that evenly covered its sedimentary rocks: drama in the landscape derives from a few great rivers and their tributaries that have dug out deep valleys, characteristically with one high bank (on the outer edge of a meander) looking over a broad flood-plain. From time to time the Russian plain appears distinctly hilly: north of the latitude of St Petersburg, where limestones and clays give way to older beds; in southern Ukraine, where a ridge of metamorphic rocks forms a barrier to south-flowing rivers (with important effects on the history of Rus); in the north-central area of the Valday Hills, birthplace of rivers; in the middle Volga area.

The most fundamental and visually evident distinction in the Russian landscape, however, is not a matter of elevation, but of vegetation. Northern Russia is to this day largely enveloped in a huge coniferous forest: the greatest forest in the world, stretching from Scandinavia to the Pacific. Southern Russia and Ukraine, by contrast, are quintessentially 'steppe country', where hardly a tree grows unless deliberately nurtured, formerly the realm of the tall and luxuriant feather-grass (*kovyl*) – nowadays, west of the Caspian, mostly given over to cereal crops. The distinction between untouched forest (*tayga*) and steppe could scarcely be more marked, and has been of the greatest importance to Russia's way of life and historical destiny. But these two great vegetation zones are merely the most prominent of a series of such zones, all running approximately east-west in parallel through European Russia, then – only briefly interrupted by the Ural mountains and Caspian sea – continuing with slight modifications for thousands of kilometres through Siberia, Kazakhstan and Mongolia. They are the distinctive features of the vast, thinly-populated landmass (birthplace of large empires) that the modern geo-historian David Christian has named 'Inner Eurasia'.

The 'outermost' zones, to north and south, are hostile to settled habitation, impossible to cultivate, and never formed part of historic Rus. The northernmost is tundra, fringing the Arctic Ocean in a fairly narrow belt (broadening in Siberia). It is treeless (though there is plenty of plant life, including dwarf shrubs) and the subsoil is permanently frozen: such 'permafrost' should not be simply equated with tundra, however, since areas of permafrost extend further south into many parts of the forested tayga, particularly in the more mountainous regions of eastern Siberia. Despite its being under snow and ice for two-thirds of the year, and considerably waterlogged the rest of the time, the tundra is not wholly unproductive: its land supports reindeer and innumerable water-birds, its seas are rich in fish, seals and walruses; it has a thin scatter of inhabitants (Nentsy and other 'Eskimo' peoples). The

*Plate 1   Northern Russian landscape: Kondopoga on Lake Onega,*
*with the Church of the Ascension (1774).*

southernmost zone, equally uninhabitable to Rus, is desert: though
more characteristic of Central Asia than Europe, it curls round the
north and west of the Caspian Sea towards the Caucasus. Though true
desert is wholly unproductive, its oases and in particular the lower
course of the Volga cutting through it produce intensively-grown
southern crops, notably melons, that Rus valued highly. The broad

subzone of semi-desert that stretches northward and westward from the desert proper has patches of rough grazing or 'wormwood steppe', and can support pastoralists; there are also extensive salt-pans that were exploited from Muscovite times onward. It should also be mentioned that south of the steppe and desert zones European Russia nowadays reaches the north slope of the Caucasus, with its mountain vegetation; around Sochi it retains a strip of Black Sea coastline protected by mountains, giving a narrow but significant band of Mediterranean or subtropical conditions, where, for example, tea and citrus fruits can grow.

The great zone of the coniferous *tayga*, occupying all the Russian territory from a little south of latitude 60° to the tundra that fringes the Arctic Ocean, has undergone human interference and settlement from before Kievan times, yet remains entirely recognizable even to the modern traveller and still gives the impression of a landscape where humans have an insecure foothold. In European Russia fir, pine and spruce predominate – beyond the Irtysh, larches. Where trees are cleared some agriculture is possible, particularly along river-valleys and by lakes. However the growing season, though warm, is short – less than five months – and even the hardiest of the cereals, rye, is a marginal crop; the meadows can produce enough grass and hay for livestock and dairy products, predominantly at the southern fringes of this zone. But the main antagonist to settled agriculture is not so much the climate as the condition of the land (for which climate is largely responsible). Much of it, when not frozen solid, is very swampy: partly as a result of irregular scouring of the landscape in glacial periods, partly because the soil itself, the so-called *podzol*, is generally thin and sandy: its minerals leached out to form an impervious rocky 'hard pan' of ironstone, hindering drainage, a little below the surface. These conditions are magnified to the north of the imperceptible watershed separating river systems that drain west or southwards (into the Volga and ultimately the Caspian; into the Western Dvina, Neva or Dnieper), from those leading north to the Arctic (in European Russia, chiefly that of the Northern Dvina; in Siberia all the main systems save the Amur). Northward-draining rivers thaw from their sources while their lower reaches are still frozen, causing huge spring floods. Evaporation, too, is naturally less in northerly regions.

The northern forests, where agriculture is at best marginal, are thus over-provided with water; by contrast the southern steppe zone, which in recent times has largely gone under the plough, is generally too dry. The steppe is potentially very fertile: its characteristic soil is *chernozyom*, the famous 'black earth', enriched with humus sometimes to a depth of many feet, created from the growth and decay of the tall wild grasses. Their thick and tangled roots conserved moisture: when they were broken up (which could only be done extensively with modern ploughing equipment) dustbowl conditions could all too easily develop. As elsewhere in Russia, the overall precipitation is low and often falls in a few late summer storms, which are useless for the growing season and may well knock down the harvest. Where conditions are right, however – particularly in the few large river-valleys – the steppe is excellent grain-growing country: wheat exports from these rivers were the chief cause for early contacts between the Greek world and the lands that would one day be Russia. Early Russians knew the steppe, travelled over it, cast longing eyes upon it but found it impossible to encroach upon it more than marginally with farming settlements. The reasons were not so much to do with climate as with security. The steppe is ideal country for horses, with their speed and their ability to cover considerable distances between watering places and to feed off the countryside. A succession of nomadic or semi-nomadic peoples, mostly Turkic, utilized this with often devastating effect, making surprise raids on the fringes of Russian settlement and interrupting over-extended trade routes. Only in the late eighteenth century did Imperial Russia at last manage to secure all its southern flank. Rus, nearly a thousand years earlier, did in fact succeed in establishing one lasting outpost in the steppe zone[3], significantly on a defensible site: the peninsular of Tmutorokan, between the sea of Azov and the Black Sea on the Strait of Kerch. This somewhat mysterious principality was an integral and valued part of Rus, but proved untenable well before the end of the Kievan period, probably at some time in the early twelfth century.

Squeezed, as it were, between uncultivable *tayga* and untenable steppe, Rus might well seem to have been scarcely habitable – let alone suitable to be the cradle of a great nation – were it not for two more

---

[3] Historical atlases often indicate early Rus as extending as far as the north-western segment of the Black Sea coast, roughly between the Crimea and the Danube delta. Early Russian tribes, the Tivertsy and the Ulichi, certainly occupied the valleys of the major rivers of the area (Bug, Dnestr, Prut) but one may doubt if their settlements impinged much on the steppe proper; there are no other Kievan Russian towns identifiable until well into the wooded steppe, at least 200 miles inland from the sea: see the map in M. Tikhomirov *The Towns of Ancient Rus* (Moscow, 1959) pp. 312–13, and fig. 6. However, the Primary Chronicle does specify that the Tivertsy once 'inhabited the banks of the Dnestr almost to (*ole*) the coast' (at this point the zone of steppe is quite narrow). Note that Cross's translation of the Chronicle (see above, note 2) is seriously misleading here, since it introduces the misprint 'east' for 'coast'. Apart from Tmutorokan, however, a single town regarded as Russian in the eleventh century is known to have existed in the steppe zone: Oleshye, at the mouth of the Dnieper (modern Aleshki), guarding the crucial trade route.

narrow but crucial zones of vegetation that provide the transition between them. The irregular southern fringe of the coniferous *tayga* does not end in open countryside: it becomes a mixed forest, with a high proportion of trees like hazel, alder, oak, lime and above all birch. The mixed forest zone, broad to the west where it encompasses the whole of Belorussia, funnels eastward into a narrow strip that nevertheless continues (in Siberia, as 'sub-tayga') along the southern edge of the entire forest belt. Between it and the steppe country comes another narrow zone known as 'wooded steppe' – basically open countryside with large broad-leaved forested massifs within it. Together, these two intermediate zones are disproportionately significant in the establishment and further history of Rus, and in the Russian imagination: a welcoming, undulating, often surprisingly 'park-like' landscape. Less waterlogged than the *tayga*, less arid than the steppe, these regions have a growing season just about long enough (around five and a half months) to make cereal crops feasible, with quite high summer temperatures. Though much of the mixed forest soil is still the thin *podzol*, in many places the annual decay of broad leaves has built up good humus, and 'brown' or 'chestnut' soils approach the 'black earth' in fertility. Mixed and deciduous woodlands were somewhat easier to clear for agriculture – though much forest remains in these zones to this day. Rus seems first to have exploited the wooded steppe (at the northern edge of which Kiev, the first capital, stands), then to have moved steadily into the mixed forest – site of the next two capitals, Vladimir and Moscow. Between these two cities, it should be noted, there occurs something of a geographical anomaly: a large, irregularly oval area, whose long (north–south) axis measures some 80 miles, between the rivers Klyazma and Volga. It was known historically as Opolye (from *pole*, 'field') and is a relatively treeless area of good fertile soils – a sort of northern outlier of the wooded steppe. Its fertility led to the early growth of towns (Rostov, Suzdal, Vladimir, Aleksandrov, Pereslavl, Yuryev-Polsky) in and around it.

The vegetation-zones, then, constitute the 'face' of Rus; if this is the case, then waterways are its nerve system. The rivers and lakes, large and small, were the chief pathways by which the far-flung parts of Rus kept contact with each other. They structure the Russian landscape: if one were to draw a sketch map of Rus, one would have to begin not with its rather amorphous frontiers, but with its main river systems. Each of the seas that the early Russians knew had a great river, with its source in the mixed forest zone of middle Russia, flowing into it: the Northern Dvina/Sukhona into the White Sea; the Volga, fed by the Oka, into the Caspian; the Don into the Sea of Azov; the Dnieper into the Black Sea; the Lovat/Volkhov/Neva into the Gulf of Finland (to which one may add the Western Dvina flowing into the Baltic, though its lower course was outside historic Rus). The Volga, Don and both Dvinas each had a port-city near its mouth; the Neva and Dnieper had to wait until the eighteenth century to get theirs (St Petersburg, Odessa). But of course the tributaries to the main rivers were equally important: a glance at the map shows the crucial location of Kiev, immediately downstream of the point where Desna, Pripyat, Teterev (which in turn have important tributaries of their own) funnel into the Dnieper, giving good communications within a huge area of the wooded steppe and mixed forest belts in the middle of which Kiev stands – characteristically, on a hilly escarpment overlooking the river and floodplain beyond.

Even apparently insignificant rivers have historically been important for communications in Russia. The Moscow (Moskva) River, hardly noticeable on the map, has enabled Moscow to become and remain a major inland port. Mostly slow-flowing and without impediments (the Dnieper rapids are a notable exception), Russian rivers can be navigated by small craft to a point close to their sources – not, admittedly, all the year round (in winter they freeze, in late summer their level may drop low), but above all in early summer when they are swollen by meltwater. From early in the history of Rus a series of well-defined portages between the headwaters of various rivers was established. These

*Plate 2   Central Moscow, showing the Eastern range of the Kremlin wall (fifteenth to seventeenth centuries) and the church known as 'St Basil's' (1558) dominating the one-time port and trading district.*

portages would take the form of short roads, paved with brushwood and logs, over which small boats would be hauled on rollers (the word for 'portage', *volok*, a frequent ingredient of placenames, is related to the word for 'to haul' or 'drag'). Sometimes watersheds between several river-systems had a quite exceptional role as a centre for portages. One such area is the neighbourhood of the great circular 'White Lake' (*Beloye ozero*) in northern Russia, one of the earliest Rus outposts on the edge of the coniferous forest, where the Sheksna river system represents a northward extension of the Volga basin, abutting the Sukhona-Dvina system to the east and feeders of Lake Ladoga and eventually the Neva to the West, as well as the less important northward flowing Onega River. But the most significant such group of portages is in the area of west-central Russia between Novgorod and Smolensk known nowadays as the Valday Hills. The Russian Primary Chronicler knew this as the Okovsky Forest, and brings it into his memorable description of what he calls 'the way from the Vikings to the Greeks' (i.e. from Scandinavia to the Byzantine Empire) – about which we shall have more to say. Here the headwaters of the Dnieper, the Volga, the Western Dvina and the Lovat (tributary of the Volkhov-Neva) come close, while feeders of the Oka and Velikaya (flowing to Pskov) are not far away. Early Western cartographers imagined there must be a range of mountains here to give birth to so many rivers; instead there are lakes, marshes and irregular moraine hills reaching a little over 1000 feet above sea level – poor agricultural land, without towns, and on the borders of different Old Russian principalities. Later, Russian explorers were to find that much of Siberia offered even simpler portages than Rus proper, permitting easy (if protracted) lateral progress through a country where the main rivers flow south to north.

Overland travel in the pre-modern age was everywhere more expensive, arduous and usually slower than by water, and in Russia with its great distances and often marshy soils more obviously so than elsewhere. In winter good progress could be made across the frozen landscape by sleigh, save where there was thick forest, but winter also presented its own obvious difficulties: short daylight, snowstorms and bitter cold. Roads of any kind were impracticable in the *tayga*, and there are few in it to this day. With the gradual clearance of the mixed forest from the late Middle Ages roads became more significant, particularly around Moscow. A series of moraine ridges running west through Smolensk provided higher, better drained ground than elsewhere for Muscovy's main highway to Western Europe. Eastward, the ancient road called Stromynka (later trodden by convicts) ran through the Opolye towards Vladimir. But the best roads, or tracks, ran to the south of Moscow: the ancient military routes called *shlyakhi*, keeping mostly to the dry watersheds between the rivers that flow through the wooded steppe. The Tatar horsemen used these, and their Golden Horde has left its name in the ancient radial street in the southern part of Moscow still called Ordynka. Everywhere in Russia, long roads through thinly populated country put travellers at the mercy of highway robbers in the pre-modern period, if not later. Waterways where available remained safer as well as cheaper.

## The Human Landscape

In outlining the physical characteristics of the land of Rus, we have already unavoidably touched on several aspects of its human geography. Before we move to specifically historical questions about the formation of Rus as a people and a political entity, it is worthwhile examining this human geography a little more closely, establishing some of the constants of the pre-modern (at times, indeed, even modern) way of life in Russian conditions: how people lived, worked and fed themselves, how they occupied and exploited the land, what difficulties or opportunities they encountered.

Between the end of the last glaciation (over 10,000 years ago) and the appearance of anyone whom we could call, even speculatively, 'Russians', other peoples made use of the steppe, wooded steppe and even mixed forest zones (there is some evidence, incidentally, that these zones were less sharply distinguished in prehistoric and early medieval times than they have since become – both for climatic reasons and because of human intervention). There is a scattering of Palaeolithic, Neolithic and Bronze Age sites throughout central and southern Russia; we may focus, though, on what is known from about 500 BC onwards. This is the period at which recorded history begins as far as southern Russia is concerned, when Herodotus and subsequent ancient historians took an interest in what lay beyond the Black Sea littoral on which Greek colonies had been long established. At that period the Pontic (i.e. Black Sea) Steppe had fairly recently come under the control of an extensive empire of people of Iranian origin who still led a largely horse-based nomadic life, the Scythians. Herodotus lingers on the richness of the steppe country, and in particular on the great rivers full of fish that cut through it, and the fertile land in their valleys. The Scythians left material witness to their wealth and cultural level in the astonishingly intricate gold objects that accompanied their burials, mostly discovered after Russian power was established in the steppe country (including the trans-Caspian Kazakh steppe) during the eighteenth century. They mingled with Greek colonists and were partly Hellenized. Their traditions to some extent continued when they were gradually displaced by another people also of Iranian origin, the Sarmatians, in the second century BC. The Sarmatians seem to have been a looser coalition of tribes of varied ethnic origins, some of whom were predominantly agriculturalists, already exploiting the wooded steppe, while the Samartian rulers on the steppe proper were still mounted nomads. It is likely that Slavs, forebears or at least relatives of the East Slavs who were later to become Russians, were among them: in particular there are good grounds for believing that a tribal coalition called the Antes (though this does not sound a Slav name) contained a large Slav element. Grave goods and villages associated with the so-called Chernyakhovo urn-field culture are widespread in (largely) the wooded steppe between the Prut and the Donets rivers, and are considered by some archaeologists to represent the material remains of Slav agriculturalists whose descendants would be the core population of Kievan Rus.

Meanwhile, in the same period (from about 500 BC to the middle of the first millenium of our era) the mixed forest zone of what was to be Central Russia, particularly between the Volga and the Oka, sees the development of hill-forts, located usually overlooking the bends of rivers, that betoken a different type of civilization with different pottery styles and burial customs from those further south. Their builders were primarily hunters, gatherers and stock-breeders, using arrowheads of bone and knives of sharp stone: though a few iron objects made their way to them, their civilization could not be said to have entered the contemporary Iron Age then, or indeed for a long time afterwards. These people were evidently forbears of the many Finno-Ugrian tribes that, coming from the east, have occupied areas of the two forest zones until modern times, and have left their political mark in the contemporary states of Finland and Estonia (there is a distant relationship with the Hungarians too). The classic example of these hill-forts is at Dyakovo, overlooking the Moscow River on the eastern outskirts of the city of Moscow.

Thus in the early centuries of the first millenium we see a threefold exploitation of what would fairly soon become Rus, by peoples of different ethnic origins, corresponding with ecological distinctions related to the major vegetation zones we have described. Rus, when it materialized as a culture and state, would add a fourth mode of exploitation embracing all three regions: long-distance trade in high-value products. In this respect it reinvigorated the traditions of the Scythians, with their exports of wheat, honey, wax and slaves to the Greek world. Russians however could not (as we have seen) reliably subdue the steppe, and did not – though they sometimes tried – adopt for their own purposes the horse-based, pastoralist, mobile culture appropriate to the open grasslands: until, that is, 'Cossack' communities began to form in the 'Wild Field' on Muscovy's southern frontier from the late Middle Ages onward.

By contrast Russians were highly successful in taking over and exploiting the realm of the hunter-gatherers, first in the mixed forest, quite soon on the fringe of the *tayga* too. We can only guess at the nature of, and reasons for, the early stages of this process. There is a strong indication, however, that it was by and large peaceful: the vast majority of ancient names (particularly river names) in Central and Northern Russia are of Finno-Ugrian origin.[4] Where one people violently displaces another people (as, for example, South Saxons displaced Celts in what became Sussex) it generally has to bring in a new nomenclature: only when peaceable relations exist for some considerable time between peoples living side-by-side do many local names pass from the one to the other. Doubtless the proto-Russians encroached on the forest zones in the process of opening up new land for agriculture, not seriously interfering with the rather sparse populations of hunter-gatherer-pastoralists – indeed cooperating and no doubt intermarrying with them, while clearly learning new skills for the exploitation of the forest.

Nobody nowadays seriously disputes that the primary occupation of the people who were to become Russians was settled agriculture, at first in the wooded steppe. Nineteenth-century historians (it should be mentioned), headed by the great Vasiliy Klyuchevsky, often saw things in a different light: for Klyuchevsky the Russian peasant from the earliest times was essentially a wanderer, unlikely to live where his grandfather lived, in fact no better than a 'ravager' of the land, subjecting it to slash-and burn farming before moving on. Winning new farmland through slash-and-burn (or 'assartage') certainly had a role in the colonization of the nothern forests (and subsequently Siberia). It implies cutting down a section of forest, burning the scrub and branches, and sowing onto the unploughed ash for a few seasons until fertility declines. It requires the availability of at least ten times as much land as is in use at a given moment, and it has been calculated that around forty-five man-days per hectare need to be invested in each clearance operation, so it is hardly an uncomplicated business. But it is inconceivable that slash-and-burn could have operated in the wooded steppe in historic or even late prehistoric times, particularly in the regions around Kiev where there is abundant evidence of an ancient settled farming tradition with carefully demarcated field and landholding boundaries, and cropping methods

---

4 In West-Central Russia, and above all in Belorussia, the linguistic substratum for river names is Baltic (i.e. related to modern Lithuanian): see map on p. 95 of M. Gimbutas *The Slavs* (London, 1979).

that allowed a proportion of land to lie fallow.[5] Nevertheless the comparative poverty of the soil north of the vulnerable 'black earth' belt encouraged extensive rather than intensive farming practices, and the spread of colonists over the great plain of Russia testifies to this. It should be noted that this spread was not an even one, but much more apparent at certain times and in certain places – a notable example is the increase of population in the Volga-Oka region (*Zalesskaya zemlya*, i.e. the 'land beyond the forest') in the twelfth century, undoubtedly assisted by the warmer climatic conditions that obtained over northern Europe in the early Middle Ages.

What factors encouraged or hindered human existence in the Russian land, and how did its inhabitants exploit it? Not in the reckless, happy-go-lucky way that some nineteenth century historians seem to have assumed: knowledge of agricultural techiques and, of course, of hunting and gathering had been built up over millennia of prehistory and could

*Plate 3 Central Russian landscape: Lake Nero at Rostov the Great, one of the most ancient towns of the 'land beyond the forest', close to a Viking-period fort (Sarskoye gorodishche).*

5    There has been endless debate about the introduction of the 'three field system' (itself an imprecise concept) into Russian agriculture: it certainly existed, in some form or another, in the late Middle Ages, but it is hardly to be doubted that the advantages of rotating crops and allowing some land to lie fallow were appreciated many centuries before.

only keep life going in Russian conditions with enormous popular accumulation of knowledge and skill. Russia has a 'continental' climate, marked by a great range of temperature between warm and cold seasons (coupled with low precipitation, as we have seen). This continentality is exacerbated by its notably northerly location, which tilts the balance of climate so as to give predominance to the cold season over most of Russia. It is worth mentioning that Canada – the country geographically and climatically most similar to Russia – has virtually no population at all at the latitude of Moscow and Central Russia generally, while almost all its agricultural land is south of the latitude of Kiev. The Russian climate, incidentally, gets notably more continental (and in winter, colder) as one moves eastward: in the Moscow area – even more so in St Petersburg or Novgorod – there are still sufficient effects from the weather systems of the rest of northern Europe to add some unpredictability to the climatic conditions; the warmth of the Atlantic ocean that makes Scandinavia habitable also has a certain effect, so that Russia's only reliably ice-free port, Murmansk, is also (rather bizarrely) its northernmost, far above the Arctic Circle.

The northerly location of middle Russia gives little daylight in midwinter: conversely, early summer provides long days that not only encourage many plants into swift growth but allow more time for the intensive labour that Russian peasants need to put into the early part of the farming season. Ploughing and sowing must be done rapidly: the traditional Russian plough was the light *sokha*, a horse-drawn, forked, wooden contraption (though its points might have iron tips) that

*Plate 4 Manuscript illumination (*The Life of St Sergius, *c.1600): ploughing with a* sokha, *the age-old peasant forked wooden implement that scratches, rather than turns over, the soil.*

scratched, rather than turned over the soil, but covered a large area quickly. It was ineffective in breaking up the hardpan that forms under (leached) *podzol* soils, and thus there could be a wide difference between the viability of different plots of land in the same area: it is not surprising that the communal redistribution of land was a feature of Russian village life. Equally, shared labour has always been a necessary aspect of central and northern Russian agriculture – fully individual farming has proved attractive only in the south.

The basic working team has in most parts of Russia been the nuclear family (in some remoter parts, this comprised an extended family in a single large home), whose senior male member would be the *bolshak*, 'boss', symbolic distributor of the bread at family meals, who would represent the family to the village gathering or *obshchina* ('community'). There has been a good deal of controversy as to whether there was any historical continuity between the ancient *obshchina* and the form it took, more often under the name *mir* (literally 'world'), in recent centuries. Slavophiles have stressed the Russian age-old tradition of grassroots democracy, others have simply seen the *mir* as a convenient and deliberately fostered intermediary between state (imperial) power and the people. Be that as it may, a tradition that cannot be doubted is that of Russian peasant self-reliance. Many landholdings were in tiny hamlets or scattered farms, remote from centres of population: any families that could not be self-sufficient, in food production and storage as in other areas of everyday life, would starve or disintegrate before winter was out. The Russian peasant would in later centuries often be blamed for conservatism, for sticking to traditional crops and age-old farming practices: many a landowner after Peter the Great's time would try to introduce new agricultural methods and plant varieties, only to be ignored at best, at worst resisted violently. But tried and tested methods, in a climate which, if harsh, was at least fairly predictable, would from the peasants' point of view be their only bulwark against possible disaster. There was no margin for error, corner-cutting or speculative experiment. So while Western European grain yields began steadily to rise from about the thirteenth century, Russian returns on sown grain remained at medieval levels until recent times. What, after all, could be done with a grain surplus save distilling it into alcohol? There were no readily accessible markets to mop up any substantial overproduction. Though there were many towns in early Rus, their populations seem to have been small (with the solitary exceptions of two major urban centres, Kiev and Novgorod) until the later rise of Moscow. Russia, in other words, had organized for itself a successful, even remarkable subsistence agriculture that until modern times could not, because of its very structure, become a great creator of wealth.

An appropriately down-to-earth example of such conservatism was the peasants' reluctance to grow potatoes. In a famous jibe, Boris Pasternak compared the official propagation of the poet Vladimir Mayakovsky's reputation after his death to that of 'potatoes under Catherine II'. The sting is somewhat drawn, though, when one realizes that no state or private efforts in the eighteenth or early nineteenth century to encourage potato growing had any noticeable effect on the Russian peasantry. Only from the later nineteenth century did the potato begin to acquire the major place in the Russian diet that it holds today. Conditions in Russia are in fact good for potatoes, with their relatively brief (3–4 month) growing period and their tolerance of light soils. But in earlier times the peasants had calculated that a potato crop was more labour-intensive, maybe also riskier, than cereals (and they probably failed to understand the importance of storing it away from light and from frost). In any case there were perfectly good root vegetables – turnips and beet – that Russians grew extensively and without difficulty, and felt no need to displace. Who knows if the peasants' apparently excessive caution in making an investment in a promising new crop may not have saved them from the unexpected visitation of potato blight and perhaps a disaster of the proportions that struck Ireland in the 1840s?

What the Russians grew, from the earliest times, was predominantly of course grain. As elsewhere, the most highly rated but temperamental cereal was wheat. It was scarcely a viable crop north of Central Russia, and even there could not be relied upon. Rye could be grown further north, though its yields are lower; dark rye-bread became the characteristic Russian bread, enjoyed even at the Tsar's table. Oats were grown, particularly for animal feeds, as well as some barley, millet and, later in the Middle Ages, buckwheat, which gave rise to a type of *kasha* (steamed grain or porridge) that remains a tasty and characteristic Russian dish. As well as their obvious purpose in providing bread, all cereals were widely used in such steamed dishes, in soups, stews and even jellies (*kisel*), for pastry, dumplings and pancakes (*bliny*). Peas and beans were used, but did not occupy a prominent place in the diet; flax and hemp seeds were either cooked or crushed to provide vegetable oil.

Overwhelming reliance on grain for the bulk of the diet carried obvious dangers. Grain harvests can fail anywhere, for a variety of reasons, and in other parts of medieval Europe (particularly the Mediterranean) considerable efforts were made by those who controlled the supplies, notably the Venetians, to secure various sources of grain as a hedge against failure in any one place. In Russia, distant from other sources of supply and with long lines of communication, crop failure could quickly become catastrophic. Famine would often lead to outbreaks of disease, of which the most dramatic was ergotism, as people ate grain infected by the poisonous fungus ergot that would otherwise have been discarded. Since Russian grain yields were low (probably averaging a ratio of 1:3) until recent times, there was little margin between a poor harvest and a disastrous one. When, however, there was a surplus, grain could be 'conserved' by being fermented into alcohol. Beer was known from the most ancient times; distilled vodka, which could keep more or less permanently, seems only to have reached Russia (from Western Europe) in the middle of the sixteenth century.[6] But there was and is another ancient, and characteristically Russian, drink made from grain (usually rye): *kvas*. Fermented but scarcely alcoholic, like 'small beer' in early England, it is agreeably astringent, supposedly health-giving and of particular value where drinking-water supplies were hygienically questionable. It can even serve as the basis of a cold herb soup (*okroshka*).

Vegetables, crucial for their vitamins, included many wild plants such as ramsons (wild garlic) and sorrel – but the dominant Russian vegetable from ancient times to the present day has been cabbage. This is treated in two main ways: pickled in brine for winter use, or as the main constituent of the most universal of Russian dishes: the variety of green soups that go under the generic title *shchi* (red soups made with beetroot, *borshch*, are somewhat more characteristic of Western Russia, as of Ukraine and Poland). Small cucumbers or gherkins (eaten fresh in summer) are the other characteristic pickled vegetables that have always provided much-needed vitamins in winter. Pickles with vinegar could provide the 'sour', acidic element that Russians have always appreciated in their diet (ascorbic acid is vital for health, of course); lemons in brine, another such source, were an early luxury import into Rus. Root vegetables have been mentioned; cottage gardens also provided onions, garlic and herbs, of which the most characteristic is dill. Herbs might also flavour vodka or *kvas*, as might fruit; apples, pears, plums and gooseberries have long been grown, though usually less successfully than in milder climates, while the Opolye district between Moscow and Vladimir is noted for its cherries.

Livestock was essential for the Russian peasant economy, though hard to keep during the long winter: a large amount of hay would be needed and the animals would be out of condition by the time they could be turned out onto the spring grass (traditionally on St George's Day, 23 April; there was a second St George's Day in November, marking the end of all agricultural operations). A horse rather than an ox would

---

[6] Historical writers have speculated unrestrainedly on when and whence distilled spirits reached Russia; the evidence is summed up judiciously in R. E. F. Smith and D. Christian *Bread and Salt* (Cambridge, 1984), pp. 88–9.

normally pull the *sokha*. Pigs and sheep were of course kept, but not in great numbers, nor did they grow large, and generally meat was not much eaten except on special occasions. If animals were slaughtered in early winter, however, their carcasses would in most years remain conveniently deep-frozen until needed. Chickens, ducks and geese were ubiquitous in the Russian village. Cows and goats – again, small breeds – would be kept for the many milk products, from excellent soured cream (*smetana*) to various yoghurts and soft cheeses (harder cheese was not widespread till modern times) that are so characteristic of the Russian diet. The livestock on a farm would produce the much needed manure to raise the quality of at least some of the peasants' thin *podzol* soil.

The Russian diet was importantly supplemented and varied by the natural products of woodlands, lakes and rivers: particularly in the northern forests which could support hunter-gatherers and where normal cultivation was anyhow unrewarding, but also throughout the historic Russian lands. A productive tract of forest can yield an awe-inspiring quantity of edible berries, fungi, and hazelnuts (up to 500 kilos of berries or of fungi per hectare has been estimated). The fungi most highly rated were, and still are, those that can best be preserved (particularly russula and boletus species) – either pickled or dried and hung up in strings: they are often a constituent of the soups that are so substantial a feature of Russian cooking. Berries too would be preserved in honey or sugar, and made into jams of various kinds that later came to be the standard accompaniment to tea. The most valuable forest product though – one exploited and indeed exported from ancient times – was honey, which has an important by-product in the form of wax. Obviously peasant families could and did set up their skeps or hives, but 'honey-trees' (*borti*), where bees nested in hollow trunks, producing wild honey, were numerous, well-known, individually owned and highly prized – not only by humans, of course, but also by bears, whose name in Russian (*medved*) means 'honey-knower' – probably in origin this word is an apotropaic euphemism for a feared creature. Honey was not only a concentrated and durable source of calories: from the most ancient times it was fermented into mead and other drinks. Wild birds, such as ducks, were caught in nets; the consumption of creatures killed in snares, however, was frowned upon officially (as were black puddings made with blood) – a reflection of Old Testament dietary laws.

The greatest source of inexpensive protein in early Russia was, naturally, fish, with which its innumerable lakes, pools and rivers teemed. Fish can be caught even in winter with lines lowered through holes drilled in the ice. Once again, fish was and is often the basis for the sort of soup (*ukha*) that was a meal in itself. The finest of Russian fish were the various members of the sturgeon family, whose availability increased as Russia secured more southern territory from the mid-sixteenth century, since the best species of sturgeon inhabit the lower courses of southward-flowing rivers, particularly the Volga. Sturgeon were valued not only for their caviare, but for their firm and tasty flesh that takes well to being smoked or salted. In so far as Russia has an indigenous traditional cuisine (as is surely the case), it is founded on fish rather than meat dishes. Fish cookery was encouraged by the large number of official fast days (around half the year in total) designated by the Orthodox Church: strict fasting, however, might mean avoidance of fish too.

Russians traditionally cooked in the stove or oven that provided indispensible warmth to the living-room of the peasant house. Such stoves, in early times semicircular and primitive in construction, reached their modern cubic form from around 1600. Thus traditional Russian cookery is characterized by pot-roasts, stews and pies rather than boiled, fried or grilled dishes; baking was well developed with a wide range of tasty breads available in towns. Indeed, in Rus a meal would open with a course consisting of samples of bread, with salt and maybe a cold soup; 'bread-salt' (*khleb-sol*) is a famous and ancient Russian term for 'hospitality'. Later, probably as late as the eighteenth century (with German and Scandinavian influence) the first course that we have come to regard as characteristically Russian, *zakuski* ('snacks') developed: a range of items such as pickled mushrooms, pies, salted fish, caviare, cold meats, 'Russian salads', washed down with glasses of vodka and a 'chaser'. Anyone interested in the image of rustic gastronomic abundance, as conceived (and doubtless exaggerated) by a writer of the first half of the nineteenth century, should turn to Nikolay Gogol's short story 'Old World Landowners', though it could well put one off one's food.

Nobody would imagine that the everyday Russian peasant diet would be other than skimpy and monotonous, as it has been in most places at most times of history. Instead of Gogolian lavishness it might normally consist of little more than black bread with some salt and raw onion or garlic, as well as soup or gruel. Yet feasting, not to mention carousing, was also an integral element in Russian life at all levels of society from the earliest times. Feasts would in the first instance, of course, be linked with major Church festivals, and as elsewhere the pre-Lenten binge could take on spectacular dimensions (foreigners were advised to keep off the streets of Moscow for their own safety). More structured feasts existed, however. Some were organized by fraternities (*bratshiny*), recorded since Kievan times, that seem to have developed their social role as discussion-places early, maybe holding some judicial powers as well. There are several documents from Muscovite times seeking to prevent state officials from imposing themselves on such feasts as uninvited guests and consuming too much.

Within the family too there were feasts, no doubt from the most ancient times, marking great life events: births, deaths, marriages, the completion of harvest. The ritual character of much Russian feasting, together with its associated merrymaking and disorderly goings-on, was long evident, and in the Muscovite period – particularly in the seventeenth century – greatly disturbed churchmen because of its pagan connotations; the state authorities too worried about the possibility of disturbances. The state, however, somewhat compromised its position (if it wished to discourage drunkenness) when it discovered the revenue benefits of establishing a monopoly in the sale of spirits, early in the seventeenth century, less than a hundred years after the introduction of distilling to Russia. Indeed the drink-shop (*kabak* – as distinct from the *korchma*, inn, where food would be provided), which was controlled by the authorities, had become a feature of Russian town life even earlier, in the reign of Ivan IV. As R. E. F. Smith strikingly puts it: 'The monstrous appearance of such drinking establishments influenced the entire subsequent history of the Russian people.'[7] The social consequences hardly need spelling out, and have continued through the Soviet period to the present day. With the increasing circulation of money from late Muscovite times, carousing at the *kabak* could spill out from special festivities into everyday life; any agreement or job done might be sealed with vodka (as happens to this day). Overall alcohol consumption per capita was doubtless not significantly higher in Russia than elsewhere: it merely took place more publicly, unrestrainedly and often destructively. From the 1850s there was a reaction in the form of grassroots temperance movements (that also worried the government). Tea, introduced from China in the seventeenth century, was imported in rapidly increasing quantities from the 1790s onward, providing a low-key alternative to carousing that soon picked up (particularly among the merchant class) a characteristic ceremonial coloration of its own.

A certain ceremoniousness still pervades drinking and to some extent eating in Russia to this day, even at quite a crude or humble level. Vodka tippling in whatever in whatever circumstances has its unbudgeable rituals, including toasts (themselves formalized) and the obligatory consumption of some kind of food, however exiguous: Westerners have looked on in wonder to see Russian drinkers, half seas over, stumble out to look for edible herbs in the garden, or carefully cut a boiled sweet into three with a penknife, so as to have a symbolic meal with their drink. Peasant hospitality retains its laws: the stranger at the door is settled

7 Smith and Christian *Bread and Salt*, p. 90.

down to be given 'bread-salt', a meal or refreshment, before being asked his business. Formalized eating revolves round the single important meal of the day: *obed*, dinner, that can take place at any time from late morning till evening (mid-afternoon is the preferred time, as in eighteenth-century Western Europe, if there is a free choice) – its immediately distinctive feature is a soup course after *zakuski*. *Zavtrak*, breakfast, *vtoroy zavtrak*, lunch ('second breakfast') and *uzhin*, supper are by comparison insignificant and haphazard meals.

Returning to the past, we can see the importance of ritualized carousing at a state level at various moments of Russian history. Peter the Great, for all his reputation as a 'Westernizer', had much in his makeup that harks back to older Russian patterns of thought and behaviour. Several modern historians and semioticians of culture have given renewed scrutiny, in particular, to his strange institution the 'All-Drunken Synod' that engaged a remarkable amount of his time and attention from before he was 20 till his death over 30 years later. Its mixture of blasphemy, obscenity, parody, theatricality and public hooliganism has been variously interpreted: as an imitation of Western 'Hell Fire' clubs, as a political gesture in the direction of modernization, as an aspect of Peter's private pathology, as relaxing horseplay (its name has been softened into 'The Jolly Company') after a hard day's work. But the ritual, archaic and indeed pagan aspects of Peter's 'antibehaviour' (Yury Lotman's term) can scarcely be in doubt, particularly when one takes into account the importance Peter himself gave it, and the linking of carousels with significant times of the year (see also p. 129).[8] Ivan the Terrible, in many ways Peter's acknowledged predecessor, was another 'ritual carouser' – particularly in the company of his *oprichnina*, the quasi-monastic gang of troubleshooters whom he used to terrorize the populace and with whom he set up an 'alternative realm' within Muscovy. Maybe we should re-examine the famous words of Vladimir I – who converted Rus to Christianity but was a notable carousing monarch – when (according to the Primary Chronicle) he turned down Islam as a possible state religion: 'Drinking is the joy of Rus: we cannot exist without that'. This might be taken as a skittish or self-ironizing comment on the part of Vladimir or of the chronicler, a touch of folk-tale buffoonery (Vladimir apparently fancied the idea of the Moslem paradise in other respects). But perhaps there is a quite serious

---

[8]   There is a remarkable concise study of Peter's 'antibehaviour' by B. A. Uspensky 'Historia sub specie semioticae' in B. Khrapchenko et al. (eds) *Kulturnoye naslediye drevney Rusi* (Moscow, 1976), trans. in L. Lucid (ed) *Soviet Semiotics* (Baltimore, 1977). See also Smith and Christian *Bread and Salt*, p. 172.

sub-text: Vladimir had to choose a developed religion for his people that would not not necessitate doing away with age-old feasting rituals. Further interesting descriptions of Vladimir's feasting habits, and their public dimension, are provided by the chronicler in his entry for the year 996, while for further remarks on feasting within the pre-Christian ritual world see Chapter 3, Belief Systems (p. 99).

Russian peasants, of course, extracted more than just products to be eaten or drunk from their environment. In fact, save for the tiny urban or moneyed class of Rus, hardly anyone needed anything that was produced outside the country, or indeed outside the immediate neighbourhood. Fine cloth would be imported, but for ordinary purposes there was plenty of flax and hemp that grew well even at a latitude where grain would be unreliable. Though leather was produced and used for shoes in towns, peasants generally wove their own footwear from strips of birch or lime bark (since these would wear out quickly, on a long journey the peasant would normally walk barefoot with shoes slung over the shoulder on a stick, to be put on when the destination was reached – such sights could be witnessed into the twentieth century). Iron was obtained from the boggy and sandy *podzol* areas of northern Russia – yet was little used in the peasant household: perhaps only for the points of the *sokha*, for sickles and knives and for that most fundamental of peasant tools, the axe – even spades were normally of wood. There was even less demand for other metals: they would probably be encountered only in items of church furniture such as icon-casings, lamps etc., in coins and in rings and personal adornments. Even the pigments used in icons and wall paintings would mostly be earth colours obtained by grinding up locally-found minerals; the few exceptions (cinnabar, from mercury; verdigris, from copper; white lead; gold leaf; lapis lazuli, imported as a semi-precious stone from the Near East) would be needed only exceptionally and in small quantities. Pottery was required only for a few cookery-vessels and, late in the Old Russian period, stove tiles. Mica, found in the Northern Dvina area, was generally used in Rus rather than glass.

One important item that the peasant household could not usually obtain by its own efforts was salt.[9] It was in demand as a necessary ingredient of diet (particularly for livestock stalled in winter), as a savoury condiment, and in particular – given the long Russian winter – for preserving all kinds of food (even melons from Astrakhan, a favourite Muscovite treat, were pickled in brine). As has happened in many countries through history, the government organized the salt industry

[9] There is a fascinating analysis of this trade in Smith and Christian *Bread and Salt* Chapter 2, to which my account is indebted.

and raised revenue from it. Central and southern Russia were poor in sources of salt (though there was rock-salt in Galicia, an area that after the Tatar invasion passed into Lithuanian control, and there were salt-pans in the deserts around the lower Volga: these areas became Russian only in the 1550s and anyhow presented considerable transport difficulties). So brine had to be drilled for in various often remote areas of the north and east, where there were reserves sometimes at a depth of several hundred feet – a remarkable, expensive technological effort in 'backward' pre-Petrine Rus. The alternative was to evaporate sea water in the unpromising climatic conditions of the White Sea. This was indeed done, apparently from very early times, though the problems associated with the supply of firewood and of grain to feed the labour force were great. For much of the Muscovite period this salt trade was a crucial economic mainstay of the North generally and of its monasteries (particularly the great monastery on Solovki Islands) more specifically. Vologda prospered in its role as probably the greatest Russian salt entrepôt. Siberia when it was opened up provided some new sources of salt, but not very significant ones ('the salt mines of Siberia' are a myth). The importance of the industry was dramatically shown when the government of the young Tsar Aleksey made some unwise upward adjustments to the system of salt taxation in 1646; not only did this lead to a large-scale uprising, the 'Salt Revolt' (*Solyanoy bunt*) in Moscow a couple of years later, but to the loss of large quantities of inadequately salted fish and of salt stockpiles that dissolved away, as the early seventeenth-century German traveller Adam Olearius recounts.

Of all the products of the Russian land – or at least of the *tayga* and mixed forest zones – animal furs were the most glamorous and financially rewarding, over a vast span of time from the beginnings of Rus onwards. They were equivalent to a currency: they gave their names to certain early units of money; even in the later seventeenth century Russian ambassadors set off for Western Europe with a stack of pelts to meet their expenses (they would have to set up stalls and sell them, to the astonishment of the host population). Some fur-bearing animals (e.g. beavers, otters, bears, wolves, hares) were at least until early-modern times quite common in the central and more populous parts of Rus; the really valuable ones, such as arctic fox, marten and above all sable, had to be sought in the cold and trackless stretches of the *tayga*, to meet whose climatic conditions their fur would grow luxuriantly. The most important and abundant all-purpose fur was squirrel. Not surprisingly, the Muscovite authorities established control over the fur trade for their own profit: in the seventeenth century it was the biggest single contributor to state revenues. Before the 1470s it had been largely in the hands of the merchants of Novgorod, who had established a vast 'empire' of dependent, scarcely populated territories in the northern *tayga* – stretching as far as, indeed a little beyond, the Urals – so as to exploit it. But however much others profited by it, fur-hunting also gave a chance for low-born but enterprising people to do well for themselves. Ordinary peasants would be more likely to wear sheepskin than furs – but would probably eat the meat of the bears, squirrels or hares that they caught.

As time went on the more highly-prized creatures had to be sought in ever-remoter regions. Astonishing as it may seem, Russians began colonizing Siberia from the north, along trade routes leading from the former Novgorod lands. and set up stockaded towns at Arctic latitudes on either side of the northern Urals and the Ob-Taz estuary system. The furthest and most remarkable of these was Mangazeya, in the early seventeenth century evidently a rip-roaring frontier town, a 'second Baghdad', full (as its governer reported) of 'fugitives . . . tax-evaders, debtors, robbers and other criminals'; in a desperate attempt to stop unofficial trading with foreign merchants, the government ordered the closure of the northern route to Siberia in 1619 (the customs posts it had earlier established were evidently ineffective).[10] Nowadays many of these fortified outposts are ghost towns, or have been reclaimed by the *tayga*; Mangazeya itself, after a fire, was relocated as 'New Mangazeya' at Turukhansk on the Yenisey. To open up these vast territories – from the earliest Novgorodian operations onwards – required close contact with the indigenous peoples who, thinly spread throughout the forest zones, could provide indispensible guidance and often did the actual hunting, paying for Muscovite protection through a *yasak* (fur tribute). If they converted to Orthodoxy they, too, would be considered Russians; not surprisingly, the government was unenthusiastic about missionary endeavours. Eventually the hunt for furs was to lead Russian explorers and settlers across the Bering Strait to colonize Alaska and the American west coast down to Fort Ross in California.

Furs were not, as it happens, the only high-value animal products obtained from the remoter parts of the north and east. Ivory – strange as it may seem – was a significant Russian export from Kievan times on; it was obtained in the first place from the walruses that were caught by Russian and indigenous fishermen in the White Sea and Arctic Ocean (the 'Breathing Sea', as they evocatively called it from its heavy and frequent mists). When Siberia was opened up, an even more surprising source of ivory became available in the form of fossilized mammoth

[10]  On Mangazeya, and much else concerning the Russian colonization of northern Siberia, see A. and Y. Opolovnikov *The Wooden Architecture of Russia* (London, 1989) p. 114ff.

tusks from the terraces of tundra rivers: incredible quantities are reported to have passed through the annual Yakutsk fair.[11] Ivory was not just exported: it was used in Kievan and Muscovite Rus for delicate carved artwork, particularly small personally owned icons. Semi-precious stone was similarly used, and also, for example, for the floor of the Annuciation Cathedral in the Moscow Kremlin: the Urals, once they were fully in Russian control, proved a rich source of such materials as also of minerals such as copper and silver.

## Wooden Russia

In the exploitation of the Russian landscape's natural resources, nothing could rival the importance of wood, and it is worth going into some detail on the subject. In a continental climate such as that of Rus, trees grow slowly but often very tall; their wood is dense and durable.[12] With the axe (saws were not much used till late in Muscovite times), maybe with the help of wedges to split logs and of adzes, early Russians made an amazing number of objects of everyday life. Agricultural implements – even spades and harrows, though these might be tipped with iron – and domestic ones for the processing of yarn and production of cloth would all be wooden; so would all storage vessels for liquids or substances such as flour, together with buckets, churns, scoops, spoons, plates and so on; so of course would be all furniture, made without the use of screws or nails; the domestic icons were painted on wooden panels. Means of transport – boats, sledges, skis, snow-shoes and carts – were of wooden construction; boats capable of carrying considerable loads were in early times (and still in the sixteenth century) hollowed out of a single great oak trunk. Bast made from birch or lime bark was woven into many household objects: bast shoes have been mentioned, but it was used too for mats and even ropes, depite the fact that hemp was grown in Russia. Strips of birchbark (incised with a stylus) were used for letters and similar documents by ordinary citizens in Kievan Rus and later: many thousands have been excavated from the marshy (anaerobic) Novgorod subsoil since the Second World War. Teaching alphabets were inscribed

[11]  T. Armstrong *The Russians in the Arctic* (London, 1958), p. 146, quotes an estimate of twenty tons a year.
[12]  Pine and spruce were most used for building and general purposes; oak was the chief hardwood; maple and ash provided many small domestic objects. There is an interesting table of the woods (twenty-eight in all, including some not native to Russia) used for various purposes and found in Novgorod excavations, together with a summary of the uses of wood, in R. E. F. Smith *Peasant farming in Muscovy* (Cambridge, 1977) pp. 47–51.

*Figure 2   (a) Pre-Tatar 'birchbark document' (many thousands have been found, chiefly in Novgorod, since 1945), and (b) wooden alphabet-board for teaching purposes*

on little boards. The stove naturally consumed large quantities of firewood, but a wooden spill (*luchina*) was also the usual source of lighting in ordinary Russians' houses, even though beeswax was an age-old Russian product (the church was a great consumer of candles); dry bracket-fungi from birch trees were the standard form of tinder. There were valuable by-products in the form of resin and pitch from coniferous trees. The ubiquity of wood impressed itself on Anthony Jenkinson, the English merchant, who made his first visit to Russia (via the White Sea) in 1557: the boats he took down the Dvina, 'long-builded, broad-made', carrying two hundred tons (of salt), 'have no iron appertayning to them, but all of timber'; getting to Vologda, 'a great Citie', he noted 'the houses are builded with wood of Firre trees, joyned one with another . . . without any iron or stone worke, covered with Birch barkes, and wood all over the same: Their Churches are all of wood, two for every Parish, one to be heated for Winter, and the other for Summer.'

Buildings indeed represent the utilization of wood at its most spectacular. There is something ineffably moving in the prospect of the traditional Russian village – the Old Russian town also – formed almost entirely out of the forest all around it, ready (since wood is so transitory) to return to the forest as soon as humans no longer maintain it. Of the many different types of structure that such wooden architecture comprehends (though 'architecture' is here an anachronistic term – the builders 'followed their eye', working without blueprints), the peasant house is central. In the forest zones it took, and still takes, the form of the *izba*: a cell or series of cells of horizontally laid logs, carefully matched for diameter, trimmed by the axe, the corners neatly lapped or dovetailed. The roof – in the past shingled or thatched – would have overhanging eaves and often highly decorated bargeboards and similar carved wood elements. In the south, the house was and is called a*khata*: though faced with whitewashed daub, it too is on a wooden frame. The house is merely the main feature of the domestic area, the *dvor* (inadequately translated as 'courtyard' or 'yard'): its doorway would normally give direct access not to the village path or street, but be set in the longer house wall facing the *dvor*. and be reached through a porch up a few steps. Judging by old illustrations, the ancient *izba* had a steeper-pitched roof than is normal nowadays with smaller, plain windows, that would be closed by a sliding board. Chimneys were rare until fairly recently: smoke from the stove would simply have to find its way out through the unglazed windows or a *dymnik* (smoke stack) in the high ceiling (the atmosphere was less oppressive than might be thought: the smoke formed an insulating layer above head height). In the one heated room the family would live, work, cook, eat and sleep, in the winter months at least. This main room was properly speaking the *izba* itself (a word thought to be a prehistoric Germanic borrowing, related to the modern German word *Stube*, 'room'): its counterpart was *seni*, unheated room or rooms, sometimes not much more than a corridor through which one had to pass from the heated room to the outside world. The house would probably also have a basement for storage, and often unheated attic rooms, sometimes with a whole upper storey; in northern Russia, as so often in peasant societies, accommodation for livestock and haylofts would be contiguous with the back of the house. These houses would be – would have to be – excellently insulated, with sphagnum moss or some other wadding filling the interstices of the logs, yet at the same time the timber construction would allow it to 'breathe'.

Town houses were little different: they could be put up at great speed from prefabricated modules. Even in important towns there were very few stone or brick domestic buildings in pre-Petrine Rus, though these do become rather more numerous (particularly in Moscow where remains of over 100 masonry domestic buildings survive from pre-Petrine times) during the course of the seventeenth century. Often a wooden superstructure – in which people preferred to live, considering it healthier – would surmount a brick foundation-storey. But completely wooden structures too could reach a high degree of complexity and ornamentation, particularly in the latter couple of centuries, and particularly where various merchant or craft activities would take place under the domestic roof, with a more extended family living there. With the comforts of chimneys and glazing came a good deal of attention to the decorative aspect of window surrounds (*nalichniki*), carved in imaginative lacy variations on pediments based on classical motifs. Old Russian palace architecture in wood must have been even more fantastically decorative, but nothing of it has survived, with one precious exception: the scale model in wood made at Catherine II's direction when the great wooden palace at Kolomenskoye, near Moscow was dismantled. This had been built mostly in 1667–8, and presented an amazing, fairytale assemblage of disparate and picturesque linked elements, over 200 rooms in all. It was Tsar Aleksey's favourite place of relaxation in his latter years – both the climax and the last product of its tradition, a showpiece anthology of its constructors' skills.

Within its protective fence – a guard against the depredations of bears and wolves – the Old Russian village too was in its way an anthology of the woodworker's arts. Beside the more or less sizeable *izba*, the individual *dvor* would have its outbuildings and stables (some of which might be under the same roof as the house), its neatly stacked logpile, its store room raised on legs, its counterpoised wood-built well, and finally a phenomenon almost universal in Russia to this day: a miniature house, with its own woodstack and (nowadays) chimney, located at the far end

*Plate 5 Aleksey Venetsianov* Threshing Floor *(1821, Tretyakov Gallery): first a portraitist, Venetsianov (1780–1847) later devoted himself to genre paintings of a calm and idealized Russian countryside, the first major artist to do so.*

of the vegetable garden, or by a lake or riverside if available. This would be the bathhouse (*banya*), stoked up usually once a week for all to steam in, flagellate themselves with birch twigs and maybe then roll in the snow. The ritual is so time-honoured (doubtless going back to the indigenous Finno-Ugrian inhabitants of the forest zones) that it is described, somewhat tongue-in-cheek, in the early pages of the Primary Chronicle as a spectacle St Andrew supposedly witnessed in Novgorod and then recounted to incredulous listeners in Rome: 'I saw the land of the Sloveni and while I was among them, I saw their wooden bathhouses. They warm them to extreme heat, then undress, and after annointing themselves with tanning-acid they take young branches and lash their bodies . . . Then they drench themselves with cold water and are thus revived . . . they make of the act not a mere washing but a veritable torment.' The bathhouse was more than merely a convenient location for weekly ablutions. It could be a spare guest room, a meeting room, a drinking place, a birthing place. It carries a strange web of ancient associations in folklore. Yury Lotman (with his predilection for binary modelling in the analysis of culture) put it strikingly: 'Buildings like bathhouses, barns and smithies are interesting examples of the fate of pagan temples in the Christian world. There is reason to believe that the perception of these places as 'unclean' is connected with their special sacral significance . . . as family or domestic temples . . . The bathhouse also appears as the traditional place of divination, sorcery, magical cures and of course incantatory healings; the cult role of the bathhouse also shows up clearly in the marriage rite, where bathhouse rituals are no less important than the church ceremony: each complements the other.'[13] In the little cosmos of each village household, then, the bathhouse stands at one, 'pagan' spiritual pole; at the other is the 'fine corner' (*krasny ugol*) of the main room of the house, on the far right from the entrance, where the household icons would stand, to be greeted on arrival by visitors, who would be seated and entertained in the same part of the room. In Russian towns and cities of modern times, incidentally, the bathhouse has not disappeared but taken on another form – as a large public institution, the people's meeting and relaxation place, spawning its characteristic urban folklore (as exemplified in many stories by the remarkable Soviet satirist Mikhail Zoshchenko, 1895–1958).

Outside the town or village, there were still any number of timber structures: watermills, windmills raised on high bases to catch the wind above the trees, hunters' cabins and gamestores on tall poles, dependent summer hamlets deep in the forest, wayside crosses and shrines, weirs and bridges – often large and elaborate. Once the Russians began expanding into potentially hostile territory, forts and trading posts acquired formidable timber stockades. Such defences once stood on top of massive earthen banks, which can usually also be seen at the centre of many medieval towns in the Russian heartland, though none of the timberwork survives. Apart from such fortresses – which in Muscovite times were sometimes replaced with impressive brick kremlins (e.g. at Smolensk, Novgorod, and several other places – Tula, Kolomna etc. – guarding the southern borderland), and maybe some streets with timber paving, there was little in pre-modern times to distinguish a town from a village. Even the city of Moscow – which from the sixteenth century covered a vast area, as foreigners frequently testified – was largely built up on the 'courtyard' principle of the village or rural estate: full of gardens, sheds and livestock (the cattle would be driven out to pasture in the country each morning, to return spontaneously to their homes for milking each evening). Away from provincial capitals, the rustic quality of places that appear on the map as considerable urban centres can even

---

[13]   Yu. Lotman and B. Uspensky 'Binary Models in the Dynamics of Russian Culture', English trans. in A. D. and A. S. Nakhimovsky (eds) *The Semiotics of Russian Cultural History* (Ithaca, 1985), p. 38.

nowadays surprise the visitor. In such places there are no built-up streets of continuous shops or offices, no obvious 'town centre', merely one or two haphazardly placed Soviet concrete housing-blocks and a dusty space serving as market-place among the detached and totally rustic log houses with their ample gardens. In Old Russia there was scarcely any sense of town life as being qualitatively different from that of the country (save maybe in Novgorod, till its enforced decline), no sense of privileged urbanism among its inhabitants, who on the whole shared the same obligations and limitations on their rights as the peasants, until the nineteenth century: the concept of city dwellers as free and self-governing, that developed early in many parts of Western Europe, and was known in Kievan Rus, was entirely foreign to Muscovy.[14]

At the heart of each traditional village was the *pogost*, a term that originally designated the district or parish as a whole but over time narrowed to mean the churchyard area – another world-within-a-world, usually surrounded by its own timber wall (and nowadays often meaning just a graveyard).[15] Churches (generally in pairs, one smaller and heated for winter use, as Jenkinson noted, above) were the most spectacular of wooden buildings: monumental beyond their dimensions, they towered not just over the crouching village houses but over the undulating landscape, punctuating it in 'a peaceful invasion of space' (D. S. Likhachov's phrase). Towns too once had such wooden churches on each street or in each quarter, but these were nearly all replaced in brick or stone (usually after fires) during the seventeenth and eighteenth centuries. The grander wooden churches rose in a series of diminishing storeys, octagonal or square in section, to a 'tent' or spire with one or more small decorative domes, the whole often reminiscent in silhouette of some great fir tree. These churches were virtuoso products of folk creativity, made with the axe and without a single nail, following age-old techniques but always reinterpreting them. The origins of such buildings are mysterious: the Novgorod chroniclers recall a wooden church, predecessor of the present stone cathedral of Santa Sophia, built at the end of the tenth century 'with thirteen tops' (decorative domes? Interior cells? Since all such buildings have long disappeared, we can only surmise). If there is any direct connection with the medieval 'stave churches' of Scandinavia, it has yet to be elucidated – there are too many differences of design principles, at least when we get to the late medieval Russian structures that are the earliest that have survived to our day. In Russian wooden architecture the logs were always laid horizontally; pine

14  See J. Blum *Lord and Peasant in Russia* (Princeton, 1961) p. 270.
15  On the *pogost*, the *trapeznaya* etc., see Opolovnikov *The Wooden Architecture of Russia*, pp. 143ff.

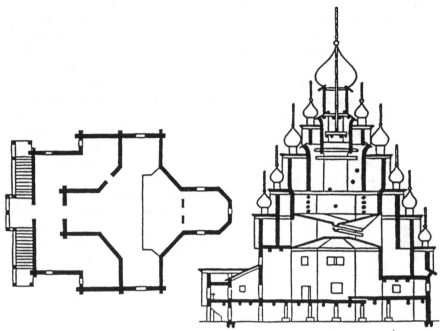

*Figure 3    Ground plan and cross-section of wooden Russian
church of the Transfiguration, Kizhi, 1714.*

was the commonest timber, but oak or larch, more resistant to rot, might
be used for the lowest courses and for carved pillars, and other woods for
details, silvery aspen notably for roof shingles.

The climax of wooden church building was reached in 1714, with the
construction of the towering (38 metre high) Church of the Transfiguration on the island of Kizhi in Lake Onega. It is a pyramid bearing no less
than twenty-two decorative domes, and built on the virtuoso 'twenty-
walled' ground-plan: i.e. an octagon with projecting cross-arms and
porch. Legend has it that its builder, Nestor, flung his axe into the lake
when it was finished, with the words 'There was not, is not and will not
be another such one.' Kizhi was an important parish, trade and
administrative centre, with many other fine wooden buildings – since
the 1950s others have been dismantled and reassembled there from
villages in the area. Yet Russian wooden architecture is more than a
matter of individual fine buildings that can be shifted around and
'museumized' (urgent as it undoubtedly has been to give them loving
restoration and safeguard them from fire and dilapidation). It represents
as we have seen a unique and all-encompassing built environment –
whose traditions are, as a matter of fact, still viable and indeed alive

today (particularly since the end of Soviet rule and the legalization of private property rights). The living heart of this environment in Old Russia was the *pogost* itself, with its paired churches, its bell-tower, clergy-house, ceremonial gate in its roofed wall and cemetery. It was the setting not just for services, but for processions, in some places for mystery plays and wooden sculptures of saints, and most importantly for parish meetings and even feasts: churches were built with a large western porch or terrace, sometimes a whole lower storey, which served as the *trapeza*, the meeting-room for the locality. The church, its icons and its rituals were a great living calendar that marked out not merely the main life-events but the seasons of the year, and linked them with universal culture and with eternity: we shall have more to say on this later. The graveyard itself, beside its great grave-markers, once had standing tomb-structures in the form of a miniature wooden house (*domovina*), through whose tiny window food and gifts could be passed: the ultimate symbolization of generational continuity in the Russian countryside.

# 2

## Rus As People And As State

### The East Slavs

In previous sections we have tried to examine those aspects of life that remained more or less constant for Old Russia (and, often enough, Russia subsequently): in particular its geographical setting, the necessities of, and possibilities for, settled existence within it. Even when we concentrated on the permanent coordinates of the Russian experience, it was not possible to avoid any mention of historical factors. When we move to the scrutiny of Rus as a people, and how that people organized itself socially, the historical dimension will be in the foreground – though conjecture and inference will be involved as well as demonstrable fact. A question such as 'Who are the Russians?' looks simple enough – but how would we recognize a satisfactory answer? Even when we project it back towards its origins, and ask 'Who (or what) were, or was, Rus?' the same problem remains. Would we most readily accept an answer in the geographical, or racial, or cultural, or linguistic, or some other terms? Geography is crucial, as we have seen – but frontiers are fluid, people are mobile (in Russia notably so), and indeed they modify their environment. In so far as racial characteristics are a meaningful field of enquiry nowadays, they are so only in the light of modern gene studies – which can give hard evidence about the relative isolation, movement or mixing of populations (usually confirming what was known or guessed already, e.g. that the Basques have remained a remarkably self-contained people, and once spread over a larger part of Spain than today), but do not provide any grounding for the notions of clearcut racial definition that were so naively and dangerously taken for granted in the nineteenth and early twentieth centuries. Culture – the sum total of such features of a shared way of life as received social attitudes, folk wisdom and customs, notions of justice, symbolic systems, religion and so on of a people – seems promising, but is too fluid and complex for well-defined answers, particularly if investigated diachronically.

So answers to questions about the identity of peoples – and self-definitions of where one 'belongs' – are most often given in terms of language. Languages, though naturally always evolving, represent an unbroken and clearly-discernible thread leading back at any rate to their earliest written records (in Russia, this means over 1000 years). What is more, language, the most fundamental feature of human consciousness, plays an exceptional and pervasive role in any discrete culture; as the influential linguist Edward Sapir (1884–1939) and his followers argued, a given language is a unique determinant of its speakers' mindset. Pinning down such a mindset, whether through grammatical phenomena, proverbs, turns of phrase, resources of vocabulary or whatever can however prove elusive or contentious. It must be admitted that for all their durability and (often) conservatism, languages are not eternal: a group of speakers may occasionally change their language (sometimes with bewildering speed) and remain a recognizable cultural or national unit. The Cornish, it could be argued, are no less a distinct people for having lost their language in the eighteenth century, nor conversely are the Swiss for having four languages of equal official status. Furthermore ostensibly 'dead' languages often have a shadowy afterlife as a substrate affecting the forms and patterns of their successors. Nevertheless it remains the case that 'Russianness' from the point of view of ethnicity, or nationality, is most obviously and closely bound up with the Russian language itself. Before passing on to the complex question of the origins of Rus, we may with advantage first look at the origins and characteristics of the Russian language. In doing so we are following the Primary Chronicler, who pays a good deal of attention to the linguistic map of Eastern Europe immediately before he discusses how Rus arose.

Russian is of course a Slavonic (or Slav, or Slavic) language, a member of a great and close-knit language family whose speakers occupy most of Eastern, Central and Balkan Europe. Over the course of the last millennium and more these languages have, as is natural, grown away from each other and developed their own idiosyncrasies, yet it may seem surprising how much they retain in common (for everyday purposes they are often intercomprehensible). The process of linguistic differentiation is not yet complete: Ukrainian and Belorussian have separated themselves from Great Russian in a gradual process from the late

Middle Ages to the establishment of independent literatures in the nineteenth century; Macedonian only became widely recognized as more than merely a dialect of Bulgarian a generation or two ago, while it is today a moot (and politically sensitive) point as to whether Serb and Croat should be considered as separate tongues. It is normally nowadays reckoned that there are eleven or twelve living Slavonic languages, divided into three sub-families (the Western – Polish, Czech, Slovak, Sorbian; the Southern – Serbo-Croat, Bulgarian, Macedonian, Slovene; the Eastern – Russian, Ukrainian, Belorussian). The Slavonic languages form one of the major branches of a yet greater language family (the greatest, indeed, in the world: stretching from North India to the Atlantic, and since colonization from Europe across the Americas and Australasia), the Indo-European family. The Slavonic languages are on an equal footing with, for example, the Romance, the Germanic, the Celtic or the Iranian branches of this family, as well as with solitary languages such as Greek, Albanian and Armenian, which are unique surviving representatives of their own 'branches'. To characterize the Slavonic languages in any detail would be outside the scope of this work, but it is worth mentioning that they retain many more grammatical features of early Indo-European (so far as this can be reconstructed) than do, say, the living Germanic or Romance languages. The Slavonic languages are highly inflected: in other words their verbs, pronouns and (save in Bulgarian and Macedonian) adjectives and nouns have a range of case endings to indicate grammatical relationships within the sentence, while the verb system makes great play with the category of 'aspect' – indicating not the temporal sequence of actions but their quality of completeness or duration. Nouns are subject to the apparently arbitrary (but grammatically determined) category of gender. Word-building in these languages proceeds rather logically, with simple 'roots' modified by prefixes and suffixes – in this as in several other respects a learner may find that a grounding in Latin or Ancient Greek is a good preparation for the structures of Slavonic languages. Among the other Indo-European language families the Slavonic is usually considered to stand closest to the Baltic languages (Lithuanian, Latvian, the extinct Old Prussian), which conserve an even more archaic grammatical system, and it is postulated that the proto-Slavonic language must have developed in proximity to the Baltic family for some considerable period.

That such a common Slavonic language once existed, even though it has left no written relics, cannot be in doubt: it has been simple enough for historical linguistics, extrapolating back from the later languages, to reconstruct much of it. But working without the benefit of modern scholarship, the Primary Chronicler at the beginning of the twelfth century was well aware that the Slavs once spoke a single language and still formed a close-knit language family. Referring to the late ninth century, he writes: 'There was one Slavonic people [*yazyk*], ('people' here is literally 'language'): the Slavs who were settled along the Danube and were conquered by the Hungarians, and the Moravians, and the Czechs, and the Poles [*lyakhi*], and the Polyane who are now called Rus'. The earliest common Slavonic territory of which the chronicler was aware was in the neighbourhood of the Danube, from which, as he describes it, several tribes moved outwards to other locations – for example to the neighbourhoods of the Morava and Vistula rivers, to Carinthia, to the forests and fields of southern Russia and to the area of Lake Ilmen.[1] There was indeed such an expansion of Slav tribes as the chronicler recalls in the middle centuries of the first millennium of the Christian era, taking them westwards as far as the River Elbe, southwards into the Balkans even beyond the Gulf of Corinth, and eastwards into Russia. Thus arose, of course, the three sub-families of Western, Southern and Eastern Slavs whom we have already mentioned – whose linguistic distinctions nevertheless took many centuries to become more perceptible than mere differences of dialect.

Modern specialists disagree with the chronicle account in one significant respect – the area from which the Slav expansion or waves of migration began appears not to have been on the banks of the Danube, but further north, around the upper course of the River Vistula in modern Poland, and probably reaching eastwards towards the Dnester and Pripet. The evidence is to some extent archaeological, but mostly linguistic: this is an area where the river names – usually the most archaic and persistent names in any landscape – are of Slavonic origin; it is also an area where trees such as birch and oak, known by similar names in all later Slavonic languages, are native species, but which lies beyond the range of others (e.g. beech, yew) whose Slavonic names turn out to be very early borrowings from the Germanic or other language families, and must therefore have been unfamiliar to the proto-Slavs. This reasoning is ingenious, but it is unclear whether it is fully backed by historical climatology; in any case there is every probability that the Slav 'homeland' at different times expanded or shrank in the period before recorded Slav history in response to pressures from other, more mobile populations in the area. Thus there is no *prima facie* reason to doubt that there was at least a strong Slav element among the Antes or Antae who (as we mentioned Chapter 1) once formed part of the Sarmatian confederation and survived on the wooded steppe for several hundred years until they were obliterated by the Altaic Avars at the beginning of

---

[1] The ancestors of the Novgorodians are often referred to as 'Ilmen Slavs' (*Slovene* or *Sloveni*), though of course they are only one Slav tribe out of many.

the seventh century. The first historians unambiguously to describe the Slavs (Procopius, Jordanes, and the Byzantine Emperor Maurice – to whom is attributed the *Strategicon*), all writing in the sixth century, believed in the kinship of Slavs and Antes, and in their linguistic identity with the Venedi of the Vistula basin.[2] In any case it seems clear that in the turbulent years of the early part and middle of the first millennium the Slavs, until their great migrations began, were well rooted in their east-central European homeland, despite the violent movement of Huns, Bulgars, Avars, Goths and other peoples across the area. Their devotion to agriculture was doubtless their strength. As Marija Gimbutas puts it: 'The invaders, having camped wherever there was good grazing ground for horses, returned to their plains after every campaign, however successful . . . It was the Slavs who did the colonizing; in travelling on foot in vast numbers, they constantly sought an outlet for their population surplus.'[3]

It is the southward thrust of Slav migration that is best documented, since from quite early in the sixth century till the middle of the seventh their raids and major population movements intermittently affected the Eastern Roman (or 'Byzantine') Empire, whose commentators reacted to them with horror mixed with curiosity. Fortified cities could usually withstand Slav attacks, but infiltration in the countryside was another matter. The South Slavs sometimes made common cause against the Byzantines with the Avars, but their most lasting and remarkable alliance was with another Turkic people, the Bulgars. In their wanderings westward this people had split into two groups, each of which (somewhat confusingly) continued to carry the same name. One group moved upstream along the Volga, founding a settled state – that was to play a role in Russian history – in the neighbourhood of the later city of Kazan. The better known branch of the Bulgars moved across the Pontic steppe and over the lower Danube in the late seventh century, imposing its rule on the Slavs who were already there. Their small warrior elite soon adopted the Slavonic language, and thus was born Bulgaria, a powerful medieval state, at times a rival to Byzantium, an important neighbour to old Russia, a nation that has of course lasted into the modern world. The Slavs' expansion westward and eastward by contrast seems to have been a quiet business, and not merely because

---

[2] 'Venedi', that later gave rise to forms such as 'Wendish', is, however, a widely used tribal name that has historically been applied to peoples other than Slavs; it became, apparently, a frequent component of names in several Slavonic languages, e.g. Venceslav or 'Wenceslaus', Vyacheslav, the ancient Russian tribe of Vyatichi.

[3] M. Gimbutas *The Slavs* (London 1974) p. 98.

there were no professional historians to record it: they were moving into relatively empty territory that could absorb a greater settled population. In both south and west the Slav tide eventually receded somewhat from its furthest extent. In most of what is now Greece, the Greek language reasserted itself over Slavonic, though many place names of Slav origin remain (as also in modern Romania, where a language derived from Latin somehow survived). The extent to which the modern mainland Greek population descends from Hellenized Slavs was a matter of controversy in the nineteenth century but is, perhaps fortunately, unknowable (there are Thracian and Illyrian substrata there too). Even more evident Slav place names are found in the eastern parts of Germany, and there two pockets of a Slavonic language (Sorb or Lusatian) are spoken to this day to the west of the River Oder. From the early Middle Ages onward considerable efforts were made to reverse the Slav thrust and to settle Germans east of the Elbe, particularly in the regions close to the Baltic Sea; this eventually took on the character of a partly religiously motivated crusade, whose advance guard was halted by the Russians only in the mid-thirteenth century when it was already close to Novgorod and Pskov.

The sixth-century historians who have just been quoted used the terms 'Sclavini'/'Sthlavenoi' to refer to Slavs. Later these were considered, in Mediterranean Europe, as derivatives of the late Latin *sclavus*, slave, and in a somewhat derogatory way it was often assumed that the Slavs acquired their name from having been frequently enslaved; it is more likely that things were the other way round (*sclavus* < Slav). Doubtless the late antique slave-markets of the Middle East and of Constantinople often had Slavonic victims for sale: this was a standard and profitable way of disposing of prisoners of war. However, there is no reason to think they were more numerous than any other linguistic group in such sad circumstances, and certainly their name is not derived from *sclavus*: the 'c', 'th' were merely added in deference to the phonetic systems of Latin and Greek, which do not tolerate an initial 'sl'. There have been several more or less ingenious explanations of the *slav-/slov-* root that is so widespread among local subdivisions of the Slavonic peoples and provides their overall name. The most obvious derivation remains the most plausible: from the cognate roots, among the most persistent in all the Slavonic languages, *slava* ('glory') and *slovo* ('word'). Nothing could be more natural than a self-designation involving the concept of the 'word' (which has a broader sense than in English, including 'discourse') that is the palpable tie with one's fellows. It is significant that a widespread and ancient designation for 'German' (originally, it would seem, all foreigners) in the Slav languages is *nemets*, 'a person who cannot speak' (cognate with Russian *nemoy*, 'dumb'). The *Slov-* root appears in several Slav tribal names, from the Slovenes at the south-western corner of the Slav world to the Ilmen *Sloveni* of Novgorod at its north-eastern extremity. Equally ancient and also widespread is the root appearing in *Serb* and *Sorb*, possibly cognate too with *khrvat* ( = 'Croat'), which has been interpreted as meaning 'guardian' (probably, of livestock).[4]

All these matters are of historical interest, obviously, but point also to something that seems to have permanent political and even perhaps emotional significance: the long-standing awareness among Slav nations of their familial relationship. 'Pan-Slavism', a political and cultural offshoot of nineteenth-century Romanticism, has in fact deep roots that go back to the Middle Ages (we shall return to the concept of a common Slav literary language in Chapter 4); it was given its modern impetus by the seventeenth-century South Slav traveller in Russia, Juraj Križanić. Awareness of close kinship has not, of course, led to undying affection between the Slav peoples: a glance at Russo-Polish relations since the seventeenth century, or Serb-Croat (and Czech-Slovak) relations in the twentieth century, makes this all too clear. But as irritant or inspiration it is always there in Slav peoples' dealings with each other. On the whole Russian relations with Southern Slavs – notably Bulgarians and Serbs – have been close and cordial, particularly after the Turkish conquest of the Balkans (late fourteenth to fifteenth centuries) and during the nineteenth century national independence movements. But despite rivalries there was also much cooperation between Poland and Russia from the later seventeenth to the early eighteenth centuries, and indeed a considerable Polish influence on Russia at this important turning-point of its cultural and political history. Russia was important to Czechs as a counterweight to Germanization at the time when they were struggling to preserve their culture and eventually to set up a state; to the earlier Croat Juraj Križanić (mentioned above), as to the even earlier South Slav thinker Konstantin of Kostenets (early fifteenth century), Russia seemed the repository of true Slav culture.

To return to the expansion and migrations of the early Slavs: our primary business in tracing the history of what were to become the Russian language and the land of Rus itself is with the easterly wave of expansion (though it is worth noting that specialists have proposed, on the grounds of certain features in the dialects of Novgorod and Pskov, that a lesser component of West Slavs reached that area too through the

[4] There are vexed problems surrounding both the origins of these names and the first nations – in central, rather than southern Europe – to have been designated by them: see for example F. Dvornik *The Making of Central and Eastern Europe* (London, 1949), Appendix I.

Baltic lands). As we have seen there was probably a Slav presence on the wooded steppe of what is now Ukraine in Sarmatian times; however the great easterly thrust of Slavs onto the Russian lands had to await the middle centuries of the first millennium, since it was effectively blocked in the early centuries of the Christian era by a powerful and warlike people who occupied the important corridor between the southern Baltic and north-western corner of the Black Sea: the Goths. This highly mobile East-Germanic nation (that has left its name in Gothenburg and in the Baltic island of Gotland) divided into two main branches, of which one, the Visigoths, became a notable menace to the later Roman Empire (their westerly migration took them to Northern Italy and as far as Spain); the other, the Ostrogoths, controlled East-Central Europe till their power was broken by the invasion of the nomadic Huns from the steppe in AD 375. Eastern Slavdom abutted on the Ostrogothic territories over a long period, and a few important Germanic loan words, including some in the areas of domestic, financial and military life, probably date from the period of that encounter. The Gothic language (that provided the earliest written Germanic texts) soon faded from Western Europe, but survived in the East for many centuries; its last stronghold was the Crimea, where it was still spoken in the eighteenth century. From the fifth century, however, the Gothic presence was no longer (after the East-West passage of the Huns) a barrier to the East Slavs in their fateful expansion.

If the primitive Slav society was familial or based on clans, by the time it moved east it was coalescing into larger tribal units, doubtless many thousands strong. The Primary Chronicler names about a dozen such tribes (it is not always clear where two names apply to the same basic group), and is able to distinguish them clearly not only from the Finnic, Baltic and Altaic peoples next to whom they settled, but also from the various West and South Slavs (*Lyakhi* or Poles, Czechs, 'White Croats' etc.). Tribal units, after their eastward wanderings, settled down more or less fixedly in territories often defined by river basins; sometimes they subdivided, established citadels that might become towns and began to be regarded as political rather than kinship entities. The chronicler identifies, and to some extent describes, in the first place, his forebears the Polyane ('field people'), who settled the area of Kiev on the middle Dnieper. South-west of them dwelt the Tivertsy (who, squeezed out by steppe invaders, later moved to the sub-Carpathian area of modern Ukraine). A little inland were the Buzhane, around the River Bug, who later became known as the Volhynians when their territory became a political unit. North-west of Kiev, on either side of the Pripet marshes, were the Derevlyane ('forest people') and the Dregovichi. Due north were the Krivichi, whose headquarters was to be Smolensk, and further north still the Ilmen Sloveni of Novgorod. To the north-east were Radimichi and Severyane (who sprang from the Krivichi, we are told). The spearhead of East Slav expansion was represented by the Vyatichi, who moved into the then remote regions of the northern mixed forest between the Oka and the Volga. Thus a great wedge of East Slav tribes, thinly spread but in direct contact with each other, moved a thousand or more kilometres north-eastwards from the Baltic-Black Sea corridor.

Scattered among and adjoining these Slav tribes (who as we have seen were basically agriculturalists) were the earlier inhabitants of the country, primarily hunter-gatherers and stock-breeders. Evidently all were few in number and able to coexist with the Slavs (indeed to intermarry) without excessive competition for resources. Many of these mostly small peoples were incorporated into Rus as it was consolidated, and the chronicler, after setting out a (shortened) list of Russian tribes of Slavonic tongue, goes on 'And these are the other peoples (literally 'tongues') who pay tribute to Rus: Chud, Merya, Ves, Muroma, Cheremis, Mordva, Perm, Pechera, Yam, Litva, Zimegola, Kors, Norova (=Narva) and Lib (=Livonians): these have their own languages.' These peoples – all Finnic or Baltic – include some that are still well-known (the Chud were the forebears of the modern Estonians); the chronicler might also have included the *golyad* or Galindians, an isolated Baltic tribe who remained identifiable at least till the twelfth century in the very middle of Rus, on the Protva River between Moscow and Smolensk.

The chronicler's ethnographic interests extend to an examination of the customs of the individual East Slavonic tribes that went to make up Rus. Warming to his theme, he then widens the investigation to anecdotal accounts of various nations ancient and modern, primarily through a quoted passage from the Byzantine historian George Hamartolos (whom he cites by name). But the account of East Slav tribal customs remains more interesting and valuable, even though it is presumably based on hearsay and tradition largely relating to the already distant pre-Christian past. The Polyane (who, living where Kiev was later to be, were doubtless the chronicler's own ancestors) come out best:

'Each of these tribes had individual customs and ancestral laws and traditions, and each its own temperament. The Polyane retain the mild and peaceful habits of their forefathers, and modesty towards their daughters-in-law and sisters, towards their mothers and parents . . . Whereas the Drevlyane lived in bestial fashion, lived like cattle, used to kill each other, ate all sorts of unclean things, and they had no marriages but used to abduct girls by the water, while the Radimichi, the Vyatichi and Severyane had a common tradition: they lived in the forest like wild animals, ate everything unclean and spoke indecently in front of their fathers and daughters-in-law. And they had no marriages, but they used to hold village festivities, used to meet together at these festivities for dancing and all sorts of devilish singing, and there they used to abduct wives for themselves with their agreement: they had two or three wives each. And if anyone died, they would organize a funeral feast, and then build a great pile of wood and lay the corpse on it and burn it, and afterwards would gather up the bones and put them in a little urn and set it up on a post by the wayside, as the Vyatichi do to this day. This sort of custom was maintained by the Krivichi and other pagan people who did not know God's law, but created law for themselves'.[5]

A migratory expansion such as that of the early Slavs (as later, *mutatis mutandis*, of the Vikings and Mongols) is a dynamic process that unavoidably produces changes in the society that undergoes it. Once they were settled on more or less defined territory, what should their property rights and socio-political order be? How would they relate to the international circumstances that their own migrations had played a part in creating? Could (or should) the small units of clan-based or tribal society overcome – or be forced to overcome – their differences and sink their independence in larger political entities? What systems of authority and belief-system were appropriate, and how could they be established? Each of the three great branches of Slavdom (not just the Eastern one) faced such questions from the eighth century onwards (whether or not they were consciously formulated in such terms). Each of the three had historical moments when it was, or might have been, possible to weld their peoples into a large and powerful single state. In no case has this endured permanently; the East Slavs came closest to realizing such a project. The West Slavs attempted it first, with the alliance of princedoms that formed 'Greater Moravia' during the eighth to ninth centuries on the modern Czech, Slovak, Hungarian, Austrian and some adjoining territories; the arrival of the Magyars (*c*.900) on the Hungarian plain caused its disintegration. A little later there arose the possibility, never quite realized, of a joint Czech-Polish state that would have been a formidable bulwark against Germanic expansionism.[6] In the south, the Bulgarians twice formed powerful Balkan empires, but the most promising attempt came in the fourteenth century with the Serbian ruler Stefan Dushan, whose early death frustrated it. The East Slavs formed a greater, more or less united state as Kievan Rus – at least at first – and again only from the late eighteenth to the early twentieth century. It hardly needs saying that the historical destiny of Russia, and much of

---

[5]　Later anthropological sources attest to the survival of some of these marriage and funeral practices (as also to such details as incest with daughters-in-law and abduction 'by the water'). As for 'unclean' foods, the chronicler subsequently (with reference to the Polovtsians) gives 'hamsters and marmots' as examples. It may or may not be relevant that these animals were subsequently carriers of the plague.

[6]　See Dvornik *The Making of Central and Eastern Europe*, Conclusion.

the theme of this book, is tied up with this enterprise, and it remains a painfully relevant matter at the time of writing.

## The Origins of Rus

The Primary Chronicler, it would seem, was interested in the historical moment when the East Slavs' migrations had ceased (or slowed down) and a unified system of rule was soon to be imposed. Three times in his opening pages he introduces a new topic with the curious phrase 'When the Polyane were living separately/apart/by themselves . . . ' (the old Russian word is *osobe* – Cross uses the two latter translations). It has been acutely argued that what is undoubtedly meant is 'were leading an independent tribal existence';[7] on one occasion we are given the additional information that they were controlling their own clans and living on their own pieces of land. This is immediately followed by an account of the founding of the city of Kiev (supposedly by one Kiy, his brothers and their sister). It seems more than merely symbolically relevant that the founding of a strongpoint that would become a city is stressed at this point: such strongpoints, giving protection from the raids by steppe nomads (or indeed other Slav tribes) were a prerequisite for settled life. A Bavarian geographer writing in the eleventh century (i.e. before the Primary Chronicler) cites improbably large numbers of towns among some of the tribes exposed to the south – these could have been no more than simple *refugia*, but had the potential to grow into towns as we understand the concept: trading, craft and administrative centres with significant permanent populations. When in the eighth to the ninth century Viking adventurers came to know Russia, they called the land *Gardariki*, 'Land of Cities'; an ironic designation in view of the notoriously rural nature of Russia through most of its history, of its tiny proportion of urban population and general lack of separate urban institutions, but understandable if 'city' here meant something more like 'enclosure' or 'stockade'. Incidentally the story of how Kiev was founded shows the chronicler as an intelligent critical historian: he gives different accounts of the tale and explains why he accepts one of them (the same happens at other points in his narrative).

More significant still, however, is the famous passage, also introduced by the words 'When the Polyane were living independently . . . ', where the chronicler places Old Russia in a world-geographical context. This passage, extremely important for our understanding of how Rus saw its

---

[7] D. Ward 'From the Varangians to the Greeks' in *Gorski Vijenac*, a Festschrift for Dame Elizabeth Hill (MHRA, London, 1970).

place in the greater scheme of things, mentions the Vikings, the Byzantine Greeks and the central Asian powers which together made up the great triangle of cultural and political forces within which (and in tension with which) Rus developed its own civilization. Since it has been often misunderstood by commentators, it is worth providing a translation that attempts to stick as closely to the Old Russian text as possible, though using modern place names, with a few glosses.

'When the Polyane were living independently on the hills [i.e. around Kiev], it was possible to travel from the Vikings to the [Byzantine] Greeks, and from the Greeks along the Dnieper, and at the headwaters of the Dnieper there is a portage to the Lovat, and along the Lovat to get to the great lake of Ilmen; out of this lake flows the Volkhov, and flows into the great lake Nevo [i.e. Ladoga], and the estuary from that lake flows into the Viking Sea [i.e. the Baltic]. And by that sea one can go to Rome, and from Rome arrive by the same sea to Constantinople, and from Constantinople get to the Pontic [i.e. Black] Sea, into which the River Dnieper flows. Now the Dnieper flows out of Okovsky Forest, and flows southwards, while the Dvina flows out of the same forest, and goes towards the north and flows into the Viking Sea. From the same forest the Volga flows to the east and enters the Caspian Sea through seventy mouths. In this way one can go directly from Rus along the Volga to the Bulgars and to Khorezm [i.e. Central Asia], and eastwards reach the lands of Shem [one of the sons of Noah, progenitor of the Semitic peoples], and along the Dvina to the Vikings, and from the Vikings to Rome, and from Rome to the people of Ham [another of the sons of Noah – Africa is meant]. Whereas the Dnieper's estuary flows into the Pontic Sea – on whose shores St Andrew, the brother of St Peter, once taught, so they say.'

Rich in information as it is, this passage does not stand in isolation; nor, self-evidently, is it merely an account of a trade-route called 'the way from the Varangians [i.e. Vikings] to the Greeks', as commentators tend to take it. It is placed immediately following the account of how, after the Biblical flood, the world was divided between the three sons of Noah (Ham received the southern lands, Shem the eastern, Japheth the northern and western), and of how the Slav tribes (from the line of Japheth) migrated from their supposed Danubian homeland. It is immediately followed by the remarkable tale of how St Andrew, preaching at Sinope and Kherson (or Chersonesus) on the Black Sea, conceived a desire to travel to Rome by a huge circuitous route: from the estuary of the Dnieper, past the hills on which Kiev will one day stand (he blesses them and foretells Kiev's great future), past Novgorod where he observes the bathhouses and to Rome where he makes his curious and comic disquisition on the Novgorodians' bathing habits (quoted earlier, p. 32); he completes his great circular journey round Europe by returning to Sinope. It cannot, I believe, be merely accidental that the only two stopping-points of the saint that merit any description are Kiev and Novgorod – not only are they (and the route between them) the axis of the Old Russian state: given the pagan cult connotations of the bathhouse that were described earlier (p. 33), a contrast between the pagan and Christian heritage of Rus must surely be intended (this would be a microcosm of the overall structure of the Primary Chronicle about which we shall have more to say).

The Primary Chronicler's 'symbolic geography' thus sees Rus in dynamic terms – first in terms of the movement of Slav peoples eastward, then in terms of the north-south and south-north movement of people between the Greek and Viking lands, and also as one sector of the great journey round the periphery of Europe. Then, however, he focusses on Rus itself, and views it in terms of the connexions southward, northward and eastwards from its heartland, the Okovsky Forest with its portages between the headwaters of its great rivers. In the myth of St Andrew's journey there is also, surely, a subtle foreshadowing (as often in the Primary Chronicle) of a later great event: in this case, the Christianization of Russia under St Vladimir. Andrew's journey takes him from Kherson (Chersonesus) via the site of Holy Kiev to pagan Novgorod; Vladimir, while still a pagan, will reverse the journey, coming from

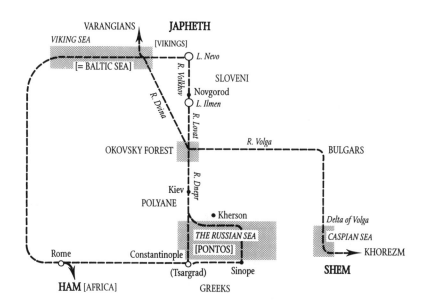

*Figure 4   The Primary Chronicler's 'symbolic geography' (based on the account in early pages of the* Tale of Bygone Years*).*

Novgorod to the throne of Kiev and going to Kherson to receive
Christianity.

When we look outwards from Rus at the beginning of its history, then
we see three major directions to which its attention turned: north-
westwards, southwards and south-eastwards; and three major (non-Slav)
powers that constituted a 'triangle of forces' within which its early
development could take place: respectively, the Vikings, the Greeks (i.e.
the Byzantine Empire) and the Khazars. The Vikings first penetrated Rus,
as other parts of Europe, with a view to plunder or trade; they gave it
large horizons, central rule and a certain dynamism. The Byzantine
Empire exercized its influence mostly at a remove, though for much
longer, providing Rus from the late tenth century onwards with the
matrix in which its subsequent culture developed. About both Byzantines
and Vikings we shall have more to say. The Khazars are less known, and
fade into insignificance during the tenth century, but have an interesting
place in early medieval history. The descendents of Turkic steppe peoples
who (as was to happen again and again) exchanged a nomadic for a
settled life, by the beginning of Russian history they had established their
state on a broad wedge of territory from the Caucasus northwards,
encompassing the lower courses of the Volga and Don (and with them a
variety of ethnic groups). For a couple of hundred years the Khazars kept

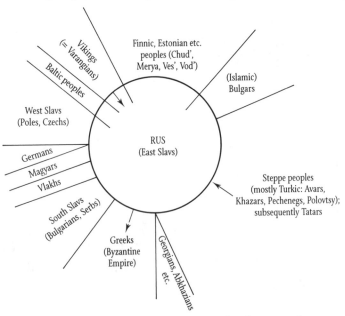

*Figure 5   Diagrammatic representation of early Rus and
neighbouring peoples (from a Rus viewpoint).*

the peace in the steppe country (this period in the eighth and ninth centuries is sometimes termed the *Pax Khazarica*, on the lines of *Pax Romana*). The Khazars absorbed and in 737 turned back the northward thrust of the great two-pronged Arab attack that in the century after the death of the Prophet carried them through the Near and Middle East to Central Asia, Persia and Anatolia. The synchronous westward thrust of course went the length of North Africa, through Spain, and was halted, also in the 730s, by Charles Martel in Central France: without the Khazars, would not the armies of militant Islam have penetrated equally far into Eastern and Central Europe? Some at least of the East Slav tribes were tributaries of Khazaria, and it is interesting that early rulers of Rus took on the Khazar title of 'Khagan', suggesting they saw themselves in some sense as the Khazars' successors. They also adopted a trident-shaped *tamga*, authority symbol, widely used by Khazar rulers (it has now become the badge of modern independent Ukraine). To put a stop to the last payments of tribute, the Russian ruler Svyatoslav marched against the Khazars in the 960s: already weakened, their international power was destroyed. Rus could not, however, hold down the steppe corridor, along which other mobile invaders (Pechenegs, Polovtsians) could now move unhindered and harass its southern flank.

Khazaria was important to Rus as an exemplar of the benefits of controlling long-distance trade routes in a well-ordered, multi-ethnic state. It was also a cultural melting pot. The Byzantines (until Khazaria's decline) favoured it as a bulwark against possible threats to their north-eastern outposts along the Black Sea: they sent engineers to construct its fortress-city of Sarkel on the lower Don, and harboured hopes of its Christianization. Some Khazar vassals – notably the Bulgars on the middle Volga – converted to Islam. But the religion that made most headway among the previously pagan Khazar ruling class – apparently from the time of the Arab invasion, though becoming dominant only in the ninth century – was Judaism. Khazaria thus presents the unusual picture (since Judaism was not normally a proselytizing faith) of a large, officially Jewish state a good thousand miles distant from Palestine. The ultimate disintegration of Khazaria is poorly recorded, and some historians (most famously the late Arthur Koestler) have speculated that the large medieval Jewish population in East-Central Europe is at least partly a Khazar legacy.

The Khazars and (a little later) Byzantine Greeks exercised their pull on the nascent Russian politico-cultural consciousness from a distance: the Vikings, the third group of outsiders involved, were there at its birth. The problem of Viking participation in the establishment of Rus is so important, and has been so contentious that it must be examined in some detail. By 'Vikings' (a term whose origin is still in dispute) we mean the people of Scandinavia – Denmark, Norway and Sweden – otherwise known as 'Norsemen', 'Normans', in their remarkable expansionist phase, lasting for approximately the ninth, tenth and to a lesser extent eleventh centuries. 'Viking' seems primarily a Western European term – in the East the Scandinavian adventurers were known as 'Varangians' (Greek *varangoi*, Russian *varyagi*), which may derive from *vaeringjar*, 'trading agent' or 'wanderer'. The reasons for the Viking expansion (as with other such great expansionist episodes in history – e.g. that of the Mongols later on and indeed that of the Slavs earlier) is rather mysterious. The Scandinavians were not threatened with displacement by some other people – a frequent cause of mass migration. Population pressure in their northerly lands with limited agricultural resources must have played a part (to the south they were blocked by the strong Frankish kingdom that became Charlemagne's Holy Roman Empire in 800). In any case, success bred emulation, once it became clear what power a fairly small number of tough and ruthless warriors swiftly transported in longboats could wield. The early Viking adventures in the West were generally raids of plunder (north-east England was an early victim of these, from the 790s); sometimes these were accompanied by wars of conquest. Soon the Vikings were appearing in the less destructive roles of colonizers and traders: the spread of Islam and consequent crisis in the Mediterranean trade gave northern Europeans new opportunities in the latter role. The most advanced of the Scandinavian peoples were the Swedes, and it is likely (from archaeological evidence) that they had already ventured across the Baltic to lands on its eastern seaboard in the pre-Viking period. They reached the territories that would become Rus via the Gulf of Finland: a sign that their original trading interests lay in an easterly direction, towards the Volga and the Caspian Sea; had they wished in the first instance to reach Constantinople, routes via the Gulf of Riga or even further west would have been much shorter. In any case the lands at, and beyond, the head of the Gulf of Finland were thinly populated and they could establish themselves there without meeting much resistance. Their first major base seems to have been at Aldeigjuborg, now Old Ladoga, on the river Volkhov close to where it flows into Lake Ladoga. This is the junction of the greatest early Viking river-routes: eastwards through Lake Onega and the White Lake to the Sheksna, a tributary of the Volga, and southwards past the minor impediment of the Volkhov rapids to Lake Ilmen, at whose outflow Novgorod was to develop in the tenth century as a great entrepôt and meeting-place of Vikings and Slavs. At the opposite (south) end of Ilmen stands the ancient town of Staraya (=Old) Russa, whose curious name has suggested to some historians that it must be the site of one of the earliest urban centres of Rus. Beyond it, rivers flow from the area of the

Valday Hills and Okovsky Forest, where there are portages giving access to several other river systems, in particular that of the southward-flowing Dnieper. This river is reached in the neighbourhood of the later fortress-city of Smolensk, whose ancient predecessor at Gnyozdovo appears to have been another Viking base. But, despite the discovery of Viking cemeteries in Rus, we have no evidence of peasant colonization by Norsemen as in parts of Western Europe, Iceland etc.[8]

Viking leaders whose names have come down to us (Askold and Dir – in Scandinavian, probably Höskuld and Dyri) established themselves among the Slav Polyane tribe at Kiev, on the middle Dnieper, in the mid-ninth century: thence they launched their celebrated surprise attack on Constantinople in June 860 – which may be considered the entry of Russians into the historical record. In the aftermath of this raid, incidentally, the Byzantines succeeded (if we are to believe the Patriarch Photius) in converting a substantial portion of the attackers to Christianity. By that date they (and maybe their land too) were undoubtedly known by the name 'Rus'. How long this name had already been current, and how it arose, is far from clear, however. There are some tantalizing fragments of evidence, at any rate two of which refer to the period before 860. The earliest of all is a strange and circumstantial account in the Western European (Frankish) Bertinian Annals, referring to an episode that took place in 839, when there came to the Carolingian court at Ingelheim some envoys sent by the Byzantine Emperor Theophilus, who

'also sent with them certain men who said they were called Rhos, and that their king, known as chacanus [i.e.khagan], had dispatched them to him [Theophilus], for the sake of friendship, as they had asserted. He [Theophilus] asked . . . that the emperor [the Frankish Louis the Pious] allow them to return home across his possessions since the roads by which they had come to Constantinople were cut by wild and ferocious tribes and he [Theophilus] did not want them to face danger in case of returning by the same route. The Emperor [Louis] investigated diligently the cause of their coming and discovered they were Swedes by origin'.[9]

Several points are worthy of attention if we wish to use this account to

[8] For an up-to-date account of the state of archaeological knowledge on these matters, see S. Franklin and J. Shepard *The Emergence of Rus* 750–1200 (London, 1996), Part 1. Shepard stresses the importance of Arab silver coinage for the eastward Viking expansion. There is a judicious summary of the state of the debate about Viking expansion in R. H. C. Davies *Early Medieval Europe* (London, 1988) 2nd edn only.

[9] Translation from G. Vernadsky *A Source-book for Russian History I* (New Haven and London, 1972), slightly amended with reference to J. L. Nelson (ed.) *The Annals of St Bertin* (Manchester, 1991) p. 44.

help us pinpoint the origins of Rus. First, though the Bertinian Annals are in Latin, the Greek form 'Rhos' is used (a form deriving from the Hebrew *Rosh*, as Dvornik established – see note 1, Chapter 1); either the author of this part of the annals (Prudentius, Bishop of Troyes) quotes the form of the name used by Theophilus and his Greek envoys, or the Swedes themselves, when interrogated, used the name by which they had been known in Constantinople, rather than in any Scandinavian form or in Latin (which seems odd). Prudentius' text reaches to the year 861, so it could be subsequent upon the date of the first Russian attack on Constantinople, when 'Rhos' was (as we have seen) used of the attackers. These Swedes' king was a 'khagan', an Asiatic title: thus either they were in the service of the Khazar ruler, or their own ruler had adopted a Khazar title (as some later princes of Kiev were to do). It is also clear that in 839 Rhos/Rus was a name unfamiliar in Western Europe – otherwise the interrogation would have been superfluous. Evidently the Byzantine Theophilus was well disposed towards the men, which suggests they were envoys in the service of the Khazars, though presumably with their roots still in Sweden if they wished to return there. History does not relate whether they managed to do so, incidentally: the Holy Roman Empire was far from friendly towards Vikings, who at the time were harassing its northern flanks.

The incident related in the Bertinian Annals lends itself to various interpretations. The Scandinavian scholar A. Stender-Petersen saw it as implying the existence of a 'Kaganate', an organized state, in Northern Russia at the time. This seems to me far-fetched, though clearly it (and a couple of Byzantine saints' lives that refer, less reliably, to 'Russian' raids in the Black Sea area in the same century) reflect Viking exploration of the Volga and Don river systems; these rivers come close enough to each other in the southern steppe for easy portages between them to be possible at any time of year. Another very early source, the 'Book of Routes and Kingdoms' by the Arab ibn-Kurdadhbih (*c*.846–7), surprisingly identifies the 'Russians' not as Scandinavians but Slavs: 'The Russians are a tribe of Slavs. They bring furs of beavers and black foxes, as well as swords, from the most distant part of the land of the Slavs to the Black Sea where the ruler of the Greeks collects a tithe. If they like, they go via the Slavic River [the Don] to Hamlih [on the Volga], a city of the Khazars.'[10] It would appear that as early as the first half of the ninth century there was a regularized Slav-Viking trade network set up with both Khazaria and Byzantium, long before the famous Russo-Byzantine

[10]   G. Vernadsky *A Source-book for Russian History* p. 9; T. Lewicki *Zrodla arabskie do dziejów slowlańszczyzny* I (Warsaw, 1956), p. 77 (text in Arabic and Polish).

trade treaties of 911 and 944 whose terms are recorded in the Primary Chronicle. By the tenth century, of course, there are many references to Rus or Rhos in non-Russian sources. The majority seem to refer to Scandinavians: most famously, the list of the Dnieper rapids provided by the Byzantium Emperor Constantine Porphyrogenitus in his work *On the Imperial Administration* (usually known as *De administrando imperio*, though it was written in Greek), of the mid-tenth century, provides both 'Russian' and 'Slavonic' names, of which the former are indisputably Old Scandinavian.

Nevertheless we cannot simply follow the Primary Chronicler and say that Rus was the name of a tribe of Varangians on a par with Swedes, English (*sic*) or Gotlanders, so that 'on account of these Varangians the Russian land received its name' – and not just because of counter-indications in sources such as Ibn-Kurdadhbih and occasionally in the Primary and Novgorod Chronicles themselves. The name 'Rus' is unknown as a tribal name in the Viking lands; curiously, it seems early to have been attached rather to the area around Kiev rather than that around the Gulf of Finland where the Vikings actually arrived. The difficulties are reduced if we cease looking for a specifically ethnic, or indeed territorial, meaning for the word. Here the Finnish name for the Swedes, *Ruotsi*, is a useful clue. It appears to derive from a Scandinavian/Germanic root *rod-*, implying 'to row [a boat]', so to the earliest inhabitants of the area of the Gulf of Finland – and by extension to the Slavs whose migrations took them to the same area – Swedes or Vikings were perceived in their role of 'rowers' (the modern English 'row' and 'rudder' are cognate) or water travellers. 'Rus', in short, when the term arose some time before the mid-ninth century, seems to have had dynamic connotations as a cooperative venture of Vikings, Slavs and Finns – later some Turkic people too – who had come together to exploit natural resources and trading (to some extent colonizing) possibilities on the eastern side of the Baltic: it meant the establishment of a new kind of political entity in early medieval Europe. At its very inception, then, Rus was multi-ethnic, and the implications for later Russian history are not negligible.

## The People and Government of Rus

Much attention has been devoted by Western (perhaps even more than Russian) scholarship to the socio-political history and institutions of Russia. This volume certainly cannot aim to compete with the specialists in the field, and its general orientation is anyhow somewhat different. Nevertheless there are good reasons why, having looked quite closely at the origins of the state of Rus, we should trace – if only in outline – its subsequent destiny. Russian self-perception and cultural status are clearly bound up with questions of the nature of Russian government and society. Russia provides an intriguing model of historical development eccentric to the more familiar European (or, for that matter, Asiatic) patterns. This may not be an unmixed historical success story, but equally it does not deserve to be regarded (in the simplistic terms towards which even some of the best-known commentators have tended) as a kind of Dostoyevskian political morality tale of an inexorable progression from unlimited freedom to unlimited tyranny. The structures of government that grew up and underwent radical modifications in Russia over the course of its long history were often oppressive, occasionally bizarre, but generally represented a response to massive external or internal threats that had somehow to be met. An ever-present factor in Russia's socio-political history was its great size, with its concomitant difficulties of communication, unstable frontiers, thinly spread population and risk of ungovernability. Even Catherine II in her 'Great Instruction' (*nakaz*) of 1767 – an astonishing, comprehensive and highly educative digest of libertarian political ideas – assumed that Russia, on account of its size, had to be ruled with absolute powers.[11]

The early Slavs (if we are to believe the sixth-century historians mentioned earlier; see p. 41) made decisions democratically. When the forebears of the Russians, having migrated eastwards, settled down to a 'tribal' existence (whatever that may have meant) they doubtless had some social differentiation and certainly had leaders, but not much more can be said for lack of contemporary evidence. Many modern historians consider that the customary law recorded in writing from early Kievan times goes back to the period before the concept of 'Rus' arose, and the same may be true of the *obshchina* or village commune. According to some early chronicles a legendary leader called Gostomysl invited Viking rulers into northern Russia, saying that the land was rich but had no order in it: such events however are a mythic commonplace in the supposed early history of various lands and their dynasties. To equip the Viking adventurers who began administering Rus in the ninth century with adequate credentials to secure their prestige, the chroniclers fitted them out with a fantastical pedigree from an invented brother (Prus) of the first Roman Emperor, Augustus. The legendary 'invitation' to the Vikings gave rise to a literary comic masterpiece in the nineteenth century (that is more than just comic): A. K. Tolstoy's ballad 'History of the Russian Land from Gostomysl to Timashev'. The reputed founder of

[11]   For a translation of the *nakaz*, see P. Dukes (ed.) *Russia under Catherine the Great: Select Documents* (London, 1977–8)

the Varangian (i.e. Viking) dynasty Ryurik – not recorded in any source earlier than the *Tale of Bygone Years* – was accompanied by his two brothers Truvor and Sineus whom he supposedly settled in Izborsk and Belozersk (on the White Lake) respectively: again no doubt a mythic motif, signalling the importance of the trade routes leading not just south from Novgorod, but south-westwards and eastwards. A later chronicle, known to contain a good deal of hearsay material that did not get into the *Tale of Bygone Years*, briefly records an unsuccessful rebellion in Novgorod led by 'the brave Vadim' against Ryurik's Varangians, an episode controversially exploited by nationalistic Russian writers from the late eighteenth century onwards.[12]

Generally, though, the establishment of the Varangians' rule seems to have taken place without causing serious tensions between themselves and the Slavs, Balts and Finnic peoples with whom they established Rus as an enterprise and political entity. Presumably it brought security and a growth of prosperity without causing any great cultural disturbance or economic rivalries. In Richard Pipes's striking formulation, the Norman (i.e. Varangian or Viking) state in Russia 'resembled the great merchant enterprises of seventeenth- and eighteenth-century Europe, such as the East India or Hudson's Bay companies, founded to make money but compelled by the absence of any administration to assume quasi-governmental responsibilities'.[13] The first two rulers who seem to have had a more sophisticated concept of Rus as a state were also the first two to be Christians – the regent Olga (who in the mid-tenth century put tax-gathering on a systematic footing and established a defensive network of forts) and her grandson Vladimir I. Between them came Svyatoslav, who despite his Slav name was a true Viking wanderer-warrior, and briefly (late 960s) controlled the first 'Russian empire' – a vast and untenable territory stretching from the Bulgars on the Volga to those in the Balkans and from the Baltic to the steppe-lands of Khazaria. He had so little sense of Rus as a defined geographical location or a state in the modern sense that he left relatives to keep order in Kiev and other towns while setting up his own capital at Pereyaslavets (somewhere on the lower Danube), since, as the chronicler quotes him, 'that is the centre of my realm and all merchandise is brought there: gold, silks, wine and various fruits from the Greeks, silver and horses from Hungary and the Czechs, and from Russia furs, wax, honey and slaves'. The small detached Russian principality of Tmutorokan by the Black Sea may be a legacy of his conquests.

It has often been suggested that the Ryurikids regarded the manage-ment of Rus as a family business: at the end of each reign there was often

[12] See A. Wachtel *An Obsession with History* (Stanford, 1994).
[13] R. Pipes *Russia under the Old Regime* (London, 1974) p. 31.

*Figure 6   Early Rus, with main pre-Tatar towns and centres of principalities (eleventh century) indicated.*

fierce competition among relatives for the chief prize of Kiev, leading to frequent internecine warfare. A prince of Kiev would appoint (generally) his brothers to other principalities, among which Chernigov and Pereyaslavl were reckoned the senior (apart from Novgorod, where special considerations applied). At times it looks as if a lateral system of succession, from brother to brother (with other princes 'moving up' a step), was operated – but if so it took place quite informally and inconsistently. Indeed an unwelcome aspect of the Varangian heritage in Russia was its lack of a formalized and equitable succession system: it can be argued that over a millennium, from the mid-ninth to the mid-nineteenth century, the occasions on which there was a smooth and unchallenged succession to princely or monarchical power were rare, and the various attempts to arrange a trouble-free succession system all ran into difficulties. Unigeniture never made much headway either on a royal level or among the population at large: even Peter the Great could not enforce it permanently. Another baneful legacy of the Ryurikids (much stressed by Pipes, though not all historians are as insistent on it as he is) was a 'patrimonial' attitude towards their dominions, regarding the land and its people as resources to be exploited rather than as a sacred responsibility – though it should be said that from time to time rulers appeared who took a more statesmanlike attitude and clearly enjoyed popular legitimation. Already in the eleventh century a concept of the 'Land of Rus' as a nation with its own integrity and divinely ordered destiny is reflected in the Primary Chronicle, where under the year 1097 a vivid and detailed account of the kidnapping and blinding of a minor prince, Vasilko of Terebovl, condemns the squalid episode as a stain on the land of Rus (invoked half-a-dozen times in the course of a single page).

Unlike the 'tribal' East Slavs, so-called Kievan Rus has left a great deal of written information on the ordering of its society. The trouble is that no-one is quite sure how to interpret much of it: we have the words for many different social classes, but often little more than tantalizing hints as to how they related to each other. It is generally agreed that there were bondsmen (*kholopy*) – maybe of several kinds – whom some commentators regard as slaves: they were often members, sometimes crucial members, of the princely household. Bondage might be voluntarily entered into, particularly by debtors, and worked off. Whether serfdom, such as later became characteristic of Russia, existed separately is a moot point: probably it did not. It is however clear that the bulk of the population consisted of free farmers, able to migrate at will. At the top of society those who served in the various princes' retinues were also completely free to change their allegiance and place of residence. The retinue or *druzhina* was both a bodyguard and an advisory council to a prince – the progenitor of the later 'boyar council' that persisted until Peter the Great. Some popular oral literature and early chronicle tales reflect a society when access to the *druzhina* must have been in principle open to anyone of sufficient bravery and quick-wittedness (the epic 'golden age' of Vladimir I, known in folk poetry as the 'Bright Sun', is so presented); quite soon though it must have become a self-perpetuating aristocracy. During the tenth century the Viking element in the Ryurikid family and its retinues must have been 'slavicizing' itself more and more, in habitual Viking fashion; as Allan Brown, the historian of Norman England, put it, Normans tended to 'assimilate themselves out of existence'. Yet we cannot nowadays even say what language predominated at the court of Yaroslav, Vladimir's son (1019–1054). Despite his Slav name and his reputation as a beacon of Orthodox Slavonic learning, Yaroslav appears frequently in the Norse sagas, married a Swedish wife, and Vikings stayed regularly in his capital on their way between Scandinavia and the Byzantine lands. Northern European connexions were kept up by the Ryurikids till well into the twelfth century (Vladimir II Monomakh, Prince of Kiev 1113–25, married the daughter of Harald, last Saxon king of England). But the signature of Anna, Yaroslav's daughter, who married King Henry I of France and subsequently the Count of Valois, survives in Cyrillic script (her husbands were illiterate).

An important role was played in the society of Kievan (and, to a lesser extent, later) Rus by the various classes of townspeople. At the top were travelling merchants, who might be (or be accompanied by) armed warriors; there were also sedentary traders and craftspeople, some of them members of the free guilds, some indentured; and there were the churchpeople, including not only priests and monks but, for example, cantors, teachers and doctors. Old Russian towns may have been nearly all very small in population by modern standards, but were vital for the economic viability of so extensive and vulnerable a realm. George Vernadsky has tellingly pointed out the differences in Rus from the situation in Western Europe, where incipient feudalism was centred not on cities but on a manorial system with institutionalized serfdom. The main Old Russian towns were the capitals of principalities, in which after the mid-eleventh century various branches of the Ryurikid family were tempted to put down roots to form their own local princely dynasties. Rus became a loose federation of more or less independent territories, some of which (Novgorod, Polotsk) developed their own foreign policy. The throne of Kiev remained the chief prize for the ruling dynasty, however, until Andrey Bogolyubsky (1157–74) decided to keep Vladimir in the north-east as his seat of power and sent a force to sack the old capital (1169). Kiev was never the same again; but when Andrey tried to subdue Novgorod the following year he was unsuccessful, and the defeat of 'the men of Suzdal by the men of Novgorod' became a defining moment of Novgorodian self-consciousness, to the extent that it was the subject of many later icons.

In fact Novgorod experienced something of a golden age in the twelfth century and demonstrated the clearest instance of interesting political processes that took place throughout Rus in the later Kievan period: the growing power of the popular assembly (the *veche*) and corresponding limitation of the authority of princes. The *veche* seems normally to have been an open-air assembly, to which all heads of families had access, held in the capital city of the principality (so evidently not of much use to countryfolk). It would be summoned by the ringing of a bell – when Novgorod lost its independence to Moscow, the *veche* bell was taken away: it is uncertain how its proceedings were conducted, though decisions were meant to be unanimous. It seems that most twelfth century princes made a verbal agreement with their local *veche* on taking office. In Novgorod and two territories that originated from it, Pskov and Vyatka, things went still further. Novgorod became effectively a *veche* republic from 1136. Earlier the senior princes had tended to save the principality of Novgorod for their eldest sons: this meant no local princely dynasty could permanently establish itself there. By the mid-twelfth century the citizen assembly was powerful enough not only to make a contract with the incoming prince, but to dismiss him at will, to insist that he reside outside the city and to deprive him of almost all authority save that of army commander (in fact an important role, since Novgorod had only a small urban militia of its own). The city was run by elected officials (who tended to form an oligarchy), with its archbishop as effective head of state. There is no doubt that the mass of citizens of 'Lord Novgorod the Great' (as the 'republic' styled itself) were proud of, and anxious to preserve, its institutions and status – though whether it, at least theoretically, formed part of the Grand Prince's patrimony was never satisfactorily settled till Moscow forced the issue in the 1470s. As the eastern entrepôt of the Hansa community, Novgorod had commercial interests stretching from the northern Urals and Arctic Ocean to the port of London: a northern counterpart to those of Venice, reaching in turn from London round southern Europe to the Near East, and up the Black Sea to the Crimea and the southern fringes of Rus. A comparison between these two city-states, with their own commercial 'empires' and with trade networks that between them embraced the whole circumference of Europe, is instructive. As for Vyatka, founded by Novgorodian hunters and river-pirates in the later twelfth century, it never had princes at all, but was a republic from its inception.

When the Mongol or Tatar horsemen reached Rus in the thirteenth

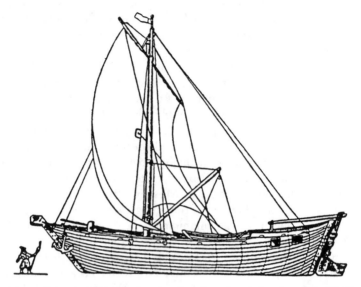

*Figure 7 Koch (Old Russian Arctic sailing-boat): by the second half of the seventeenth century all parts of the Arctic coastline and the Bering Strait were known to Russian adventurers.*

century they found it rather easy to pick off the major Russian cities one by one. The sack of Kiev in 1240 is generally considered to mark the beginning of 240 years of *tatarshchina*, Tatar rule. Their first great leader Genghis (pronounced 'Jengis'; Russian and Mongol 'Chingiz') Khan had, according to legend, been ordered by the Sky God to conquer the world to the limits of the grasslands. His forces would appear, often unexpectedly, outside a city and demand submission: if this was not forthcoming they would destroy everything without mercy, a form of 'total warfare' unfamiliar to Rus. Sometimes a whole nation would submit – for example the Uighur Turks of the ancient trade route, the 'Silk Road', who gave the Mongol Empire its literacy and bureaucratic expertise. In Rus the young prince of Novgorod, Alexander Nevsky (the surname derives from the River Neva) averted a Tatar attack by paying tribute and generally showing himself to be cooperative, while saving his military efforts for a successful resistance to the advance of the German Teutonic Knights and the Swedes. Other parts of western Rus (nowadays Ukraine and Belorussia), to which the Tatars did not penetrate quickly, came under the control of the growing Lithuanian principality, which in the fourteenth century made a dynastic alliance with Poland, and lived a separate 'Central European' cultural life until its piecemeal reabsorbtion into Muscovite and Imperial Russia from the mid-seventeenth century onwards.

The Tatars' rule in Rus differed from their rule in China for instance – in fact, they hardly 'ruled' in a modern sense at all. They installed a small number of overseers (*baskaki*) in the cities, laid down their demands for tribute and skilled personnel, but left the governmental structure intact. It was possible for Russians (as Halperin has recently pointed out),[14] whether because they were traumatized by the conquest or because of genuine incomprehension, to ignore its reality and write as if the Tatars were just another set of steppe raiders. But the political and economic situation could not help but change. As the princes became tax-gathering agents confirmed in power by their overlords, popular power (save in Novgorod and its dependencies) waned. Trade at first was badly disrupted, and city life declined: Rus was forced back to a subsistence economy. The already existing tendency of principalities to subdivide into smaller, scarcely viable 'appanages' gathered pace with each generation: for the Tatars it was a convenient way to 'divide and rule'.

## The Service State

The complex society and economy of early Rus together with its loose and rather casual political structures left it vulnerable to the well-organized assailants who arrived across the steppe: even without the Tatars its integrity was being undermined by the fragmentation characteristic of the twelfth to thirteenth centuries. Yet it was 'warmly cherished in the popular memory', as Vernadsky writes; 'there must have been something in Kievan Russia which made people forget its negative side and remember only its achievements'. That 'something' was the spirit of freedom – individual, political and economic – which prevailed in the Russia of that day and to which the Muscovite principle of the individual's complete obedience to the state was to present such a contrast.'[15] The Varangian founders of Rus had, it would appear, only the most rudimentary notion of the state, and most of their successors, viewing it in terms of 'patrimony', were scarcely more perceptive. The Tatars were to teach the Danilovich branch of the Ryurikids (who constituted the grand-princely dynasty of Moscow) about the effectiveness of well organized and centralized authority. Thereafter, throughout

---

[14]  C. Halperin *Russia and the Golden Horde* (Bloomington, 1987)

[15]  G. Vernadsky *Kievan Russia* (New Haven, 1948) p. 18. Note that political fragmentation did not preclude a fair degree of economic prosperity and cultural vigour, as Franklin has recently argued (see note 8).

Russian history up to the time of writing in the late twentieth century, centripetal and centrifugal forces have been locked in a dynamic and unstable relationship without either establishing a permanent dominance.

The Tatar period of Russian history lasted 240 years, roughly the same length of time as those of the free Kievan Rus and of free Muscovy before and after it. In Russian 'mythistory' it is often presented as a 'dark age', when Rus absorbed and reeled from countless blows that would otherwise have struck at Western Europe, emerging from this self-sacrificing experience free, proud and despotic, but disastrously backward in its historical development. As usual with such mythic pictures, there is something to it, but matters were really more complicated. 'Dark ages' do not last that long, and the later fourteenth and fifteenth centuries turn out to have been a time of ferment in the political, religious and artistic life of Rus, while economically there was enough of a revival for the diminished Byzantine empire to send high church dignitaries to Moscow soliciting alms. From the Byzantine point of view Russia was still part of its 'commonwealth', the Orthodox *oikoumene* or civilized world; in a famous missive of the 1390s the Patriarch Antonios reproached the Moscow Grand Prince Vasiliy I for leaving the Emperor's name out of prayers and saying 'we have a church but not an emperor'. But on the whole the Byzantines supported the claims to ecclesiastical seniority of the north-central lands, under the dominion of the Tatar 'Golden Horde', over those parts of western and southern Rus (including Kiev) that were now controlled by Lithuania, and this played its part in confirming Moscow's hegemony.

The rise of Moscow from an obscure sub-principality of the Vladimir lands at the end of the thirteenth century to its position of unassailable power before the end of the fifteenth has been much discussed, generally with an assumption of its inevitability that smacks of historical or geographical determinism. Yet well into the fifteenth century there were still significant rival centres: the huge Polish-Lithuanian state that probably contained a larger proportion of the Orthodox Rus population than the northern and central territories; the principality of Tver, well located for trade on the Volga; above all Novgorod the Great, enjoying a 'silver age' on the profits of its Hanseatic links, ideologically self-assertive and jealous of its traditional liberties. Moscow, however, had been steadily increasing its territory and economic base by absorbing neighbouring appanage principalities through persuasion, force, purchase or inheritance. The Moscow princes dealt cannily with the Tatar problem, at first acting as servile and efficient agents and usually being awarded the coveted title (*yarlyk*) of Grand Prince, even marrying into, and involving themselves closely in, the Golden Horde; then, under Dmitriy Ivanovich, surnamed 'Donskoy', risking acts of insubordination that culminated in the defeat of a large Tatar army at Kulikovo near the headwaters of the Don in 1380. The Tatars sacked Moscow soon after, but Dmitriy retained his position, and it is clear from his will (of 1389) that the end of the *tatarshchina* was envisaged: 'And if God brings about a change regarding the Horde and my children do not have to give Tatar tribute to the Horde, then the tribute that each of my sons collects in his patrimonial principality shall be his'.[16] When in 1480 Tatar rule in Rus came at last to a low-key end, with the stand-off or 'non-battle' on the banks of the River Ugra, Ivan III followed this principle and simply pocketed the Tatar tribute (finding himself wealthy enough to undertake the rebuilding of the Kremlin).

The last great Tatar raid took place in 1408; thereafter the Horde grew weaker and fragmented, with several Tatar nobles going into Moscow's service (with or without conversion to Orthodoxy). There is evidence in the early part of the century that there were dreams of a restored Kievan-type federation of Russian principalities, respecting each others' liberties, while the Trinity Monastery of St Sergius became for a time an all-Russian cultural centre: the great Trinity Chronicle of the early fifteenth century – probably composed by Yepifaniy the Wise (see p. 160–2);[17] its manuscript was lost in the 1812 fire of Moscow – seems to have deliberately projected an all-Russian view of events. But a good deal of uncertainty surrounds the ideological currents of the eventful fifteenth century, and indeed many of the events themselves: though we have numerous historical sources, they are generally more or less skewed towards the interests of later Muscovite propaganda (which, for instance, built up Dmitriy Donskoy's victory into a huge and heroic struggle against the infidel, supposedly blessed and encouraged by Sergius and his monks).

A protracted and messy civil war for the throne of Moscow occupied the whole second quarter of the fifteenth century. It had several consequences for the political culture of Rus. It put an end to any likelihood of reinstating the practice of 'lateral' princely succession common in pre-Tatar times, though the concept sporadically and unsuccessfully resurfaced on a few occasions subsequently; it was a salutary reminder of the horrific and debilitating dangers of internecine feuds; it must have been a formative childhood experience for the future Ivan III (sometimes called 'the Great'); it proved an ominous foretaste of

[16] R. Howes (ed.) *The Testaments of the Grand Princes of Moscow* (Ithaca, 1967), also partly in D. Kaiser and G. Marker *Reinterpreting Russian History: Readings 860–1860s* (Oxford, 1994) pp. 87–90.

[17] G. G. Kloss 'Determining the Authorship of the Trinity Chronicle' in M. Flier and D. Rowland *Medieval Russian Culture* vol. II (Berkeley, 1994).

what was to come for the Novgorodians, who backed the wrong side at a late stage, were defeated and fined (1456) by the victorious Vasiliy II and forbidden to conduct an independent foreign policy. When Ivan III came to the throne (1462) it was not yet clear that he intended to subdue and incorporate the last independent principalities: but the logic of what appears to have been his driving ambition, to assert the authority of his grand-princely position over his whole 'patrimony' of Rus, pointed in that direction. Novgorod had economic problems (the collapse of the European squirrel-fur market) and social tensions; one leading party in the republic was rash enough to parley with Lithuania, Moscow's chief rival; its delegates did not address Ivan by his preferred title. It could neither reliably feed itself nor defend itself. Ivan moved in for the kill in 1478, abolished the republic's independent institutions, hauled off the *veche* bell to Moscow, soon closed down the Hansa offices, sacked the archbishop and installed a Muscovite strongman, and, most significantly, forcibly resettled several thousand of the better-off citizens in other territories, replacing them with a smaller number of Muscovite servitors. All these people henceforth held their land not as *votchina*, heritable and saleable property, but as *pomestye*, landholdings conditional upon service, and indeed these lands were intended primarily to provide the means wherewith the servitor could equip himself to undertake military tasks. Ivan and his successors continually extended the *pomestye* system, then insisted that *votchina* holders must also serve, under the threat of expropriation. The extension of *pomestye* made it hard for the Muscovite landowning class to put down local roots. Appanage principalities began to revert to the Grand Prince after their rulers' lifetime. After the fall of Novgorod, it was without much difficulty that the remaining independent territories of Rus were 'gathered in' by Ivan III (Tver, Vyatka) and his son Vasiliy III (Pskov, Ryazan).

The promulgation of conditional land-tenure in newly liberated and vastly expanded Muscovy looks like the belated institution of European-style feudalism, and many historians (particularly Marxists, for whom feudalism represents a necessary stage of social development) have so regarded it. Feudalism was indeed known in Lithuania; but in Muscovy there were such significant differences that it seems better to speak in terms of a different model, that of a 'service state'. Western feudalism had developed in connection with weak central power and the enserfment of the rural population: Ivan III was a centralizer and organizer closely comparable with such a 'modern' monarch as Henry VII of England (his slightly younger contemporary), while serfdom – later considered so characteristic of Russian society – was still well in the future (it crept in during the second half of the sixteenth century). Russia had no sub-infeudation, nor was there a feudal contract laying obligations on the greater as well as the lesser party. The Muscovite service state grew out of specifically Russian conditions: a vast country with a sparse, rather mobile population; very long, often indeterminate frontiers that demanded constant defence (and later, expansion) to west, south and east; an economy with little spare cash but with great resources of land – though often without workers to exploit it properly – to reward servitors; a class of recently dispossessed boyars and princes; memories of the Moscow civil war and the long experience of Tatar rule, strengthening (as national misfortunes generally do) a sense of nationhood in the disparate parts and people of Rus; an international situation wherein, after the fall of Constantinople (1453) to the Ottoman Turks, Muscovy soon became the only significant free Orthodox nation and bastion of Orthodox culture.

The processes involved in the setting up of the service state (which itself is a modern term) were complex and gradual – there were no general decrees establishing it or, for that matter, its subsequent concomitant institution, serfdom. From the servitors' point of view the most significant change was the disappearance of independent territories in Rus other than Muscovy and Lithuania: hence the impossibility of exercising their ancient right to choose freely where and whom to serve. Lithuania, having converted to Catholicism (1386) and having entered a dynastic alliance with Poland, was regarded as hostile, and defection to it from Muscovy was seen as treason. Of course a few such defections nevertheless took place, a late and celebrated case being that of Prince Kurbsky, when Ivan IV's reign of terror was just getting under way (1564) – it probably helped to fuel Ivan's paranoia, and gave rise to a remarkable correspondence between the two in which the duties and authority of a ruler are for the first time in Russia extensively argued out.[18] Under Ivan IV the Muscovite ideology of sovereignty reached its fullest form: for Ivan, as he made clear in correspondence with other rulers (including Queen Elizabeth I of England) a ruler was either an autocrat (*samoderzhets*, a 'possessor in one's own right'), ruling by right of inheritance, or a mere hireling, ruling on others' suffrance (memories of the old situation in Novgorod and elsewhere must have conditioned this idea). This attitude was bound up with vestiges of the possessive patrimonial attitude to power of his Ryurikid Viking forebears: the ruler was basically a mighty landowner (rulers had always anyhow paid close attention to their private estates), Rus itself being the one true *votchina* remaining.

---

[18]   J. Fennell (ed.) *The Correspondence between Prince Kurbsky and Tsar Ivan IV of Russia* (Cambridge, 1955). Attempts to show that the correspondence is apocryphal have not met with general acceptance.

The service class represented only about one in three hundred of the population: an inconsiderable number of people to supply the bureaucracy and military elite of a vast country. Most of them were far from rich (this remains true of the landowning class in later centuries) and their obligations, starting at the age of fifteen, could be onerous. The first Muscovite law codes (of 1497 and 1550) even attempted to prevent them selling themselves into bondage, which evidently sometimes seemed a lesser evil.[19] In the early decades of the formation of the service state, the bulk of the population, the peasants, were freer, though like all except servitors and churchpeople they carried the burden (*tyaglo*) of having to pay tax in money or kind (e.g. army conscription or public works). Peasants had the guaranteed right of changing their employer during the two weeks adjoining St George's Day in late November. In times of crisis this right was abrogated by the government, and in the late sixteenth century, after bad harvests and much rural depopulation, it ceased altogether: if the government were to make a policy of handing out conditional grants of land, there had to be hands to work it. So serfdom (first mentioned as a fact in the law-code of 1649) came into being. Much later, in the eighteenth to nineteenth centuries, both Russians and Westerners would often write as if the serf were in fact a slave: indeed the degree of control exercised, at least in theory, by serf-'owners' made the two conditions look similar. But there were important distinctions. Serfs were tied to the land, not to an individual landowner (though landowners represented authority to them, and paid their taxes: in exchange, the serf had to work a certain number of days per week for the landowner or pay 'quit-rent', *obrok*). In reality, they were performing state service of a special kind, and in Muscovy were regarded as being under the special protection of the government. Living in their own homes and communities (that effectively policed and regulated themselves), able unlike slaves to dispose of the products of their labour, the serfs, as various Russian and foreign observers noted, had a dignity, sense of humour and self-worth that did not suggest slavery; they did not form an exclusive and identifiable caste, they were of the same race, language and religion as the rest of the population, and indeed there was some movement into and out of serfdom. *Obrok* serfs – mostly in the north, where farming was unprofitable – would often, with permission, spend part or all of their time in the cities, joining one or another craft

---

[19]  The early law-codes, from Yaroslav's time onwards, have many similarities with Frankish and Anglo-Saxon laws, and are mostly concerned with fines and monetary damages for injuries: see G. Vernadsky *Medieval Russian Laws* (New York, 1947). There are, however, considerable textual problems: see Franklin and Shepard *The Emergence of Rus*, Chapter 6:2.

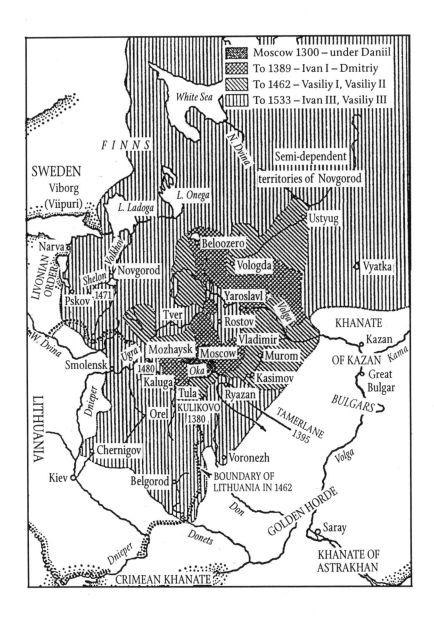

Figure 8   Muscovite Rus (sixteenth century; based on Riasanovsky).

guild (*artel*), maybe sublettling their land or themselves employing labour (serf millionaires were not unknown in the nineteenth century). In the early nineteenth century it was generally agreed they were better off than the Irish rural poor or many English industrial workers. Curiously, the serfs seemed to consider that in some fundamental sense they owned (as well as their homes) the land they worked, even while accepting that their landlords owned *them*: from the legal point of view both assumptions were mistaken.

It is a common error to assume that all Russian peasants before the Emancipation in 1861 were serfs. Actually the latter never constituted much more than half the rural population (they were most numerous in the richer south-central agricultural areas). To the end there were substantial numbers of 'free peasants' on so called 'black' lands that had not been allocated to servitors; there were communities of fishermen and hunters; in Siberia and the far north serfdom was virtually unknown. Free peasants were inscribed in their villages and had to get permission to move, but were otherwise able to arrange their own lives. Muscovy also had substantial free communities on its southern, steppe-land fringes: *odnodvortsy* ('single-homesteaders') deriving from the soldiers who manned an elaborate southern defensive line against the Crimean Tatars, and beyond them Cossacks, recorded from the fifteenth century onwards, many of whom were the descendants of runaway peasants from Ukraine and Russia. They settled in militarized, self-governing 'hosts' on the lower courses of the great southward-flowing rivers and gained a reputation as freebooters and hardy warriors. They were prepared to cooperate with Moscow if their traditional rights were respected, played a large part in opening up Siberia (a Cossack adventurer, Simon Dezhnev, navigated the Bering Strait as early as 1648), but their provocation of the Turks and Poles brought Muscovy headaches, and the country's two greatest rural rebellions – of Stepan Razin in 1670, and Yemelyan Pugachov in 1774 – started among Cossacks on the Don and Yaik rivers (both leaders became mythic figures in folklore and the Russian historical consciousness generally – see, for example, Alexander Pushkin's novel *The Captain's Daughter*).

Clearly there were strong centrifugal and libertarian, even anarchic, forces at work in Muscovy, as at many other times during Russian history. The service state tried to counter these by fixing the population where possible not just to its location, but to its social role: the Muscovite law-codes and charters, more specific and punitive than their easygoing Kievan predecessors, show this. The parish clergy, for example, became a distinct caste. As Ivan IV's long reign progressed, particularly after its buoyant, successful early years (to *c.*1560), Muscovy began to look not only politically, culturally and technologically backward by Western standards, but became introspective and rigidly organized, full of simmering tensions. Soon it would become impoverished and demoralized too – from poor harvests (the climate in Northern Europe was going through a cold phase), expensive and unsuccessful wars and the tsar's excesses of cruelty (including the destruction of Novgorod in 1570, more bloody than that instigated by his grandfather nearly 100 years before and even less justified, as well as the puzzling but disastrous seven-year terror of the *oprichnina* – see p. 113). The book of household management popular in the period, the *Domostroy*, gives a hierarchical and chilly picture of the ideal family and home. The situation of women, apparently rather favourable by medieval standards in Kievan times,[20] is marked at least in the servitor and merchant classes of Muscovy by seclusion and subordination (however, in the later seventeenth century, some positive and self-willed women emerge – 'Old Believer' heroines, and above all Sophia, Peter the Great's elder half-sister, who was effective ruler, and not a bad one, from 1682 to 1689).

If any one feature of sixteenth and seventeenth century Muscovy tended to convince foreign observers of its unbending rigidity and primitive culture, it was its autocracy. The ruler appeared to have gathered absolute, and capriciously exercised, power over church and state, people and resources, into his hands; he behaved towards other rulers and their envoys with unbecoming arrogance, and demanded the slavish subservience of even his highest officials and aristocrats. As so often, though, these phenomena were more complicated than they seemed, and derived from the novel circumstances in which Muscovy found itself. After the Tatar period, the old Ryurikid concept of authority as a 'family concern' had dropped away, and urban life with its *veche* democracy had dwindled to nothingness. The resulting ideological vacuum was being filled with a set of ideas that to some extent were part of the common currency of European Renaissance pragmatic and authoritarian toughness – Ivan IV's apparently unmotivated cruelties can easily be viewed as an attack, even if unsystematic, on the old boyar class and an encouragement of 'new men' – but were, more fundamentally, Byzantine in spirit. The outward sign of this was the upgrading of the royal title. The term 'tsar' (deriving from 'Caesar') had, since proto-Slav days, referred to the East Roman (Byzantine) emperor; Constantinople was known to all Slavs as 'Tsargrad', 'Imperial City'. It was also applied by Russians to the Tatar or Mongol Khan, ruler of the other world empire they knew at first hand. Even before the extinction of both empires in the fifteenth century various South Slav rulers had aspired to

---

[20] G. Vernadsky *Kievan Russia* (1948) Chapter VI:9 gives a judicious summary; see also Franklin and Shepard *The Emergence of Rus*, Chapter 8:2.

the title of tsar, while Dmitriy Donskoy of Moscow (d. 1389) is so named in his hagiographic *Life*. Ideologists in Trnovo (the fourteenth century Bulgarian capital), Tver, Novgorod and Moscow began to suggest, with growing explicitness, that the mantle of Imperial prestige had been inherited by their own city from the first two Romes: the notorious sixteenth-century theory of 'Moscow the Third Rome' was merely the culmination of a broader process that involved the concoction of fantastical tales allegorizing such an inheritance. Ivan III adopted the Byzantine insignia of a double-headed eagle; he married the niece of the last Byzantine emperor, Zoe (in Russian, Sofiya) Palaiologina; finally Ivan IV had himself crowned Tsar in 1547 in an unprecedentedly elaborate coronation ceremony.

New outward signs and symbols were accompanied also by developments in the Russian attitude to monarchy. Various scholars, notably Mikhail Cherniavsky, have investigated the 'ruler myth' that goes back to early Kievan times and which led to the canonization of many princes (as happened in Serbia too, but not in Byzantium): it would seem that just as there might be an ideal of the 'warrior-king' or 'philosopher-king' in other societies, Rus favoured an ideal of the 'prince-monk'. To be a prince was in some sense to be a fighter for Christ, even a martyr or at least sufferer, since 'the very concept of State was introduced to Russia as part of the Christian ethos . . . there was no concept of a secular state in Russia'.[21] The famous, almost hackneyed formulation of the late-antique theorist Agapetus in his 'Mirror for Princes' 'Although an emperor in his body is like other men, yet in his authority he is like God' was well-known in Rus, and (as with many foreign ideas up to the twentieth century, as Isaiah Berlin has so often demonstrated) was taken literally and acted upon by the Russians. Incidentally this seems to constitute an ideological counterweight to the Viking-derived 'commercial' attitude to power of the early Ryurikids. With the symbolically charged liberation and unification of Rus soon after the fall of Byzantium, a responsibility not just for Rus itself but for the whole destiny of Orthodoxy and, by extension, of the world weighed on the rulers' shoulders. There seems little doubt that some of the eccentricities of Ivan IV's behaviour derive from this sense of excessive burden, including the two occasions on which he tried to 'retire': first to Aleksandrov (an event familiar from Sergey Eisenstein's great film *Ivan the Terrible*), then in favour of a Tatar princeling, Semyon Bekbulatovich, whom he installed as 'parody Tsar' and to whom he paid exaggerated respect for a few months between 1571 and 1572.

Byzantine rulers were autocrats, their power theoretically unlimited:

---

[21]  M. Cherniavsky *Tsar and People* (New Haven, 1961) p. 33.

still, they could hardly have claimed to be able to do just as they wanted, or to call their time their own. In a shadowy way, though law-givers, they were subject to the Law; much more clearly they were constrained by their position as champions of Orthodoxy. When not actually on the field of battle or away hunting, the Emperor had to spend a vast amount of time taking part in processions or in church services in Constantinople. The later Russian tsars, particularly the most 'Byzantine' of all, Aleksey (1645–76), led lives similarly more hemmed in by ritual and ceremony even than Louis XIV. For Muscovite rulers, this meant long and frequent treks between provincial monasteries, observing and being observed, as well as performing ceremonies such as 'Blessing the waters' that involved taking a dip in the frozen river at Epiphany (6th January – it supposedly led to Aleksey Mikhailovich's death at the age of 46), and the remarkable Palm Sunday procession from the Kremlin through Red Square to St Basil's (see below p. 217), with the tsar leading the Patriarch on a horse standing in for an ass. Peter the Great, impatient of such things, let his brother and co-tsar Ivan V perform most ceremonies till his death in 1696; he let the Palm Sunday procession lapse, reportedly objecting to taking the role of a groom.

Divinely sanctioned autocracy was not, however, in all ways as inflexible and oppressive as it might seem, even in its Russian form of the service state. Recent studies (particularly by Nancy S. Kollman) demonstrate clearly that the circle of senior boyars who formed a permanent advisory council for the Muscovite ruler held plenty of power and were subject to ordinary political processes. That non-Russian observers seldom noticed this, and themselves assumed the grovelling abasement even of great aristocrats before the tsar's authority, seems to be a consequence of the Muscovite adoption of one of the most fundamental of Byzantine socio-political principles – that of *symphonia*, 'harmony'. In Byzantium this principle assisted the smooth ordering of church–state relations; in Muscovy it not only led to a façade of political single-mindedness but damped down the potential for boyar inter-family rivalries, and put consensus as the most desirable of objectives. In Kollman's words 'The ubiquity of the theme of harmony and unanimity compels us to take it seriously as a principle of Muscovite politics. It is not consistent with the reality of court politics, which was marked by dissension, but it hints at limits on such fractious disputes'.[22] On its humbler level, too, the world of familial relations adumbrated by *Domostroy* and Christian texts such as *Izmaragd* (Emerald) is founded

---

[22] N. S. Kollman *Kinship and Politics: the Making of the Muscovite Political System* (Stanford, 1987), excerpted in Kaiser and Marker *Reinterpreting Russian History*, p. 156.

on the ideal of harmoniousness. Clearly when social harmony broke down – most spectacularly with the *oprichnina* (1565–72; see p. 113), the 'Time of Troubles' after the Ryurikid dynasty died out (1598–1613), and the Great Schism (1666 onwards) – the results could be bloody and anarchic. But it helped to guide the actions in very difficult circumstances of the penultimate and greatest Old Russian ruler, Aleksey, and earn him the title of *tishayshy*, literally 'most calm' (equivalent to Greek *Galenotatos* and Latin *Serenissimus)*.

The Byzantine imperial system was derived (with its added Christian element) from that of the original Roman empire. Power ultimately devolved on the emperor from the people and senate; and the Byzantine succession system, at least in theory, involved election, by acclamation, on the part of people, senate and army. Of course dynasties were in fact established, particularly in the later Byzantine centuries, and this was generally managed by the ingenious expedient of the ruler's crowning an elder son or other chosen person as 'co-emperor' during his or her own lifetime. In Muscovite Russia too this was practised, though it was not as watertight as it might have seemed (Aleksey was crowned as a child in his father's lifetime; but after he in turn crowned his favourite son the boy predeceased him, and a few years later another protracted succession crisis arose between the families of Aleksey's first and second wives). Peter the Great abolished the system and specified that the ruler should nominate his or her successor. Notoriously he failed to do so himself, and the fact that his widow succeeded him as Catherine I was partly a result of her ceremonial coronation a year beforehand. For the next hundred years the army became crucial arbiter of who should rule; court circles played some part, the people none. In Muscovite Russia, however, there was a measure of popular participation in government through the large *ad hoc* consultative body known as the *zemsky sobor*, 'Assembly of the Land', which first seems to have been summoned early in the reign of Ivan IV. The Assembly was clearly not a parliament – more a sort of 'Estates General', and little is known about its composition, agenda and influence on the many occasions it met up until (probably) 1682: but it certainly discussed, and advised on, crucial issues. Its significance as a partner in government is reflected in the formula on many edicts 'By the desire of the sovereign and all the land', contrasting with the better-known formula 'The Tsar indicated and the boyars assented'. None was more important than the Assembly of 1613, containing some hundreds of boyars, landowners, clergy, townsfolk and state peasants, that effectively brought the Time of Troubles to an end and invited Mikhail Romanov, out of a shortlist from which non-Russians were excluded, to become tsar (those commentators who claim Boris Yeltsin as the first elected Russian leader should remember that the Assembly of 1613 is still fresh in the Russian historical memory). Ivan IV also introduced a degree of local self-government by specifying the election of elders, responsible to Moscow rather than to provincial governors, who would be chiefly concerned with administering justice and tax-collection, and of assessors to keep an eye on the governors. These promising arrangements, however, did not survive the anarchy of the Time of Troubles. Had they done so, it would have been less easy for commentators on twentieth-century Russia to speak glibly of Russia's historic 'lack of civic culture'.

The age of the Service State was also a period when Russia, for all the apparent introspectiveness of its preoccupations, had to define its place with regard to the outside world – and indeed expanded mightily (on average by an area the size of the Netherlands – 35,000 square kilometres – every year for 150 years!).[23] Despite the Byzantinesque elements of their political ideology, Ivan III and his successors were wary of getting entangled in the politics of areas they regarded as outside their patrimony: Ivan turned down the proposal that he should lead an alliance of Christian nations to recapture Constantinople from the Turks. Western countries began to be interested in Rus: the Vatican had high hopes from Ivan's marriage to Zoe-Sofiya (members of her family had escaped from Byzantium to Italy, and were in communion with Rome after the Council of Florence). Muscovy set up a regular maritime trade route to the West, for the first time since the collapse of Novgorod, in remarkable circumstances when an expedition led by an English seaman, Richard Chancellor, attempting to find a northern seaway to the Indies, was washed up on the shores of the White Sea. Chancellor reached Moscow, was received by Ivan IV, and the upshot was a permanent English mission in Moscow (its building was recently located and restored), the development of the port of Archangel, the enrichment of northern towns (Yaroslavl, Vologda, Ustyug) and the setting-up in London of the first joint-stock enterprise, the Russia Company; after the news of the execution of Charles I reached Moscow, English special privileges were withdrawn. Under Ivan IV foreign specialists began to be recruited to work in Muscovy; under Boris Godunov, Russians were first sent abroad to study. But foreign contacts with Muscovy were also related to warfare: inconclusively against Poland-Lithuania and German Livonia in the West, with spectacular success (after initial difficulties) when the Tatar citadels of Kazan and Astrakhan were captured in 1552 and 1556. The whole course of the Volga was now in Russian hands (for the first time since Svyatoslav in the mid-tenth century!) and hunters, soldiers and peasants – later, convicts too – could cross the Urals more or

[23]  R. Pipes *Russia under the Old Regime* p. 83.

less unimpeded into Siberia. Historians often see the capture of Kazan as the beginning of Russian imperialism; yet Ivan somehow regarded it as part of his patrimony, and in multi-ethnic Rus the modern idea of empire (as distinct from an Orthodox realm) was yet to be born.[24]

## Aftermath

We might well have expected the service state, a basically medieval concept, by now anachronistic, to have died a natural death at the Time of Troubles – when for 15 years from the extinction of the Ryurikid line (1598) Russia was in political and economic chaos, its throne in dispute, with two foreign occupying powers on its territory, its destiny finally in the hands of a provincial citizens' army and a few fortified monasteries, its boyars having forfeited their credibility. Yet the system was reinstated, to general relief it would seem, in 1613, and proved to have plenty more life in it. Its inefficiencies made it tolerable: members of the landowning class found it quite easy to avoid service if keen and wily enough to do so, while serfs escaped in considerable numbers (the very landowners who should have policed the system and returned runaways were liable to be shorthanded – there has generally been a labour shortage in Russia – and were ready to take on new workers without probing questions). The system survived a series of varied crises in the seventeenth century, and was improved towards its end when *mestnichestvo* – a complex set of arrangements whereby boyars would only undertake duties in accordance with family and personal status – was abolished under Tsar Fyodor III (1676–82).[25] A new complication, however, was the appearance of numerous pretenders to the title of tsar – mostly quite implausible – of whom only the first 'False Dmitriy', in the Time of Troubles, was successful (and not for long). The phenomenon was linked with the concept of the 'true tsar', divinely approved and maybe recognizable only through certain secret bodily signs – there had been no such pretenders in grand-princely days. It was an oblique compliment to the system that the peasants who supported such pretenders did not wish fundamentally to challenge it, but to right

---

[24] See, for example, G. Hosking *Empire and Nation in Russian History* (Waco, 1992) pp. 5, 10. An earlier example of the extension of Russian rule over non-Russians was Moscow's acquisition of the Permian (Komi) lands in the fifteenth century (but Novgorod's 'empire' is of course earlier still).

[25] See Pipes *Russia under the Old Regime* p. 90. The system actually represented a constraint upon the power of the Tsar and the service state, at least as far as the top thirty or so governing families were concerned.

wrongs, maybe restore ancient privileges, do away with unjust bureaucrats and boyars, perhaps lift serfdom and (after 1666) restore the Old Belief. Up to the twentieth century peasants with a grievance considered they had right of access to the Tsar (and later, Lenin), who would understand their plight: the thousands of petitions Nicholas II thus received were largely sifted by a peasant, Grigoriy Rasputin.

Peter the Great, lauded by Voltaire, promoted by all the history books as a root-and-branch political reformer and 'Westernizer', would surely have been expected to do away with the service state as summarily as he did away with the Patriarchate. Not a bit of it: he refined it and managed to make it a good deal more oppressive, in the first place by making it more efficient. It became more difficult and dangerous to evade service at any level, and the service demanded was often tougher: Peter's almost ceaseless wars made terrible human and financial demands on all classes, worst of all on the peasantry, conscripted into the bewildering circumstances of army life, factories or labour battalions for such huge works as the construction of the city of St Petersburg. Not surprisingly, the able-bodied tended to escape if they could. Those left behind were subjected to a poll ('soul') tax, that raised far more revenue than the previous household tax, and was correspondingly hated. The security of the state, a constant and well merited concern of Peter's, was buttressed by the establishment of a secret police office under his ruthless crony Fyodor Romodanovsky, and by such unscrupulous means as making parish priests (who had been turned into the lowliest of state functionaries) not only swear loyalty to the regime, but reveal the secrets of the confessional in cases of potential danger to it. Late in his reign Peter followed Ivan IV's example in attempting to turn his service class into more of a meritocracy, instituting a 'Table of Ranks' on the model of some Western states, with successive equivalent rungs in the services and the bureaucracy up which the talented could climb to eventual ennoblement (though some spectacular careers were made, the old elite together with numerous foreign specialists continued to dominate the top posts). His entirely utilitarian attitude towards the population – once he told a questioner 'A noble is he who is useful' – extended to his own role as first servant of the state. Though quite unsnobbish in everyday life – Peter's image of simple tastes and hard work greatly impressed non-Russians – he made the division of society glaringly evident by ordering his servitors to shave (see p. 126–8) and wear Western-European clothing.

One need not doubt Peter's personal courage and dedication, nor even dispute that he or someone like him was needed, to question what his reforms of society and political culture added up to. He changed the appearance of many things in Russian life, from the Cyrillic typeface to

Plate 6   *Muscovite musketeer* (strelets): *drawing by the Swedish visitor E. Palmquist (1674).*

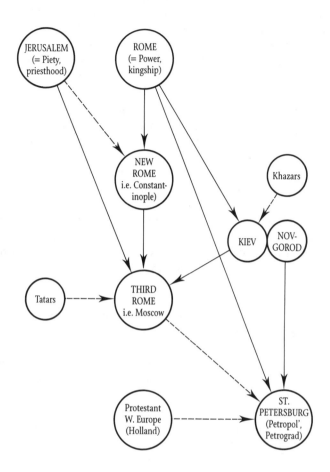

*Figure 9   'Ideological pathways' in Old and Petrine Russia
(partly based on Lotman and Uspensky).*

the façades of buildings; he widened the intellectual horizons of at least some of his compatriots; he improved the social situation of (upper-class) women. On a deeper level, though, it would seem there were only two great innovations that he brought to the Russians' inner life. One was respect for education. He insisted that his servitors should take examinations for career advancement; once again his motives were completely utilitarian, but he provided a basis on which a profounder respect for educational and enlightenment values could take root later in the century, eventually to trickle down from the upper class to the townsfolk and people generally. The second was his separation of the state from the person of the monarch, epitomized in his reported exhortation to his troops on the eve of the Battle of Poltava (1709, where the Swedes were defeated) to think not of 'Peter' but of 'Russia'. He himself thought in terms of duty to the country, to its prosperity and its potential for a leading role in the world rather than in terms of the patrimonial and exploitative attitude of his forebears. In the later part of his reign he tended to prefix his decrees with explanatory prefaces: again a sort of educational endeavour. Whether such positive achievements were worth the expense, both monetary and in the sense of the brutalization that accompanied them, is for Russians to decide, and they have been arguing passionately about it ever since. His personal example as a great voluntarist of history has been bracing, but more worrying has been the sense that such exploits must be accompanied necessarily by harshness – a lesson not lost on later figures such as Stalin or Atatürk. In place of the gradual modernization of previous decades he substituted belief in the efficacy of a single superhuman or monstrous effort to make everything new and better: a notion that has been realized on at any rate four occasions in Russian history (988, 1703, 1917, 1991) with results that were ambiguous to say the least. In place of what in retrospect seemed the relatively organic and harmonious tsardom of Rus that he inherited, he left behind him the empire of Rossiya – a legacy that Russians have on the whole found distinctly uncomfortable, and sloughed off with some relief with the collapse of the communist state in 1991 (leaving a 'Russia' whose borders were similar to Peter the Great's realm).

Peter's successors softened the toughest effects of his initiatives, but most of them lasted. The service state, so unexpectedly spruced up by the great Westernizer, had a final boost in 1730 when (in yet another succession crisis) Anna of Courland, daughter of Ivan V, was invited to the throne by a group of high aristocrats. She agreed conditions that would have made her in effect a constitutional monarch; but when the lesser gentry got wind of the arrangements they persuaded Anna to repudiate them (at a dramatic meting in the Kremlin), since they feared an aristocratic oligarchy more than absolutism and autocracy. One of the main props of the service state was kicked away, however, in the short reign of Peter III, when a remarkable decree of 18 February 1762 (confirmed by his supplanter Catherine II) liberated the entire gentry class (*dvoryanstvo*) from compulsory state service in perpetuity, save at times of national emergency. The decree exhorted it to continue to serve 'out of gratitude' and not to spend its time in 'sloth and idleness'(!) In effect, the situation did not change very radically on the surface: the old servitors continued on the whole to staff the bureaucracy and army (they

*Plate 7  View of late eighteenth-century Moscow, immediately west of the
Kremlin, featuring the grand Pashkov House (later the Rumyantsev Library)
attributed to the architect Vasiliy Bazhenov (1737–99).*

needed the money), while as landowners they administered the
countryside. In 1764 promotion up the Table of Ranks was made
automatic after service for a certain number of years, thus radically
altering its meritocratic basis; not long after, upper-class ownership of
land was affirmed.

In reality, though, a profound change had taken place. So long as it
was a functional part of a system where everyone (even the ruler) served
for the greater good, serfdom made sense: it ceased to do so – as, for that
matter, did autocracy – when the elite segment of society could do as it
pleased. The serfs understood this perfectly well, and aspired to the
condition of state peasants (whose last remaining legal disabilities were
removed in the early nineteenth century); at least they were not liable to
be shifted at a landlord's whim into domestic service, factory work or
whatever. In fact the arbitrariness of serfdom made itself felt more and
more in the eighteenth century; the educated members of society began
to feel most uncomfortable at having so anachronistic and unjust an
institution in their society, and more than uncomfortable in their
awareness of their alienation from the class which probably embodied
true Russianness in itself. Every ruler from Catherine II onwards knew

serfdom somehow had to come to an end: but it took ninety-nine years and a day for it to do so (with crippling payments for their land, the peasants were worse off when it did). Autocracy, though, drifted on like a rudderless boat, the last relic of a medieval political order that had served its time.

As for the service state, it disappeared only to re-emerge again, together with its progenitor, patrimonial rule. After the long and authentically enlightened reign of Catherine II, a ruler who worked quietly to improve things from below and with consensus, who understood human nature (unlike Peter) and continually encouraged the devolution of decision-making, the sad attempts of most of the later tsars to identify their regimes with 'Russianness' now seem farcical.

When nineteenth-century emperors, men thoroughly western in their upbringing, adamantly refused to grant their country a constitution, they were behaving not unlike ordinary property owners afraid to jeopardize their title by some legal precedent. Nicholas II, Russia's last tsar, was by temperament ideally suited to serve as a constitutional monarch. Yet he could not bring himself to grant a constitution, or, after having been forced to do so, to respect it.[26]

Something even more bizarre was to come, though, after 1917 (or rather after 1930): the fullscale, though fortunately short-lived, reintroduction of the service state in a Stalinist guise that no longer made more than a passing nod to Marxism. The Stalinist elite were a bunch of servitors jostling for non-heritable perks while preserving a façade of harmony, whereas the peasantry was re-enserfed (by the denial of internal passports) only to be 'liberated' by Leonid Brezhnev in the 1970s. Truly a strange story.

---

[26]   Pipes *Russia under the Old Regime* p. 54.

# 3

## Belief Systems

### Introductory

For medieval Russians their conversion to Christianity (988–9) was the central event of their state's history, their ticket of entry both to divine grace and to true nationhood. In the fifteenth and sixteenth centuries, by taking on the ideological heritage of Constantinople and the role of bastion against the Tatars, Russia became the self-conscious champion of Orthodoxy. Soon the resonant (but by no means transparent) term 'Holy Russia' would come into use. Russia's critical period of change in the later seventeenth to the early eighteenth centuries was accompanied by two major crises of belief: the 'Great Schism' within the Church and society at large, followed by the wholesale secularization promulgated by Peter the Great. Later, the post-Napoleonic 'Holy Alliance' of European monarchs was a Russian invention. The influential Slavophile movement of the mid-nineteenth century specifically associated Ortho-dox belief with Russian nationhood and political destiny. Subsequently (with the partial assistance of public figures and authors such as Dostoyevsky) a notion of special Russian 'soulfulness' or spirituality (*dukhovnost*) would find energetic supporters in Russia and among Western Russophiles. By contrast, among the intelligentsia of the nineteenth and early twentieth centuries militant scientific positivism, 'God-building' and atheism had a sufficiently committed following to fuel the intellectual component of the Bolshevik revolution in its early years. It is clear that the succession of belief systems, sometimes clashing with each other, that have dominated the thousand or more years of its history have had as great a determining power on Russia's culture as any other factors, if not greater. The transitions between them have on occasion been abrupt and critical, with repercussions throughout society. Questions of faith – religious, political or any other – have not been treated as matters of simply private and personal choice in Russia (many a Westerner in our own time has been startled to be interrogated by new acquaintances as to whether he or she was a 'believer'). Westerners in turn, from at any rate the sixteenth century, have been liable to subject Russians' beliefs – particularly their commitment to Orthodox Christianity – to unflattering scrutiny, on occasion denouncing them as skin-deep, hypocritical, superstitious or intellectually vacuous. It was evident to discerning observers, foreign or Russian, that 'Holy Russia' conserved much that seemed to belong to archaic , un-Christian habits of mind (just as, in our century, post-Revolutionary Soviet Russia often disconcerted foreign Communists by its less than wholehearted commitment to the ideals of the new order, save on the level of official ideology). Clearly the belief systems of Russia have been not only powerful, but puzzling, even paradoxical, and it is worth examining aspects of them.

### Russian 'Paganism' and Folk Belief

It is usual to characterize the society of Rus until the famous Conversion under Vladimir I (at the end of the tenth century) as pagan; thereafter, as Christian. What, in a Russian context, do these terms mean? (Are they indeed terms of the same order?) How did the transition take place? Does Russian paganism constitute a systematic religion comparable, say, with Greek and Roman, or for that matter Scandinavian, paganism? How much do we know about it? Is it of merely antiquarian or specialist interest?

The answers to all these questions are, of course, linked, particularly those to the latter two, which can be dealt with first. Russian pre-Christian belief is by no means an antiquarian matter, insofar as a vast substratum of folk beliefs and associated habits of mind, finding their reflection in much Russian literature and thought, is not wholly extinct even in the second half of the twentieth century. Ethnographers point to the extremely archaic nature of many aspects of these beliefs, some evidently predating not only the emergence of Rus but even the division of the early Slavs into their three main branches. Folklorists in the last couple of hundred years have assembled large quantities of data from the Russian, Belorussian and Ukrainian countryside on the beliefs, legends and rituals relating to important life events such as weddings, births, illnesses and burials, to the cycle of the seasons (particularly the agricultural year), the house and its individual features, including the bath-house (see p. 32–3 for its connotations), animals and birds, forest, river and sea and a large variety of associated supernatural beings, all embodied in a rich heritage of songs, dances, decorative art, oral epics, stories, rhymes and proverbs. Folk belief manifested itself in the rituals, language and general mindset of the Russians – and not only rural dwellers – well into the twentieth century, and probably to the present. It is frequently detectable in – and sometimes a most important component of – Russian nineteenth- and twentieth-century (even Soviet) literature.[1]

The study of Russian pre-Christian belief is nevertheless a curiously elusive topic. On the one hand, we learn quite a lot about Russian 'paganism' from the early pages of the *Tale of Bygone Years*, and there are scattered references to it throughout sources on the history of Rus and in certain works of literature (notably the *Igor Tale*); archaeology has supplied further information, though most particularly at West Slav sites such as the Temple of Arkona, on Rügen Island in Germany. In modern times, a mass of relevant ethnographic data has become available – so much so that we can feel we have too much information to form a clearcut picture of folk belief rather than too little. On the other hand, there is no systematic account of Russian paganism as a religion; though there are any number of individual myths, there is no coherent body of pagan Russian mythology; the frequently cited Old Russian 'pantheon' of gods seems to be really a modern construct, based on wishful thinking and on an anachronistic reading of the chronicles; the organizational aspect of Russian paganism remains mysterious, and we do not firmly know even if it had some kind of priesthood (as distinct from individual 'wizards' and 'sorcerers', who did indeed exist) or not.

A way through these perplexities may be found if we stop thinking of the pre-Christian belief system (which is anyhow not altogether 'systematic') as a religion in the conventional sense – and it may be, too, that we should exercise caution in using the term 'paganism', with its connotations of the officially endorsed and well-defined Greco-Roman or Scandinavian sets of beliefs. There was indeed a moment in Old Russian history when such a pagan religion was propagated, but it lasted a mere decade. That was in the late tenth century, when Vladimir I succeeded to the throne of Kiev and promptly set up a sanctuary – whose probable site has been recently located – 'with idols, on the hill beyond his residential palace: a wooden Perun with silver head and golden whiskers, then Khors, Dazhdbog, Stribog, Simargl and Mokosh. And people brought them sacrifices [apparently including human sacrifices], calling them gods . . . '

---

[1]  See, for example, L. Ivanits 'Suicide and Folk Belief in *Crime and Punishment*' in D. Offord (ed.) *The Golden Age of Russian Literature and Thought* (London, 1992).

Thus reads the laconic information provided by the Primary Chronicle; we also learn that an idol, with sacrifices, was established in Novgorod (Perun, according to some chronicles). Earlier, in the entry for the year 907, the Primary Chronicler had provided a further interesting circumstantial detail when describing the ratification of the first treaty between Rus and the Byzantine Empire: 'Oleg and his men swore an oath according to the Russian law, and they swore by their swords and by Perun their god, and by Volos, the god of cattle, and they established peace.' Volos (or Veles), known from other sources, may have been a god of the dead whose association with cattle arose later through the similarity of his name with that of St Blaise (Vlasiy); it has been suggested that, though he is not listed with Perun and the other idols on the Kiev hill top, his image may have stood below, in the market-place, as a 'popular' rather than aristocratic cult figure. Perun is well attested, and is generally thought have been a god of thunder like the Scandinavian Thor. Mokosh is thought to have been a female deity. Khors, Dazhdbog and Stribog make appearances also in the *Igor Tale* (see p. 151–5); the first two seem both to have been associated with the sun, the third with the winds, while the last two are both specifically associated with the Russians, 'Stribog's grandchildren'. Simargl is unknown elsewhere, and has been conjecturally derived from an Iranian deity (Senmurv, a magic bird) It should also be mentioned that a further (sinister) divine figure, Div, also makes appearances in the *Igor Tale* (and, more benignly, in *Zadonshchina*: see p. 154–5). The chronicler tells us what happened to the idols when Vladimir was converted to Christianity (988):

He ordered the idols to be cast down – some to be cut up, others burnt; while he ordered Perun to be tied to a horse's tail and dragged from the hilltop down the Borichev descent to the stream, and ordered twelve men to beat it with rods. This was done not because the wood could feel anything, but to insult the devil that was deceiving people in this form, so that people might get their revenge . . . He ordained that churches should be built and established them in the places where previously idols had stood. And he established a church of St Basil on the hill where the idol of Perun and the others had stood.

The chronicler's anecdotal account, interesting and circumstantial as it is, does not give us much to go on when it comes to assessing the significance of these deities, who mostly remain very shadowy.[2] We may

[2]   A single early document attempts briefly to bring some order to the history of Russian pre-Christian belief: the twelfth-century *Tale of How the Pagans Worshipped Idols*, summarized in B. Rybakov *Early Centuries of Russian History* (English edn, Moscow, 1965) pp. 53–4. It asserts that first the Slavs made offerings to vampires (*upyri*) and guardian spirits (*beregini*); then they began to make feasts for Rod and Rozhanitsy; then they began to worship Perun and other gods.

presume that Vladimir wished to establish a comprehensive and regularized cult in order to emphasize his own role and that of his capital city, to give some cultural unification and a sense of common purpose to Rus, which after all until recently had been no more than a collection of tribes with disparate customs, as the chronicler had taken pains to record (see p. 44–6). Presumably the 'idols' he chose derived from various sources: were they local totems? Perhaps (in the case of Simargl at least) they were imported from abroad for the occasion? However it came about, it is clear that the outcome was far from successful. Soon Vladimir was launching into investigations of the main international developed religions: we shall return later to what happened next. It is amusing to note, incidentally, that Vladimir retained a certain appetite for idols even after the moment of the Conversion: returning from the Greek city of Kherson, 'he seized a pair of bronze idols and four bronze horses, which even today stand near the Church of the Holy Mother of God, and which ignorant people believe to be marble'. Meanwhile, the synthetic 'pantheon', not really corresponding to the needs or prior beliefs of the people, was dismantled and physically cast into the River Dnieper with few regrets (save for some weeping for the idol of Perun by the unbaptized – so the chronicler tells us).

Vladimir's attempt to set up a specific pagan religion of Rus was artificial and unsuccessful – yet there can be little doubt that the deities mentioned in some way already existed in the popular consciousness, together with others whose names have come down to us (Svarog, maybe a powerful deity of the sun and of fire, connected with the swords by which unbaptized Russians swore oaths; Zhelya and Karna, spirits of ill-fortune mentioned in the *Igor Tale*, etc.) It seems though that they were not 'gods' in the Greco-Roman sense: rather incarnations of natural powers or personifications of feelings, aspects of 'forces' or 'force' (*sila* – it has been aptly pointed out that the concept is so fundamental, archaic and pervasive in folk belief that it is impossible to say whether it is really singular or plural, whether there is one 'force' or many). They may have existed in varied hypostases: those of Veles have been mentioned, while Mokosh seems to have represented both the well-known figure of 'damp Mother Earth' and a 'goddess' of somewhat eccentric appearance spinning out the thread of life like the Greek Fates. But clearly these divine beings did not carve up the functions of divinity among themselves in an 'Olympian' manner (no less than three of those already named are thought to be sun gods) and do not constitute a clear-cut 'pantheon'. There seems to be no clear hierarchical distinction between the deities mentioned and numerous other supernatural denizens of the house and countryside, part of the normal mental furniture of Russian traditional life till well into the twentieth century (if not to the present):

the household *domovoy*, the forest-dwelling *leshiy*, the river-dwellers *rusalka* (female) and *vodyanoy* (male), the familial spirits *rod* and *rozhanitsa* (from the root implying both 'birth' and 'clan'), as well as personifications of more abstract forces (Morena, death or plague; Lada, harmony; Yarilo, heat, sunshine and fertility), sometimes in binary opposition (Pravda and Krivda: the first representing the principle of 'truth', 'straightness', 'right' and 'justice'; the second their opposites) – in particular male/female binary oppositions can be observed. Many more specific supernatural characters (Baba Yaga, Kashchey, the Firebird, the siren-bird Sirin, etc.) are familiar to all who have come into contact with Russian *skazki* (fairytales or folk-myths, literally 'spoken things').[3]

Though we may have read, for example, 'the Russian Slavs . . . were nature worshippers' or that 'the most striking witness to the existence of

*Plate 8*  Lubok *(popular print) of Alkonost and Sirin, two mythic bird-like creatures, emblematic respectively of bad and good fortune, widely known in Russian folklore (coloured engraving, late eighteenth – early nineteenth century).*

---

[3]  For an account of 'the religious foundations of the Old Russian culture', see G. Vernadsky *Origins of Russia* (Oxford, 1959), Chapter 4.

civilization among the Russian Slavs is found in their religious beliefs, which were inspired by nature',[4] we may doubt that these beliefs were founded on any concept of 'nature' in the modern sense: primitive people are too much part of the natural world to perceive it as a distinct entity separate from themselves. Rather, folk belief is founded on such constructs as (in Yuriy Lotman's words) the 'universal theme of the opposition of "home" to "forest" – a place of temporary death'. To quote the contemporary poet and ethnographer Olga Sedakova, 'What the modern mind conceives as "nature" – the alive, non-human world – is, for the traditional Slavs, the kingdom of the dead, the manifestation of their souls', and it would be wrong to take the supernatural denizens of field, forest and river for 'spirits of nature' as did nineteenth-century and later investigators.[5] Traditional folk belief is really 'pre-religious', pre-ethical and without regularized patterns of worship – though evidencing itself in a multitude of more or less inflexible rituals, structuring everyday life from cradle to grave and beyond. Russian scholars have revived the term 'manistic', used by nineteenth-century comparitivists and implying the acknowledgement of an all-pervasive impersonal force or *mana*, to characterize this stage of belief, which is found of course in many primitive cultures.

Though elusive, all-pervasive, capable of varied visible incarnations and metamorphoses, the force or forces that characterize this belief system are not merely vague or indescribable. Certain quite well-defined concepts rule human existence within it. Probably the greatest of these is *dolya*, 'lot', a noun related to the verb *delit*, to divide or share: hence implying one's 'due portion' in life. It is symbolized or concretized by the day-to-day apportionment of bread at the family table: Sedakova interestingly notes that after a funeral a new loaf is divided among the bereaved family to indicate the deceased member no longer has a familial part to play. Another concept, that of *vek*, 'term' or 'age', but originally indicating 'strength' or 'life-force', stands in close relationship to *dolya*. To outlive one's 'age' or 'portion' is wrong; not to fulfil it, however, leads to the still more alarming consequence that one will become one of the 'unquiet dead'. A drowned person becomes a water-spirit, *rusalka* or *vodyanoy*; hanged people, *vishelniki*, caused rain to fall. *Dolya* is clearly

---

[4] S. Bolshakoff *Russian Nonconformity* (Philadelphia, 1950) p. 23; N. Andreyev 'Pagan and Christian Elements in Old Russia', contribution to 'The Problem of Old Russian Culture', *Slavic Review* (March 1962) pp. 16–23.
[5] O. Sedakova 'The Slavonic Mythology of Death', paper to Neo-Formalist conference, Cambridge, 25 March 1994. I am indebted to Dr Sedakova for many of the points I make in this section, particularly those concerning the concepts of *sila, dolya, onniy svet, nepritomniki*.

an utterly fatalistic concept, and proverbs current to the present day reinforce the notion of its inexorability (expressed often through such formulae as 'written on one's birth' – i.e. predestined – or *svoya smert*, 'one's own death', which is allotted to one). Attempts to seize a bigger portion than one's due lot run the normal risks of hubris in all ancient mentalities. However, it must be noted that for Russian folk belief there is a contrary, balancing and essentially voluntaristic principle also present in human existence, that of *volya* '(free) will' or 'liberty', an existentially prized though anarchic state of being.

Of the many such binary oppositions (male/female, right/left, even/uneven, dry/wet, near/far etc.) that structure Russian folk belief, the greatest, the most all-encompassing, is that between the worlds of the living and the dead. The dead, referred to by a variety of periphrastic, familiar or euphemistic names ('our ones', 'the souls', 'the forebears', etc.), inhabit 'that world', *onniy or tot svet* – which though very distant (the dead have a long and difficult journey to make so as to reach it) turns out to be practically contiguous with that of the living, over which it has much influence. Indeed it has also many similarities to that of the living: the dead, for example, need to be fed – hence the still universal custom of bringing food and drink as offerings to graves; a coffin is traditionally known as a 'little house' (*domovina*); babies are sometimes still buried with a note of their father's height (so they should know how much they are to grow). Those dying in accordance with their *dolya* and undergoing proper funeral rites are blessed with a *lyudskaya smert*, a 'sociable' death, beneficial to their descendants; those dying far from home, or the victims of murder or suicide, are 'unquiet', *nepritomniki*, will have difficulty reaching *zabytnoy ray*, the 'paradise of oblivion', and will be a menace to the living. Yet it should not be thought that the Russian folk attitude to the dead is generally morbid, fearful or gruesome, in say the Aztec manner. The 'unquiet' are after all a small minority. The generality of the dead are a more welcome 'presence' in everyday life, and are treated in a quite matter-of-fact manner; they sow and reap the harvest alongside their descendants and live beside them in the house. The top of the household stove must always be kept clean, because that is their preferred (the warmest!) resting-place – as it also once was of the heroes of the folk epic songs, the *byliny*. The attitude to the dead is not exactly 'ancestor worship' of the kind known in some other cultures. Nonetheless, one of the best attested and most widespread non-Christian cults in early Russia is that of *rod* and *rozhanitsa*, the familial or kinship spirits mentioned earlier, associated with a special ceremonial meal (relics of this cult have survived in Belorussia and Poland to modern times as the 'grandparents' feast'). Georgiy Fedotov points out that whereas *rod*, 'kin' or 'birth', is always a singular noun, its feminine counterpart is usually in the plural, *rozhanitsy*: i.e. the collectivity of the individual guardian spirits of the clan.[6] He links them with the belief in 'fate' and goes so far as to speak of the '*rod* religion' of early Rus. The traditional Russian awareness of the realm or realms of the dead in everyday life is not so much macabre as sociable in its essences: an apprehension less of the sad fragility of life than of its generational continuity.

## The Coming of Christianity

Our account of Russian folk belief has (apart from mention of the initiative taken by Vladimir I early in his reign) been so far largely ahistorical. One of the remarkable things of such belief systems, after all, is their formidable tenaciousness, retaining (like folk song and folk literature) their essential qualities through many metamorphoses and many generations. Nevertheless historical events did affect it, and the greatest of these was of course the adoption by the rulers of Rus of a new system of beliefs, representing a conscious and unavoidable challenge to it. The struggle between Christianity and pre-Christian belief, and more or less satisfactory accommodations between them, have characterized the Russian mindset over subsequent centuries.

Despite the drama of the famous Conversion dated by the Chronicle to the years 988–9, the coming of Christianity to Russia was actually a rather slow process. Its beginnings appear to date back to the establishment of Kiev as the Vikings' forward post on their route to the Black Sea in the middle of the ninth century. The Kiev Viking leaders Askold and Dir launched a naval attack on Constantinople in June 860 (wrongly placed by the chronicler in 866). This caused much apprehension in the Great City, and some time after it was frustrated (partly by a storm, according to the *Tale of Bygone Years*; by miraculous intervention , according to the Byzantines) the Patriarch Photius proudly announced that the Russians, who had once surpassed all nations in cruelty, had accepted Christianity and were now allies and subjects of the Emperor. How this first conversion took place – presumably as part of a political settlement after the raid – and what ultimately became of it is unknown; Askold and Dir fell victim to the forcible unification of Rus by the Ryurikid clan under Oleg in 882. It is strange that Byzantine sources speak both about this conversion and that of Olga in the middle of the next century, while remaining silent on the great events of 988–9.

[6]  G. Fedotov *The Russian Religious Mind* vol. I, (Cambridge, Mass., 1960) pp. 348–51.

However, there is some more relevant information in the texts of the two treaties between Rus and the Empire of 911 and 945, preserved in the *Tale of Bygone Years*: in the first case, the Rus envoys (whose names all appear to have been Scandinavian) were given instruction in the Christian faith while in Constantinople; in the second case, the group of envoys (still mostly Viking, but some of whom were of Slavonic, and others possibly of Estonian origin) are specifically mentioned as including both baptized and unbaptized; the former group swore to observe the treaty in the Church of Elijah which evidently already stood in Kiev. Olga, princess-regent of Russia during Svyatoslav's minority and evidently a strong-willed person, was sympathetic to Christianity from an early age and in the mid-tenth century made a state visit to Constantinople, where she received baptism (under the significant Christian name of 'Helena') from the Emperor. According to the *Tale of Bygone Years*, the Emperor Constantine VII promptly proposed marriage to his new god-daughter and received a witty and appropriate brush-off. Harder to interpret is what looks like another brush-off on a political or ecclesiastical level a couple of years later, when Olga sent a request for church personnel to the expansionistically minded German ruler Otto I (it must be remembered however that the breach between Eastern and Western churches had not yet taken place). A German bishop, Adalbert, was dispatched to Kiev, but by the time he arrived (962), Olga had probably handed over power to her son Svyatoslav, and an anti-Christian (maybe also anti-Byzantine) reaction seems to have been in progress; Adalbert turned round and went home disappointed.[7]

Svyatoslav, by nature a wanderer-warrior in the old Viking mode, had rejected his mother's attempts to persuade him to accept Christianity (so we are told in the Chronicle) lest his retainers (*druzhina*) should laugh him to scorn. The long delay in the official conversion may be connected with *druzhina* politics, and it has often been suggested that the Slav element of the urban population was disposed towards Christianity, unlike the Vikings. Be that as it may, there is a vivid account in the *Tale of Bygone Years* of the lynching of a Christian Varangian (who had been in Byzantium) and of his son, on whom apparently the lot had fallen to be sacrificed during the pagan period of Vladimir's rule. Neither the names of these first Russian martyrs nor their place of burial were recorded by the chronicler. Since this appears to have been an exceptional incident, it is likely that Vladimir's officially contrived version of paganism was no more than half-heartedly embraced by the populace and represents a somewhat desperate last attempt to breathe

---

[7]  See F. Dvornik *The Making of Central and Eastern Europe* (London, 1949), Chapter IV.

some vigour into the anti-Christian reaction. Dimitri Obolensky has pointed out that a similar revival of paganism attended the period immediately before Christianization in Bulgaria during the preceding century.[8] However, the path towards this outcome in Russia was by no means straightforward, or at least not as narrated by the primary chronicler, in what must be one of the longest and strangest accounts of such an event to have come down from any place or period.

Vladimir, we learn, was visited in the late 980s by representatives of the international developed religions of the time: Islam (from the Volga Bulgar state that lay to the east of Rus), Judaism (from Khazaria) and Christianity (from Germany, but acting on behalf of the Pope). Each representative briefly summarizes his religion, and in each case Vladimir raises witty objection. The Greeks by contrast dispatch a philosopher, who, prompted by Vladimir's questions, gives a disquisition on sacred history a dozen or so pages long and clinches his argument by bringing out an icon of the Last Judgement and explaining its awesome significance. The story does not end there, however. Vladimir consults with his retainers, and the upshot is that ten good and wise men are sent to inspect the various religious practices first hand. As every Russian knows, they came back from Constantinople with a glowing report on the beauty of Greek worship: 'on earth there is no such splendour or such beauty . . . We only know that God dwells there among men, and their service is fairer than the ceremonies of other nations.'[9] To strengthen this report his retainers point out to Vladimir that his grandmother Olga would not have adopted the Greek faith if it had been evil, since she was wiser than anybody.

Any one of these arguments – theological, emotional, rational, aesthetic and familial – might have been expected to be decisive on its own: but there are more to come (political, matrimonial, miraculous). Vladimir for unexplained reasons besieges the important Byzantine city of Chersonesus (Korsun, Kherson) on the Crimea, captures it by cutting off its water-supply (at which point he lifts up his eyes and swears to be baptized if successful!), blackmails the joint Byzantine emperors Basil and Constantine into promising him marriage to Basil's sister Anna – a reluctant pawn in the diplomatic game, though afterwards an important agent of Christianization – if he will become a Christian; the city, conveniently, will be given back to the Greeks as a wedding gift. Finally Vladimir

---

[8]  D. Obolensky *The Byzantine Commonwealth* (London, 1971) p. 83.
[9]  S. Franklin in 'Perceptions and Descriptions of Art in Pre-Mongol Rus', *Byzantinoslavica* LVI (1995) pp. 669–78, argues that the envoys' utterance was a 'later and already conventionalized - already Byzantine-tinted - view of what would have been an appropriate response' (p. 677).

succumbs to eye-trouble, which is relieved the moment the bishop of Chersonesus performs the act of baptism upon him. Once home in Kiev with church trappings and priests, Vladimir orders a mass baptism of the townsfolk in the River Dnieper, at risk of his displeasure. As N. Andreyev puts it, 'the new official religion, if the Korsun version of the conversion is to be believed, was brought into Russia much like any other trophy of a successful campaign'[10] – or anyhow of successful political manoeuvring. Reliable Arab and Armenian historical sources indicate that as part of the 'baptismal deal' of 988–9 Vladimir helped the imperial authorities to quell the dangerous rebellion of Bardas Phocas. Byzantine silence on Vladimir's conversion may reflect a degree of humiliation at being outwitted by Vladimir and at the enforced marriage of an imperial princess to a barbarian (something against which Constantine Porphyrogenitus had powerfully advised not long before in *De Administrando Imperio*.

Historians have long probed all aspects of this memorable, intricate and rather peculiar narrative. It is often pointed out that Metropolitan Ilarion's *Discourse on the Law and the Grace* composed well before the *Tale of Bygone Years*, ignores the story. There are commonplaces and apparent anachronisms (notably a hint of anti-Latin polemics) in it. The various stages of the drawn-out tale do not always hang together very logically. Yet it does not seem that there is any reason to accuse the chronicler or chroniclers of deliberate invention, still less of falsification on any significant scale. Clearly there were many anecdotes of greater or lesser credibility about the conversion current by the time the final chronicle account was compiled, and the chronicler attempted to tease those that seemed reliable into a coherent order; he certainly exercised selectivity among them (after telling us of his baptism in Chersonesus, he writes that those who are ignorant 'say he [i.e. Vladimir] was baptized in Kiev, while others mention other places'). At ten centuries' distance we are even less likely to establish the incontrovertible facts. The conversion narrative retains its powerful interest for somewhat different reasons: as the crux of the *Tale of Bygone Years* in its role as a 'shaped' literary work; as an unrivalled glimpse into the mental processes and psychological acuteness of a thoughtful early medieval historian. It is also a corner stone of Russian 'mythistory' (if one may appropriate the splendid word popularized by the Greek poet George Seferis), the first in the field as an ostentatious 'moment of change' in the destiny of Russia.

The superfluity of detail in the account of the conversion that has come down to us merely points up the fact that we have remarkably little information about the progress of Russian Christianity for another

---

[10]   N. Andreyev 'Pagan and Christian Elements in Old Russia', *Slavic Review* March 1962, p. 18.

half-century, till well into the reign of Yaroslav. The building of a few churches in Kiev and major centres is recorded. How the new Russian Church was organized is shrouded in mystery. Kiev certainly became the seat of a Metropolitan (the church dignitary next below a patriarch), and bishoprics were probably established in Belgorod (near Kiev), Novgorod, Chernigov and maybe Polotsk.[11] Presumably Bulgaria supplied some of the personnel required – it undoubtedly supplied many books in Slavonic translation. During the pre-Tatar ('Kievan') period all the metropolitans of the Russian church seem to have been Byzantine Greeks with (as far as we know) only two exceptions: the famous Ilarion in Yaroslav's time, and Klim Smolyatich (Clement of Smolensk) a century later (1147–1155). Metropolitans were in principle elected by the local bishops, but in practice the patriarch in Constantinople selected the successful candidate from a short-list of three; later (from the mid-thirteenth to mid-fifteenth centuries) an agreement was apparently struck whereby the Byzantine Patriarchate and the Russian authorities should nominate alternate metropolitans.[12] Metropolitans and bishops had plenty to do: the Russian dioceses, not to mention Russia itself, were vast. As in other parts of Europe, the Church had jurisdiction over a great swathe of family (and related) legal matters, while persons connected with Church employment had their own jurisdiction.

Christianity, in fact, brought with it far more than simply a change of belief: the conversion was essentially a great cultural package deal. Many elements came together in the package. The biggest was language itself: it had to be extended to accommodate an abstract vocabulary and syntactic structures adequate to convey the Biblical message and Christian theological thought (hence the complete transplantation into Russia of Church Slavonic as a register of the written Russian language); with this of course came an extensive literature (see Chapter 4). Reading and writing had to be propagated and a class of literate people produced through an educational system – it is significant that immediately after the Conversion narrative, the Primary Chronicler describes how Vladimir set up schools. Customary law, as has been mentioned, was fundamentally affected. Religious ritual necessitated new architectural forms and (probably) techniques, together with an utterly unprecedented and elaborate range of visual art works. An entire new music was introduced, and singers had to be trained in it. A changed conception of politics was an inevitable part of the deal, involving not only a more sophisticated

[11] See J. Fennell *A History of the Russian Church to 1448* (Longman, 1995) pp. 51–4.
[12] D. Obolensky 'Byzantium, Kiev, Moscow: a Study in Ecclesiastical Relations' in *Dumbarton Oaks Papers* (Washington, 1957).

relationship between ruler and subjects, but also access to a new system of international relations as part of 'Christendom', and more specifically of what has been called by Obolensky the 'Byzantine Commonwealth'.

The Church, once established, played a hugely important but also ambiguous part in Russian cultural (and often political) life. Through the range of innovations just listed it locked Russia into a universal, 'ecumenical' culture, and Constantinople became early Russia's 'doorway into Europe'.[13] The presence of Greek metropolitans and sometimes bishops, with their assistants, necessarily acted as a counterweight to Russian self-absorption and provincialism, particularly when trade routes with the south ceased to be much used. But from the first the Church in Russia had its own characteristics and was to play a special role or series of roles in Russian history. That does not mean that the Russians were habitually insubordinate towards the Patriarchate in Constantinople; the first documented instance of such defiance did not occur till 1448 (when Russia refused to accept the union of Eastern and Western churches arranged at the Council of Florence, sacked the pro-Union Metropolitan and chose another without Constantinople's permission). Of course there were individual instances of friction and it has sometimes – though unconvincingly – been maintained that the election of the native Russian Ilarion as early as the mid-eleventh century was an anti-Byzantine move. Generally, though, Russian loyalty to the Constantinople Patriarchate was not in doubt, and the sort of antagonisms that in Europe were to fuel the Reformation were minimized in the East by the lack of centralized authority – compared with that of the Pope – within the territory of the Eastern Patriarchates: an autocephalous church really did have a strong degree of autonomy. The Russian Church's individuality derived from its different cultural, political and economic circumstances, rather than from any innate hostility towards Constantinople, or (later) towards the West. A major aspect of these cultural circumstances was, of course, the coexistence with Christianity of the folk beliefs described above.

### Christianized Rus and 'Double Belief'

From what has been said it will be clear that the 'Christianization' of Russia was a process lasting many centuries, if not a whole millennium, within which Vladimir's 'enlightenment' at the 988–9 Conversion

---

[13]   See D. Obolensky 'Russia's Byzantine Heritage', *Oxford Slavonic Papers* vol. I (1950) pp. 37–63, reprinted in Obolensky *Byzantium and the Slavs* (London, 1971).

marked only one (admittedly important) new stage. Kiev and maybe other major cities had previously experienced some Christianization 'from below', probably more among the Slav than the Viking populace; such spontaneous and popular Christianization does not seem to have been witnessed in rural areas till the fourteenth century, and in a very different context. Vladimir and his successors imposed or encouraged Christianization 'from above', in a process starting with the building and staffing of churches in urban centres, the establishment of a hierarchy, the translation and copying of necessary texts (both with South Slav assistance), the construction of the first monasteries (close to towns) and the introduction of canon law. Not only dioceses, but parishes were very large, and in much of the remoter countryside of Kievan Rus regular church-going was scarcely a possibility, nor indeed was systematic instruction in Christian principles. Christianity, however, was associated with both authority and literacy, and was bound even without forcible measures to make gradual headway. The self-identification of Russians as 'Christian' in contrast to the steppe-country oppressors (first the Pechenegs and Polovtsians, subsequently and most significantly, the Tatars) clearly gave this process great impetus. Mostly Christianization seems to have proceeded quite peacefully, through persuasion and the application of common-sense principles rather than forcibly. This is apparent, for example, in surviving answers given by bishops of the pre-Tatar period to queries put to them as to what action should be taken when (for instance) women took sick children to a heathen healer rather than a priest, or towards 'those who sacrifice to devils and to bogs and to wells, and those who marry without blessing.' Such things should be strongly resisted, but by instruction or penance, not by severer methods.[14]

Nevertheless a few cases are recorded of violence and bloodshed in the opposition between pre-Christian beliefs and Christian authority – several of them in one of the most interesting entries in the Primary Chronicle, placed under the year 1071. The major incident recounted in that year was a revolt, almost a brief civil war, in the northern Yaroslavl-Sheksna-Belozersk area, fomented by two sorcerers (*volkhvy*) who attracted 300 followers – a fair-sized force in that thinly populated region; it was quelled with some bravado by Yan Vyshatych, whom the chronicler knew personally. In this, as in most other incidents of the

---

[14] Fennell *A History of the Russian Church to 1448* pp. 73–7, 79. The remarkable fourth surviving sermon of Bishop Serapion of Vladimir (d. 1275) makes a long and well-argued plea against the lynching of sorcerers: translation and commentary by R. Bogert in H. Birnbaum and M. Flier *Medieval Russian Culture* vol. I, (Berkeley, 1984) pp. 280–310.

kind, there are clear economic and social reasons for the popular discontent that could lead to anti-Christian reaction – generally concerned with grain-hoarding in the agriculturally marginal lands of the Russian north and around Novgorod. Might there also have been an ethnic component to the issue, insofar as the Belozersk area and the other parts of the North probably still retained at that time a high proportion of Finnic-speaking people, who may well have been the staunchest supporters of pre-Christian beliefs? We cannot be sure. There is a strange gender-related aspect to the chronicle account of the rebellion, since the sorcerers, trying to detect hoarded grain and goods, primarily targeted women: 'they killed many women and expropriated their possessions.' Modern ethnographers have noted certain correspondences with folk rituals current among the Finnic Mordva in times of famine.

A few such violent incidents apart, Christianity and folk belief seem to have found a *modus vivendi* together. The situation that often consequently arose is generally termed 'double belief' (*dvoyeverie* – sometimes rendered 'ditheism'). Some historians question the implications behind this term and avoid using it: indeed it is often unclear whether it means at one extreme a balanced (or 'split-minded') coexistence of Christian and pagan elements within a person's belief system, or a mere persistence of superstitious habits, or whether 'double belief' is taken to be consciously or unconsciously held. The influential cultural historian Dmitriy Likhachov has argued against the concept on the grounds that once Christianity has been accepted one cannot simultaneously believe in any other divine principle, and that it was pagan ritual rather than paganism as a religion that lingered on in the countryside in the post-Conversion centuries. However the term itself is no mere modern anthropological construct, but has an ancient pedigree, going back to Kievan times, and I think that (with certain provisos) it is still a useful one. Christianity and pre-Christian folk belief could, in varying proportions, coexist because – as has been argued above – 'paganism' in Russia was not really a religious entity of the same order as a 'developed' religion such as Christianity, rather an archaic mindset and series of inbred relationships within the natural and social world. Thus from an official Christian point of view such double belief was unnatural and deplorable, but not from the point of view of 'folk believers' themselves. In this context it is important, in the words of a modern researcher, to understand 'the beliefs of the Russian peasants as they existed in actual practice . . . to distinguish *religion* from *faith* as a basic, primary and practical body of beliefs. Faith was a syncretic entity in which village sorcery and Orthodox worship were dynamically fused into one indivisible creed. There was no compartmentalization between life and faith . . . Faith was a mode of behaviour that permeated everything.'[15] There was hence no ultimate incompatibility between Christian and non-Christian elements of such a synthesis (to which even Soviet 'mythic' elements and vocabulary could sometimes be added in our own century). After the seventeenth century Schism (see below) the 'Old Believers', seeking in accordance with their Christian principles to preserve old ways, seem involuntarily to have perpetuated many archaic folk traditions.

The lives of the vast majority of Russians from early times onwards were delineated and given meaning by the cycle of the agricultural year. Here Christian feast-days could in many cases be easily approximated to the pre-Christian ritual calendar. The festive season of *svyatki* marked both Christmastide (Christmas to Epiphany) and the ancient winter solstice celebrations, when meals for the departed (*bratshiny*) were held and household fires were ceremonially extinguished and rekindled. Less precisely, because of their mobility, Easter (the greatest feast of the Orthodox Church) could substitute for the celebration of the spring equinox and the start of the ancient New Year, and Whitsun for the celebration of the sun-spirit Yarilo (marked to this day by the decoration of houses and churches with leafy twigs). The greatest of early summer celebrations marked the summer solstice, in Christian terms the eve of St John the Baptist's day (24 June), known as Kupala, metonymically associated with water and hence with a desire for early summer rain, and having also erotic connotations. A memorable reenactment of Kupala rituals can be seen in Andrey Tarkovsky's famous film *Andrey Rublyov*; there was ritual bathing and great bonfires were lit. In high summer (20 July) came the less joyful feast of Elijah the Prophet, associated with thunderstorms and the power of Perun, the ancient thunder-god, who had it in his power to destroy the harvest. Particularly worrying for the Church authorities was the coincidence in September of the Feast of the Nativity of the Virgin with the traditional festival of *rod* and *rozhanitsy*.

Various Orthodox saints and holy personages, naturally, could be assimilated to folk belief, becoming protectors of the household or of particular activities. Thus the otherwise rather obscure saint Paraskeva

---

[15]  M. Mazo in W. Brumfield and M. Velimirović (eds) *Christianity and the Arts in Russia* (Cambridge, 1991), p. 77. See also E. Levin 'Dvoeverie and Popular Religion' in S. Batalden (ed.) *Seeking God* (De Kalb, 1993) which calls for a more nuanced approach to 'double belief'. On Old Believers and folk traditions, see N. Veletskaia 'Forms of Transformation of Pagan Symbolism in the Old Believer Tradition' in M. Balzer (ed.) *Russian Traditional Culture* (New York, 1992).

became one of the universally known and revered in Russia, at any rate by half its people: her day (28 October) coincided with the traditional breaking of flax, she became the guardian of spinning and weaving, and thence, by extension, of household matters, health, fertility and women's domestic work generally.[16] The word *pyatnitsa* ('fifth day', Friday) came to be added to her name (many churches are dedicated to 'Paraskeva-Pyatnitsa') and certain domestic tasks were taboo on Fridays – thus once a week lightening the heavy female burden of housework. J. Vytkovskaya points out that another 'feminine mythological image', that of 'Wednesday' (*sreda*) was 'connected with the feminine principle of uneven numbers', and 'aided in weaving and bleaching cloth, punishing those who worked on Wednesdays.'[17] Those two days, coincidentally, were also the traditional Orthodox fast-days. The most universal and venerated feminine figure of christianized Russia, of course, was the Mother of God (*Bogoroditsa* or *Bogomater*), as the Virgin Mary is always known in the Orthodox lands. She seems to have subsumed into her image the pre-Christian Mokosh, maybe also the joyous deity Lada (Harmony), undoubtedly too the revered figure of 'Damp Mother Earth', originator of all life. Her protective function was partly inherited from her Byzantine role as guardian of the Holy City of Constantinople and the Holy Mountain of Athos, but in Russia it came to be particularly associated with the feast-day known as *Pokrov* (1 October), unknown in the Western Church, translatable as the 'Protecting Veil', though often rendered as 'Intercession'. It became from the twelfth century a major feastday of the Russian church, a dedication for countless churches, signifying among other things the special protection extended by the Mother of God over the Russian land. Among other saints with particular folk relevance one may mention St Nicholas, protector of voyagers, of wealth, of children and of carpenters; St Blaise (Vlasiy), protector of cattle and livestock generally; Sts Florus and Laurus (Flor, Lavr), protectors of horses; and of course St George (Georgiy or Yuriy, whose name when he takes on folk attributes is often distorted into Yegor or Yegoriy) – as horseman and dragon-slayer a mythic protective figure, who became patron saint of Moscow and Muscovy, but who was also bound up with the agricultural year: on his spring feast-day, 23 April, animals were led out onto the new grass, and cultivation got under way, while on the second St George's Day in late November, all agricultural operations ended and labourers (before serfdom was fully instituted) could seek a new employer.

[16]  A. Hilton 'Piety and Pragmatism' in Brumfield and Velimirović *Christianity and the Arts in Russia* p. 60ff.
[17]  J. Vytkovskaya 'Slav Mythology', in *The Feminist Companion to Mythology* ed. C. Larrington (London, 1992), p. 106.

People of all classes in early Rus would normally have a 'worldly' personal name of pre-Christian or folk origin, but would also have a supplementary Christian name relating to their 'own' saint, usually the saint on whose day they had been baptized. Thus Olga, first Christian ruler of Rus, was baptized in Constantinople under the name Helena (Yelena), while Vladimir I and II both had the name Basil (Vasiliy); Yaroslav's Christian name was George (Yuriy). Monks and nuns would take a new Christian name (often beginning with the same letter as their previous name). For the first couple of centuries after the Conversion, early sources normally refer to individuals by their worldly names; gradually the Christian names became more usual. The literate upper tiers of society were obviously not so prone to 'double belief' as the peasantry, though far from always immune to it (Ivan the Terrible's superstitions and fondness for *skomorokhi* is just one indication of this). They too had 'appropriate' saints; the Archangel Michael was special patron of princely families,[18] while Sts Boris and Gleb played a complex and specifically Russian role, in part as protectors of the dynasty of Yaroslav. There is a unique and beautiful visual relic of united pagan-Christian motifs in the form of the so-called 'Chernigov Grivna', a gold disc dating apparently to the late eleventh century. On the obverse is an image of the Archangel Michael with a Greek-language text; on the reverse, a strange 'Medusa' figure with texts in Greek and Slavonic, the latter invoking God's 'help for thy servant, Vasiliy'. Such pagan images were believed to have apotropaic value, particularly in connexion with childbirth. There is a strong possibility that the first owner of this precious object was Vladimir II Monomakh, then Prince of Chernigov.[19] Vladimir's surviving writings (chiefly his moving *Testament*) nevertheless show him as a model of Christian piety. A notable prince contemporary with him, Vseslav of Polotsk, seems to have been a remarkable representative of double belief: his mother 'bore him from sorcery', according to the chronicler; he was reputed to be a werewolf and to have supernatural powers of translocation (c.f. the *Igor Tale*), and his image, transmuted into 'Volkh Vseslavych', recurs in heroic epos (*byliny*).[20]

There were several instances of Old Russian authors complaining that

[18]  N. Teteriatnikov 'The Role of the Devotional Image in the Religious Life of Pre-Mongol Rus', in Brumfield and Velimirović *Christianity and the Arts in Russia*.

[19]  For an illustration of and commentary on the 'Chernigov Grivna', see R. Grierson (ed.), exhibition catalogue *Gates of Mystery: the Art of Holy Russia* (London, 1993) pp. 118–19; cf. also D. Obolensky *Six Byzantine Portraits* (Oxford, 1988), pp. 111–12.

[20]  R. Jakobson 'The Vseslav Epos' in *Russian Epic Studies* (1949), reprinted in his *Selected Writings* vol. IV (The Hague, 1966).

*Plate 9   A gold pendant, the so-called 'Chernigov Grivna' (late
eleventh century), featuring Greek and Slavonic inscriptions, the
Archangel Michael and (reverse) a 'Medusa' figure: it probably
belonged to Vladimir Monomakh, then Prince of Chernigov.*

while churches were poorly or perfunctorily attended, the open-air folk
gatherings attracted the gleeful attendance of large numbers of the
populace. Indeed it is easy to see how much traditional folk belief could
offer the ordinary people: a secure, comprehensible, time-hallowed,
down-to-earth guide to action and set of mythic elucidations of the
world. Christianity by contrast could offer a more dynamic set of rituals
and dogmas, implying a cosmic drama continually being played out; a
set of universal moral principles according to which reward or
punishment would be meted out in the hereafter; a more subtle and
abstract conceptual world; a connection between one's own limited
horizons and the universal history and destiny of all mankind; a symbolic
system offering considerable aesthetic and intellectual gratification. The

systems obviously competed for allegiance, yet could also to a large extent occupy separate and complementary territories. There were moments indeed when the 'institutions' of the older system could come to the aid of the newer one: at times of religious persecution (the Schism of the seventeenth century, the Soviet 1930s) a grove of trees could become a church, confession could be made to Mother Earth.

### Holy Rus and the Orthodox World

The Christian Church to which Rus adhered from 988–9 onwards was, formally at least, still universal (ecumenical) and undivided. True, tensions had already surfaced between the Latin-based West and the primarily Greek-speaking East in the previous century. The Schism between them came in 1054: its pretexts were certain differences of ritual and a rather more substantial question concerning the formula by which the Holy Trinity was described. These problems might have seemed easily capable of resolution, and indeed concerned those at the top of the hierarchy rather than the mass of believers; but the rivalries between the two sides tended to deepen with the passage of time, and the several attempts to heal the Schism were all short-lived. After the sack of Constantinople by the Fourth Crusade in 1204 and the subsequent setting up of a rival Latin Church organization on historically Byzantine territory, fear and mistrust of the East towards the West became deeply ingrained at all social levels. The Church on the territory of the four Eastern Patriarchates – Alexandria, Antioch, Constantinople and Jerusalem (of which, after the rise of Islam, Constantinople was much the most important) – became known as 'Orthodox' ('right-doctrinal', in Russian *pravoslavnaya*, 'right-praising'), in distinction from the 'Catholic' patriarchate of Rome. From the Eastern point of view the Patriarch of Rome (i.e. the Pope), tracing his succession from St Peter, could claim to be 'first among equals' – but already well before the official Schism the Popes had begun to claim a universal supremacy, authority, and ultimately infallibility that the Orthodox would never accept.

Within the 'family' of Orthodox churches, that of Russia constituted an autocephalous province under the jurisdiction of Constantinople. Its head was the Metropolitan (a rank of hierarch below the Patriarch and above bishops) of Kiev, later becoming known as 'of Kiev and all Rus'. From 1299 the Metropolitans took up residence in Vladimir, centre of the principality 'beyond the forest' (*Zalesskaya zemlya*), less comprehensively-devastated by the Tatar onslaught than Kiev itself had been; around 1326 Metropolitan Peter moved to Moscow, the up-and-coming city that became – partly because of this event – successor to Vladimir and eventual centre of all the Russian lands. In the fourteenth and fifteenth centuries several attempts, with only short-lived success, were made to persuade Constantinople to re-establish a metropolitan ('of Little Russia', as the Byzantines put it) in Kiev. Ecclesiastically, if not politically, Moscow saw off its rivals (including the Archbishops of Novgorod, who enjoyed much autonomy) and eventually – under Tsar Fyodor in 1589 – engineered the establishment of a Russian Patriarchate; this however lasted only till Peter the Great suspended it in 1700, turning the Church into, effectively, an arm of state. It was restored in 1918.

What was distinctive about the Orthodox branch of Christianity, with which Russians came to identify themselves so wholeheartedly? A theological disquisition would be out of place here, but some brief comments pointing up contrasts with Western churches (Catholic or Protestant) may be of use. It should be understood that these are mostly contrasts of emphasis rather than concerning the fundamentals of faith or ritual. First and foremost, the Orthodox Church saw itself as traditionalist – the bearer and preserver of the authentic traditions of the early Church Fathers. Only the decisions of the first seven ecumenical Councils of the Church were recognized as universally valid (though of course further separate councils did take place in East and West). So it has often (though, in fact, wrongly) been thought that Orthodox doctrine was finalized by the eighth century and was not modified at all thereafter. Certainly the Orthodox Church had no Aquinas or Abelard, let alone a Dante, no careful rationalization and systematization of doctrine. Its equivalent medieval figures (notably St Gregory Palamas) operated primarily in the area of mystical theology. The medieval Western doctrine of Purgatory found no echo in the East (a fact that Lotman and Uspensky take as illustrative of the antithetical, binary nature of cultural models – in this case, as between the 'sacred' and the 'devilish' – in Old Russia).[21] Nonetheless Orthodox doctrine often seems flexible in comparison with that of the Catholic and, later, Protestant worlds, leaving some matters undefined that in the West would need to be properly clarified. The East had a broader conception of sanctity, with less rigid processes of canonization and many locally venerated uncanonized 'saints' (including, for example, *yurodivye*, 'holy fools', of which more below). As in the West, relics were venerated, though their cult does not seem to have reached quite such bizarre extremes in the East.

Certain concepts became particularly typical of Russian Orthodoxy:

[21]   Yu. Lotman and B. Uspensky 'Binary Models in the Dynamics of Russian Culture' in A. D. and A. S. Nakhimovsky (eds) *The Semiotics of Russian Cultural History* (Ithaca, 1985).

the *starets* ('elder'), a monk or hermit acting as personal spiritual adviser to a lay person; *podvig* ('feat'), of a difficult nature but with spiritual import (there is also an abstract noun *podvizhnichestvo* from this; *podvizhnik* is one who performs such feats); *sobornost* ('conciliarity'), a collective spirit that nineteenth-century Slavophiles considered to be specially characteristic of, and admirable in, Russian Christianity. Extremes of asceticism, and especially complete rejection of the body, were foreign to the Russian Church and indeed to Orthodoxy as a whole. Sexuality and its manifestations – though undoubtedly belonging to the 'profane' rather than 'divine' sphere – were treated in a more relaxed and less punitive manner in the East than in the West (as Eve Levin has shown in *Sex and Society in the World of the Orthodox Slavs*).

The Orthodox churches, organized into Patriarchates of equal status, and below these mostly into autocephalous ethnically-based units, seemed more democratic than the Catholic world in which all significant power and decision-making was centred on the Papacy. This was emphasized by the momentous decision in the ninth century to develop a liturgy and sacred literature for the Slavs in their own vernacular: this enormously assisted popular involvement in the processes of religion (but at the expense – as Georgiy Fedotov and others have pointed out – of being distanced from the treasure-house of classical Greco-Roman culture to which educated Westerners and Byzantines still had access). Not surprisingly, the ethos of Orthodoxy has been less bookish – though books were respected – than in the West (the notion of the 'intellectual silence' of Old Russia has become a scholarly commonplace, though sometimes contested). Only parts of the Bible – the Psalms, the Gospels, the Pentateuch – were familiar to Orthodox congregations; it was not until the 1490s (to counter the scriptural knowledge of heretics) that a full translation of the Bible was made in Russia at the behest of the active and aggressive Archbishop Gennadiy of Novgorod. Compensating, as it were, for the lesser bookish or intellectualized content of Orthodoxy is a heightened aesthetic consciousness expressed particularly in the splendidly organized adornment of wall-paintings and icons in even humble churches, and supremely in the 'total work of art' that is the Liturgy.

Parish priests in the Orthodox lands were generally far from being intellectuals – indeed in Muscovite Russia they were often scarcely literate (though maybe Western visitors tended to exaggerate this). They were peasants like their parishioners, and shared their way of life, usually having to till the soil to keep their families. They had to be married – another source of contention with the Catholic West, where the Popes had insisted on celibacy of the clergy since at any rate the time of Gregory the Great (*c*.600); priesthood tended to run in families. Bishops and metropolitans, by contrast, had to be unmarried, so they were generally selected from the monasteries; the only way a priest could get such promotion (beyond the rank of 'archpriest') was in the event of his wife's dying or becoming a nun. A most remarkable example of the latter event was when the boyar Fyodor Romanov and his wife were for political reasons forced into monastic life under Boris Godunov; their young son Mikhail was subsequently (1613) elected to the throne, to become founder of the Romanov dynasty, while under the monastic name of Filaret his father first endured a long captivity in Poland as a result of the Time of Troubles, then returned as Patriarch of Moscow and the power behind the throne.

Monasteries tended to be rather more closely engaged with the life of society in early Rus than might have been expected. In or close to cities, they were the chief centres of literacy, historical recording, chronicle production, Christian art and music, while their more ambitious members, whether as elders and confessors (*startsy*) or bishops-to-be, often stood close to, and were influential upon, figures of power. From the fourteenth century the situation changed somewhat, with monasteries being founded in more distant places, but monastic leaders continued to play a large role in Russian life and Tsars continued to pay them great attention (and lengthy visits) up to the time of Peter the Great, who ironically enough engineered the coup d'état that began his personal rule from the safety of the great Trinity Monastery (1689). But monasteries were (and are) also much visited by the common people – most monks were of humble origin – were the major dispensers of charity to the destitute, provided the only hospitals for the sick, and were a huge economic influence upon their localities and sometimes far beyond. There were no silent or secluded orders of monks and nuns, as in the West; indeed there were no separate monastic orders at all. The distinction of significance within the Orthodox lands was between 'coenobitic' and 'idiorrhythmic' monasteries: in the former a completely communal life was lived to the strict Byzantine Studite rule; in the latter the monks or nuns could largely establish their personal disciplines and retain some worldly goods. Within their substantial walls, monasteries functioned as citadels, were often used as strongpoints for defence and as places of exile or imprisonment. Their role in both the actual and symbolic geography of Rus was enormous. Indeed it is to monasteries, in their roles as guardians and transmitters of historical knowledge, that we owe most of what we know about early Rus – in particular to the leading Kiev monastery, that of the Caves, founded in the mid-eleventh century (the *Tale of Bygone Years* and its *Paterikon* relay a series of interesting and entertaining stories of its early monks). Its abbots had a powerful and independent voice in Kievan state affairs, and it sometimes operated as neutral territory where quarrelling princes could settle their differences. In the later period of Rus (from the late fourteenth century) the Trinity Monastery, founded by St Sergius north-east of Moscow, aspired to a similar role of all-Russian cultural centre;[22] both establishments had arisen independently of princely benefaction or of the Church authorities on the site of the hermitages of their visionary founders.

The Orthodox Churches from the first struck a characteristic balance between centripetal and centrifugal tendencies. Constantinople, the Great City, was (until the fifteenth century) at least as important an ecumenical focus of loyalty as Rome was in the West, with the difference that it remained the hub of a still extant Empire (the Roman Empire, as far as the Byzantines were concerned) and the crossroads of trade. But the foundation of individual churches generally on an ethnic-linguistic basis, together with the establishment of Slavonic as an ecclesiastical language (as, indeed, Syriac, Coptic, Georgian already were) counteracted centralization. There were also two other great focal points for spiritual loyalty, standing above politics, in the Orthodox world. One was the Holy City, Jerusalem itself, on historic Byzantine territory, which remained, even after its capture by the Arabs in the late seventh century, the goal of numerous pilgrims. The Byzantine authorities saw no need to launch crusades to recover it (after the first wave of Arab invasions, the Byzantines settled down to a fairly peaceful coexistence with their Muslim neighbours: Islam was generally regarded as a Christian anti-Trinitarian heresy rather than a new religion). The other was one of the strangest and most durable entities of the medieval, and indeed modern, world: the self-governing monastic republic of Mount Athos, the Holy Mountain at the north end of the Aegean Sea, isolated from centres of population yet at the hub of Orthodox Eastern Europe. Since the tenth century its monasteries, sketes and hermitages had become a magnet drawing monks and lay pilgrims from all the Orthodox nations, the greatest Orthodox meeting-point and centre for the exchange of spiritual ideas, the training of monks and hence bishops, for manuscript-copying and artistic production. The balance between Church and state, so full of tensions and conflict in the medieval West, was regulated (at least in theory) in the East by the doctrine of *symphonia*, 'harmony' which enjoined an effort of cooperation on secular and ecclesiastical authorities, an ideal to which both sides knew that they had at least to aspire. Generally, the Orthodox church avoided the worst episodes of savagery that punctuated the history of Western religion: the Crusades, the religious wars, the witch hunts; it disapproved (not always consistently) of capital punishment and of slavery.

---

[22]  See R. R. Milner-Gulland 'Russia's Lost Renaissance' in D. Daiches and A. Thorlby (eds) *Literature and Western Civilisation*, vol. III (London, 1973)

Two great upheavals in religious doctrine that rippled out into political life and into international relations framed the Middle Ages (if this essentially Western term can be permitted) in the Orthodox world. The first occurred immediately before Cyril and Methodius's mission to the Slavs: it was the lengthy and curious crisis, occupying most of the eighth century and part of the ninth, of 'Iconoclasm'. In the 720s the Imperial and Church authorities in Constantinople decided to ban figurative imagery from churches and shrines, in doing so following the Second Commandment (against graven images). The consequences of this policy led to bloodshed and nearly civil war; it isolated the Empire from the rest of Christendom. The causes of Iconoclasm and the underlying tensions it revealed have been discussed by historians from the most varied angles (theological, artistic, political, economic, sociological, geographical, psychological – providing a small anthology of attitudes to historical causality).[23] But it is clear that support for the icons came primarily from the common people and the monasteries, and that, against all the odds, they eventually won. The upshot, together with the restoration of the images, was a careful formulation of the role of images and their veneration; thereafter the visual component of Christian culture was a central feature of Orthodoxy (see Chapter 5 'The Iconic World').

The second upheaval came in the early fourteenth century with the formulation – particularly associated with Balkan monks centred on the Holy Mountain of Athos, whose chief voice was that of Gregory Palamas, Archbishop of Thessaloniki – of 'Hesychasm'. This word (literally translatable as 'quietism') indicated a doctrine, derived from certain of the early Fathers of the Church, whereby an individual – through repeated inner prayer, contemplation, bodily disciplines and with God's grace – might attain to apprehension of the Divine Energy, the only humanly perceptible aspect of God, conceived of as the Uncreated Light witnessed at the Transfiguration on Mount Tabor. The Hesychasts' teaching, implying a possible contact with the Divine unmediated by the processes of reason or, importantly, of organized religion, was strongly resisted not only in Western Europe among scholastic theologians but also by segments of Byzantine society, in which factions lined up as pro- or anti-Hesychast during the civil strife of the mid-fourteenth century. In the Slav lands Hesychasm was accepted readily, so far as one may judge. After bitter debate and two councils, the mystical theology of Hesychasm was confirmed as Orthodox doctrine, and remains so to this day. Hesychast revivals have from time to time reminded Russian orthodox believers of their genuinely non-authoritarian spiritual roots – notably the Hesychasm promoted by the monk and

---

[23]  Cf. A. Bryer and J. Herrin (eds) *Iconoclasm* (Birmingham, 1977).

scholar Paisiy Velichkovsky, disseminator of the influential *Philokalia* – a miscellany of ancient ascetic spiritual advice – at an otherwise low point in Church life in the late eighteenth century.

The Church in Rus underwent its own upheavals, some of which had a debilitating or disastrous effect on it. One such event, though, had remarkable and positive consequences not just for religious life but for Russia's fate as a nation. This was the so-called 'eremitical movement' wherein hermits and monks, leaving behind the 'world' in the form of large monasteries and centres of population, spearheaded the colonization of vast unpopulated forest tracts of the Russian north during the fourteenth and fifteenth centuries. Instigated by Sergius (Sergey, Sergiy) of Radonezh (1321–91) – who later as St Sergius was to be counted a patron saint of Russia – the movement remains somewhat mysterious historically: how far was it a response to the domination of the Tatars? (whose rule in the mid-fourteenth century was actually much less oppressive than in the century before); to the expansionist aims and practices of Moscow? (which soon attempted to muscle in on the fruits of colonization); to religious impulses and dissatisfactions? (it seems to be connected, though not altogether clearly, with the general mood of spiritual renewal in the Orthodox lands that also gave rise to Hesychasm). Sergius's 'wilderness' was symbolically rather than actually remote, being located among forested hills only a few miles from Radonezh – which has since disappeared from the map – and some 70 kilometres north-east of Moscow, where the town of Sergiev Posad (formerly Zagorsk) now stands. His hermitage became the great Trinity Monastery, radial point for the process that led to the setting-up of nearly 200 ever remoter religious houses in the course of a century or so. His close associate St Stephen of Perm was simultaneously responsible for the first major Russian missionary endeavour, that brought about the conversion of the Finno-Ugrian Permian (or Zyryan) people in the huge region between historic Rus and the Urals now known as the Komi Republic. Stephen, imitating Sts Cyril and Methodius, gave the Permians not only their own church organization but their own alphabet and written language; both fell victim to Muscovite centralization within a few decades. As for Sergius, he became godfather to the children of the Moscow Grand Prince Dmitriy Donskoy, supposedly encouraged the latter's defiance of the Tatars that resulted in the Battle of Kulikovo (1380) and entered the Church hierarchy when persuaded to become abbot of the Trinity Monastery; but the latter institution, the true power-house of an all-Russian culture for a few decades around 1400, attempted to stand outside the fractious inter-princely rivalries of the time. Sergius's successors in the fifteenth and early sixteenth centuries were known as the 'Trans-Volga Elders', living as they mostly did north of the great river that marks a division between central and northern Russia; they were perceived by the Church authorities more and more as a disruptive and individualistic force from *c*.1500, and were systematically repressed in the early years of Ivan the Terrible's reign, though their spirit lived on as a significant current in Russian Christianity.

Sergius's movement, attracting its following from the humbler members of Russian society, not just the educated or powerful, can be taken to mark the moment when the Russian populace (notwithstanding the long persistence of 'double belief' discussed above) seems predominantly to have identified itself as a Christian people. It was of course a clearcut way of distinguishing itself from the 'ungodly' Tatars (the Golden Horde in fact converted to Islam at about that period, though individual Tatars, even Tatar princes, were to convert to Christianity). In the following, fifteenth, century, a special destiny began to be sensed for Russian Orthodoxy: in quick succession the Byzantine leadership was perceived to have 'sold out' to the West by accepting church union at the Council of Florence-Ferrara (1438), the Russians chose a new Metropolitan without referring to Constantinople, and the Great City itself fell to the Ottoman Turks (1453). Around the beginning of the century the Grand Prince, Vasiliy I, had been reprimanded by the Patriarch of Constantinople for, apparently, leaving the Emperor's name out of prayers and claiming 'we have a Church but no Empire'. Within the next few decades various claims for a special religious (and by extension political) destiny for Rus would be put forward through propagandizing literary works: Novgorod claimed the inheritance of various 'Korsun (i.e. Chersonesus) antiquities' supposedly from the time of Vladimir's conversion,[24] as well as of the 'White Cowl' of ecclesiastical authority; Moscow claimed that sacred regalia had been conferred upon Vladimir Monomakh (whose mother was of the Byzantine Monomachos family). In 1480 Russia ceased paying tribute to the Tatars, and as the only important free Orthodox nation became the leader of the Orthodox lands, dignifying itself as 'Holy Russia'. The term is first encountered in the sixteenth century correspondence between Ivan IV and the renegade Prince Kurbsky; it becomes common from the Time of Troubles (turn of the sixteenth and seventeenth centuries).[25] Maybe it originated in a play on words, or a verbal confusion: for the expression 'Bright Russia' is encountered much earlier, and the two adjectives sound rather alike (*svetlaya Rus/svyataya Rus*). In any case, as Cherniavsky has interestingly

---

[24] See Birnbaum and Flier *Medieval Russian Culture* vol. I, chapter by A. Poppe 'On the so-called Chersonian Antiquities'.
[25] M. Cherniavsky *Tsar and People: Studies in Russian Myths* (New Haven, 1981), Chapter 4.

demonstrated, it seems to have been an expression used of the Russian people as a whole, in contradistinction to its ruling elite, to express a deeply-felt national spirit.

### Russian Orthodoxy and Heterodoxy

No sooner do we sense, with the period of St Sergius, that the Russian Orthodox church has become truly autochthonous, commanding the loyalty of the mass of the people, then we begin to detect great tensions within it. Two significant heresies arose, one in the late fourteenth, one in the late fifteenth century. To what extent either owed its popular appeal to relics of folk belief is uncertain: but it is probable that the first heresy anyhow had such elements, mingled with the influence of Bogomilism from the Balkans (a dualistic belief system related to that of the early Paulicians and of the contemporaneous Western European Cathars or Albigensians). These heretics, numerous in the Novgorod and Pskov areas of NW Russia, were known as *strigolniki* ('shearers' – the name is unelucidated). They certainly objected to various Church practices, including simony, which may relate them to religious reforming movements (e.g. the Lollards) of the late medieval West. We can say little about their doctrine, since their victorious opponents left us no clear and unbiased accounts of it. The same is true of the second of these heresies, that of the 'Judaizers' (*zhidovstvuyushchie*) – an intriguing name that was not, however, current until the eighteenth and nineteenth centuries: in its own day it was merely called (by opponents) the 'newly arisen heresy of the Novgorod heretics'. This heresy, or movement, was more successful and longer-lasting than that of the *strigolniki*, gaining a foothold in the Grand Prince's entourage primarily through an important official, Fyodor Kuritsyn. Undoubtedly it too challenged aspects of Church administration; but beyond that we are tantalizingly ignorant of the Judaizers' teaching. Even whether it contained any specifically 'Judaic' elements is open to question; if so, they doubtless came from outside, since Muscovy had no significant Jewish population at the time. Certainly its opponents (notably Joseph of Volokolamsk) later tried to discredit it by suggesting an attempt at practically a Jewish religious takeover of Rus. Several modern scholars have sought for Talmudic and cabbalistic features in what is known of the Judaizers' heritage, but these have proved elusive. The leading contemporary specialist, Yakov Luria, suggests only that they used a Hebrew method of calculating the years that had elapsed since the Creation.[26] In the late

---

[26] Ya. Luria 'Unresolved Issues in the History of the Ideological Movements of the late 15th century', in Birnbaum and Flier *Medieval Russian Culture* vol. I.

fifteenth century this was a matter of much concern, since it was thought the world would come to an end and the Day of Judgement take place at the end of the seventh millennium. Most Orthodox calculations placed the Creation at 5508 BC, so the year 1492 was awaited with much trepidation. What is clear is that the heretics were well-read in esoteric literature and had to be combated – above all by Archbishop Gennadiy – through new biblical translations and written polemics. But Gennadiy also drew the reluctant secular authorities into the fray, citing the example of the Spanish Inquisition, and when the heretics were finally condemned at a council in 1504 he managed to have some of their leaders executed.

Almost simultaneously, incipient tensions within the Russian church itself came to a head. At stake was the meaningfulness of the religious life, in particular monasticism, on an individual and social level. Joseph of Volokolamsk (d. 1515; canonized later in the century) eloquently upheld the public status, ceremonial role, patronage and charitable work of wealthy monasteries, in which the monks themselves would follow a strict rule of asceticism and obedience. To carry out their public functions the monasteries had, in his view, to be significant land-holders: hence he and his followers were usually dubbed 'possessors' (*styazha-teli*), sometimes 'Josephites'. The opposing party, or 'non-possessors', were primarily associated with the 'Trans-Volga elders', individualistic successors to the heritage of St Sergius, living alone or in small communities among the lakes and forests of the north. They believed that religious life should be founded on the renunciation of wealth, land-holdings and worldly encumbrances, and on a life of simple and unadorned piety inspired by personal motivation rather than imposed obedience. Their chief spokesman was Vassian Patrikeyev, a former nobleman and a skilled polemicist. He took as his mentor the revered figure of Nil Sorsky (1433–1508), a leading Trans-Volga holy man who had been on Mount Athos and returned a keen follower of Hesychast practices (he was eventually formally canonized in 1903). Though Nil in fact had collaborated with Joseph in combating the 'Judaizer' heretics[27] (though probably not agreeing with the harsh punishment visited upon them) he was an advocate of moderation, inner integrity and the rejection of worldly possessions; he is supposed to have attacked monastic land-holding at a council in 1503. In the nineteenth and twentieth centuries Nil has gained an extraordinary reputation as a model of principled and humane piety; Joseph has sometimes been correspondingly demonized. Under Ivan III (d. 1505) the non-possessors had at first a sympathetic hearing from the strong-willed, state-building

Tsar, to whom an overweening Church with large land-holdings was not a welcome prospect. But Joseph's later writings also supported a strong autocracy and close Church–State collaboration; the Josephites were finally victorious, and their ideas were officially imposed for more than a century.

The inflexible and highly traditionalistic Orthodox belief system that emerged as a result of the Josephite triumph set its seal upon that most characteristic age of Muscovy, the reigns of Vasiliy III and his son Ivan IV (nearly 80 years altogether). Some historians view the Church–State relationship of the age as an example of what Arnold Toynbee and others have famously termed 'Caesaropapism', the total subjection of religious to secular authority. Certainly Ivan the Terrible could behave towards Church representatives with the same rather paranoid arrogance (mingled with spasms of guilt) that he displayed towards other sectors of society. But the compact between Church and State was never wholly one-sided, nor does the caesaropapist model adequately fit it, though the case is too complex to argue here. The Church seems to have reserved an ultimate right to censure an impious or unjust Tsar, and this was dramatically exercised by the recently appointed Metropolitan Filipp in 1569, at the height of the 'reign of terror' instigated by Ivan IV, when he denounced the blasphemies and lawlessness of the Tsar's private army of *oprichniki*.[28] Filipp was imprisoned and killed for his pains, but well before the end of the century was popularly being looked upon as a saint; in 1652 the new Patriarch Nikon had his relics ceremoniously translated to Moscow, an action imbued with much symbolic significance.

From the mid-sixteenth to the mid-seventeenth centuries the Russian Orthodox church had its century of triumphs, apparently at least. Heresy had been overcome, the Non-Possessors were routed, and the Church–State compact was sealed. Byzantium had fallen, but Muscovy was free, heritor of its mantle. Since the fifteenth century the crusading German 'Teutonic Knights' no longer menaced the Baltic littoral with their armed encroachment. With Ivan IV's coronation (1547) Russia formally had a 'Tsar', an Emperor sanctified by elaborate, Byzantinesque Christian ritual. Soon afterwards Church life was put on a centralized and orderly

---

[28] The *oprichnina*, the 'place apart', refers to a puzzling episode in the reign of Ivan IV, when over the course of some seven years (from 1564) Muscovy was divided into a patchwork of territories, some under the former administration (*zemshchina*) and some controlled directly by the tsar (*oprichnina*) through a special force of *oprichniki*, charged with eliminating the Tsar's enemies, and living communally on parody-monastic lines: their arbitrariness and cruelties were notorious.

footing by the energetic Metropolitan Makariy and the 'Council of a Hundred Chapters' (*Stoglav*, 1551). Huge compendia of ecclesiastical writings were drawn up. Soon the young Tsar would embark on a specifically Russian 'crusade', wresting Kazan (1552) and Astrakhan (1556) from the infidel (in the shape of the Islamic Tatars). Everyday life was piously regulated, at least in principle, along the lines set out in a just if odiously rigid sixteenth-century volume of household management, extant in many versions, the *Domostroy*. Late in the century the Russian Metropolitan was upgraded to the rank of Patriarch. When, soon afterwards, the Ryurikid dynasty died out and political authority dissolved in the 'Time of Troubles' (*smutnoye vremya*, 1598–1613), the Church found itself equal to the challenge: Church action, centred on the main central Russian monasteries, instigated the grassroots resistance that saw off the Polish and Swedish threats to Russia's integrity. Soon after the election of the young Mikhail Romanov as tsar, the Patriarch Filaret – his father – became the most powerful person in the state. In the 1640s and 1650s a large part of the Orthodox population of the Ukraine managed to break away from Poland and adhere to Moscow. Since the 1580s the banner of Orthodoxy had been carried by Russian explorers, soldiers and colonists across the Urals and ultimately through the length of Siberia. In 1645 the long reign of that most evidently and deliberately pious of Tsars, Aleksey, began.

Not everything was as good as it seemed for the Russian church in this period, however. The fatal confrontation between Metropolitan Filipp and Ivan IV (1569) has already been mentioned. Intellectual life, never Orthodoxy's strongest suit (and still less so in Russia than in Byzantium, where the traditions of ancient philosophical rigour held sway till 1453) came to an almost total halt in the centralized and suspicious Muscovy of Ivan IV. Not a word of dogma could be challenged or critically examined, for fear of blasphemy. The chief free-ranging and humanistic intelligence in the Russian Church in the sixteenth century, in some ways heir to the silenced tradition of the Non-Possessors, a learned Greek called Maxim (formerly Michael Trivolis, who came to Russia in 1518), was officially censured and spent many years virtually under monastic house arrest till his death in 1556. Orthodoxy was hopelessly ill-equipped for the debates and confrontations with both Catholics and Protestants that by the seventeenth century became unavoidable.[29] Indeed from a Western point of view it often looked as if the Russian

---

[29]   Note particularly the formal debate with Lutheran representatives at the time of the projected marriage of Tsar Mikhail's daughter Irina to Woldemar, son of the King of Denmark, in 1644: for a concise account, see G. Florovsky *Ways of Russian Theology* vol. I (Nordland, 1979), pp. 110, 323.

church was fruit ripe for plucking: Orthodoxy as a whole seemed so far on the defensive that there was every reason to expect that the Great Schism of 1054 could be settled at last on Rome's terms. The famous Jesuit Antonio Possevino in the later sixteenth century was the forerunner of many Counter-Reformation figures who considered it feasible to cajole or subvert Russia into the Catholic fold. The Poland of Sigismund III was chief springboard for this enterprise, which could point to a remarkable success when in 1596 the Union of Brest brought a considerable proportion of the Orthodox hierarchy in the Polish-Lithuanian lands (though fewer of the laity) into the 'Uniate' church and thus under Papal control. Tensions, sometimes bitter and even leading to violence, have persisted between Orthodox and Uniats till the present. With Protestantism, relations were generally more cordial though doctrinal differences were deeper – which did not prevent Cyril Loukaris, who became Patriarch of Constantinople in 1620 after working as priest and teacher in several parts of Eastern Europe, where he knew the Muscovite Patriarch Filaret, from inclining strongly to Calvinism. With the growing tendency among Western visitors to remark on, and often mock, the perceived backwardness of Muscovy, a contemptuous attitude towards the Orthodox faith and priesthood become normal, and both Protestant and Catholic commentators sometimes doubted whether the Russians were Christians at all. Doubtless the Polish and Swedish threats in the Time of Troubles assisted the self-identification of Russians with their official religion (as had happened three centuries before, after the Tatar conquest), but as we have seen Orthodoxy itself sat lightly upon a large proportion of the population, for whom folk belief provided the natural way of ordering their lives, even if in their own eyes they were unquestioningly Christians.

What Fedotov has called the domination of regulated piety, of 'ceremonial confessionalism',[30] from the mid-sixteenth century onwards, had several unintended consequences for Russian Orthodoxy. Fedotov points tellingly to the decline of Russian sanctity as judged by the simple numerical yardstick of the canonization of saints: they become very few in the seventeenth century, and the figures concerned are local and obscure. Vasiliy III and Ivan the Terrible 'were able to talk with saints; the pious Alexis [i.e. Aleksey] could only go on pilgrimage to their tombs'.[31] The saints that Vasiliy and Ivan could have encountered, however, were less likely to be pious hermits or contemplative monks

---

[30]   G. Fedotov *The Russian Religious Mind* vol. 2 (Cambridge, Mass., 1966) p. 391.
[31]   Ibid. p. 389–90; on holy fools see ibid. Chapter XII.

*Plate 10*   Lubok *(popular print) of Saints Vasiliy [i.e. Basil the Blessed] and Maksim – two sixteenth-century Moscow 'holy fools', much honoured among the common people (coloured copper engraving, 1820s–1830s).*

than representatives of a peculiarly Muscovite way of life where sanctity intersected with popular spectacle or myth and with social action – the 'holy fools' (*yurodivye*). The concept of 'foolishness for Christ's sake' goes back to St Paul (I Corinthians 4:10) and to anti-rationalist tendencies in early Christianity; there were a few famous examples of such saints in Byzantium, performing outrageous, insulting or self-mortifying acts before the eyes of the populace so as to draw attention to worldly vainglory and to their own prophetic utterances. In Muscovite Rus such figures multiplied extraordinarily as the grip of centralized autocracy and of regulated church life tightened. Properly speaking such 'fools' were not mad or even simple-minded, but feigned insanity as part of their pattern of 'antibehaviour' (so the best-known fictional example of the type, who plays such a moving part in Musorgsky's operatic version of *Boris Godunov*, should not really be called 'The Simpleton' as he usually is). An important role of certain holy fools was to speak the unspeakable by criticizing – often in allegorical terms – the cruelties or injustices of the great, including Tsars, so fulfilling an age-old duty of court jesters and fools (as in *King Lear*) in all times and countries, but here with an added religious authority, and an added boldness since the *yurodiviye* were self-appointed. That holy fools were a distinctive and common phenomenon is attested in the comments of Western visitors to Muscovy, notably Giles Fletcher (1588): 'They use to go starke naked, save for a clout about their middle, with their haire hanging long and wildly . . . These they take as prophets and men of great holines, giving them a liberty to speak what they list without any controlment, though it be of the very highest himselfe . . . ', which 'maketh the peopel to like well of them'. But not surprisingly the church and secular authorities soon took fright; canonizations of such figures stopped, and some fools (according to Fletcher) were made away with in secret. Anyhow the whole business had got out of hand – doubtless there were impostors, subversives, opportunists or actual lunatics in their ranks. Yet holy foolishness, a truly popular phenomenon, has probably never ceased, merging with the larger number of wandering self-appointed holy men, thaumaturges and others at the fringes of the Church (Grigoriy Rasputin, neither 'mad' nor a 'monk', who famously rose to being the Tsar and Tsaritsa's 'friend' for many years till his murder by aristocrats in 1916– the only man of the people they knew – is an instructive example).[32] The most notable of the true holy fools was of course Basil the Blessed, in the reign of Ivan IV, whose name became attached to the great Cathedral of the Pokrov (Protecting Veil) in Red Square – a remarkable case of the popular 'appropriation' of the dedication of such a monumental building project.

## Sects and Schism

Towards the end of the Muscovite period, in the 1650s and 1660s, there occurred the event that shook and then fractured the rigid Muscovite belief system irrevocably: the Great Schism (*raskol*). Often this is taken to be the equivalent to the Western Reformation, and indeed some of its

[32]   A. de Jonge's *The Life and Times of Grigoriy Rasputin* (London, 1982) deals well with these matters.

consequences were similar, though not its context. But the real Russian counterpart to Western Protestantism, Sectarianism, appeared even earlier, though its roots are lost in myth and conjecture. Perhaps these go back to the Judaizers; more likely to the current of 'Transvolgan' spirituality that surfaces again in the trial for heresy of one Matvey Bashkin (1554), whose alleged views on the Eucharist and the Trinity sound distinctly Protestant. But in the second half of the sixteenth century there were anyhow plenty of actual Protestants whom Orthodox Russians could encounter on the territory of the Polish-Lithuanian state; the strong Catholicizing reaction under Sigismund III (1587–1632) drove some of them into exile in Muscovy. The most notable of the sects, and the first of which there is a historical record, comprised believers who called themselves 'People of God', but were dubbed *khlysty*, 'flagellants' –probably not because of any flagellant practices, but as a pun on, or corruption of *Khristy*, 'Christs', the name by which their successive leaders were known.

The *khlysty* dated their appearance to the reign of Tsar Mikhail, when a Kostroma peasant, Danila Filippov, proclaimed himself the Lord Sabaoth on Gorodno Hill near Murom; he and his successor 'Christs' established a following in the Oka-Volga region, and by the eighteenth century in Moscow too. During the 1730s and 1740s the government made determined efforts to root out and punish the sectarians, but they proved tenacious, breeding many further sects in the eighteenth and nineteenth centuries. Common to all *khlysty* were the extraction of a small number of basic tenets of belief from the independent study and interpretation of the Scriptures (which had become possible only from the time of the Trans-Volga Elders and Judaizers), an ideal of asceticism and chastity for the elect, democratic and egalitarian organization into independent, semi-secret *tolki* (congregations) and ecstatic, candle-lit gatherings known as *radeniya*, from the root meaning 'joy', culminating in energetic ritual dancing, outbursts of speaking in tongues and prophecy. The numbers of *khlysty* were hard to estimate accurately: they often went to Orthodox services and could pass as Orthodox. It is unlikely they numbered much more than 100,000 at any one time; yet their effect was disproportionate, and they seem to have influenced good many church people up to and including the charismatic priest John of Kronstadt (1829–1908).[33] Among the many sects deriving from, or influenced by, the *khlysty*, much shocked comment has been accorded for the *skoptsy*, self-castrators (who believed castration and clitoridectomy represented the Biblical 'baptism of fire' for the elect). Almost equally notorious were the Dukhobors (*dukhobortsy*, 'spirit-wrestlers'), whose

[33] S. Bolshakoff *Russian Nonconformity* pp. 83–91.

stripped-down Christianity and rejection of secular authority were sufficiently close to Lev Tolstoy's personal religion for him to take a leading part in financing the migration (1897) of over 7,000 of them to Canada – where for some time they continued to cause nationwide consternation through insubordination and (literally) naked demonstrations against the authorities. The rationalistic and attractive *molokane* ('milk-drinkers', so dubbed for their disregard of the Orthodox prohibition against drinking milk during fasts) split into two groups, of which the *subbotniki* (sabbatarians) were strongly influenced by Jewish writings and practices. There were many other more-or-less curious subdivisions of sectarianism, including those who believed Napoleon to be their saviour from the tsarist realm of Antichrist, and 'Old Israel' with its offshoot 'New Age', whose devotees in Dostoyevskian manner believed that immersion in a sea of sin was a necessary prelude to salvation. Sectarianism, often with an admixture of Freemasonry – strong in late eighteenth century Russia – on occasion percolated into high society, where 'fringe religion' was popular (and had court backing) in the early nineteenth century – as readers of *War and Peace* will remember – and again nearly a century later, at the *fin de siècle*. Evident West European, chiefly German, religious influence was felt from the time of Catherine II (when there was largescale German immigration) onwards: Baptists (originally Stundists) still constitute a large Protestant presence in Russia. Within Russia itself the great breeding-ground of sectarianism – as of political rebelliousness – was the recently settled south-central fringe of the steppe country, to Muscovites the 'Wild Field', and particularly the area of Tambov. The State reacted variously, and sometimes (even as late as the mid-nineteenth century) aggressively towards sectarians, often forcibly shifting them to out-of-the-way areas such as the north Caucasus, lest they should subvert the Orthodox. These tight-knit, self-sufficient sectarian communities have left a rich popular heritage of songs and hymns; a major twentieth-century poet, Nikolay Klyuyev (1884–1937), son of a peasant and a ballad-singer from the northern Olonets region, began his writing career with *Brotherly Songs* for the *khlysty*.

Significant as the sectarians are in the history of Russian culture and belief, they never numbered more than a tiny fraction of the total population. Things were otherwise with the Great Schism, which had consequences for millions. Its origins lie in the general crisis that Orthodoxy as a whole, and the Russian church in particular, faced by the early seventeenth century. One the one hand the Church had emerged from the Time of Troubles with enhanced prestige as the chief or sole unifying institution for Muscovy and for Orthodox Russophones beyond its borders; as we have mentioned, the term 'Holy Rus' becomes widely current at this time, implying a concept of Rus distinct from, sometimes opposed to, the tsarist state. On the other hand, Church life was far from healthy: the priesthood was ill-educated; 'double belief' was still widely prevalent; the rituals were largely incomprehensible (different texts would often be chanted simultaneously, while in any case the Russian spoken language was gradually diverging from Church Slavonic); errors and obscurities had crept into the sacred books; practices varied in the different Orthodox lands; the intellectual (sometimes allied to political) challenge from Catholicism and Protestantism could not be avoided, while the development of theological thought had been stunted and scholarship scarcely existed.

In the first half of the seventeenth century various tentative measures were taken by the Moscow church and state authorities to improve the accuracy of religious texts (the advent of printing as the regular method of their reproduction made their deficiencies all the more obvious). The reform of spiritual life, however, had a different and unexpected origin: as a grassroots movement known as 'Zealots [*revniteli*] of Piety' among parish clergy in the deeply provincial middle Volga area around Nizhniy Novgorod. They boldly combated laxity of observances, drunkenness, disorderliness and 'double belief' in their parishes: soon they were favourably noticed by the authorities and some were transferred to Moscow – including their senior figure Ioann Neronov (1591–1670), Stefan Vonifatyev (confessor to the young, pious Tsar Aleksey), and the two great future opponents: Archpriest Avvakum Petrovich (*c.*1620–82) and the Patriarch-to-be Nikon (Nikita Minin, 1605–81). Nikon, coming like the others from the married ('white') priesthood, joined the 'black' monastic clergy when his children died young and his wife became a nun. This opened the door to his dazzling career in the high ecclesiastical ranks: as an abbot in the north, then in Moscow, then as Metropolitan of Novgorod and (1652) as Patriarch of Moscow. In Aleksey's early years as Tsar the Zealots were in the ascendant, while the correction of service books and of corrupt ritual practices was energetically pursued by Nikon at the Tsar's behest. Such correction, however, proved in practice distinctly problematic in an age before modern textological methods or detailed historical knowledge. Nikon, a man of action rather than a scholar, decided that the right solution was to go to Greek sources (he famously declared 'by birth I am a Russian, by faith a Greek'), to obtain and discriminate among which he relied on informants who had their own axes to grind. His erstwhile colleagues soon noted with alarm that all printed Greek books derived from presses in Western Europe, were themselves inconsistent and probably contaminated with Latinisms. In any case the Greeks were scarcely to be taken as authorities in the faith, having been deprived of their Great City, Constantinople, for their sins.

As well as correcting the service books, Nikon put in hand many reforms in ritual: the one that had greatest impact on people's lives was a change in the manner whereby the sign of the Cross was to be made – a public gesture made by everyone many times daily, not only a blasphemy but a continual reminder of the enforced imposition of new ways.

Nikon's former colleagues did not object to amendments in books, or even of certain points of ritual, in themselves. What caused alarm, and ultimately revolt, were his apparently insatiable appetite for innovation for its own sake and his repudiation of Muscovite church traditions (the decisions of the Stoglav council of 1551 were condemned); his dubious associates (including scholars recently arrived from Kiev);[34] his apparent leaning towards Catholicism – he rescinded the rule that Catholic converts to Orthodoxy should be rebaptized by immersion; above all his dictatorial bossiness. He behaved like a prince of the Church, with heightened ceremonial. He instigated grandiose building works (of which the last and most spectacular was his Resurrection Monastery of New Jerusalem some forty kilometres west of Moscow – many thought the very name was blasphemous). He hinted at the superiority of ecclesiastical to worldly power; when the young Tsar went to war against Poland, Nikon was appointed regent with the title 'Great Lord'.

The story of how the Schism (*raskol*) happened has often been told, and is one that seems inevitably to engage the sympathies of the historian on one or other side. It is an epic tale, whose leading personalities seem larger than lifesize; it is probable that Nikon, Avvakum and Tsar Aleksey are the first three figures in Russian history about whom we have enough reliable information to form a good idea of their characters. Briefly, the main events were as follows. In the mid-1650s Nikon began to impose the corrected service books (starting with the Psalter, the book closest to the Russians' hearts), and new ritual forms, on the Church. The objections of the traditionalists were variously countered: Avvakum was sent as chaplain with his family on the long and heroic voyage to Dauria (see p. 162–4), effectively several years of harsh exile. However by the summer of 1658 the 'harmony' between the imperious Patriarch and Tsar Aleksey – by now growing into a self-confident and experienced, though still judicious and pious, ruler – was beginning to break down. There were personal slights, but more importantly disagreement about the politically sensitive matter of ecclesiastical authority over the newly

---

[34]   Kiev became the centre of Orthodox higher education and thought in the early seventeenth century (Moscow had no higher education till the 1680s), particularly as a result of the efforts of Metropolitan Pyotr Mogila (1596–1647), who however was regarded as being tainted with Latinism; cf. Florovsky *Ways of Russian Theology* vol. I pp. 64–78.

acquired Ukrainian territories.[35] Aleksey stopped calling Nikon 'Great Lord'. Nikon took the gamble of withdrawing from Moscow to the half-built New Jerusalem, last of his and Aleksey's great joint building projects, leaving a vacuum of authority at the summit of the Church. Aleksey kept his nerve and called Nikon's bluff: in the end Nikon (lacking enthusiastic supporters) turned out to need the Tsar more than the latter needed him. Still, the situation could not last for ever, and eventually (1666–7) the Tsar managed to convene a great Church council with the participation of two of the Orthodox Patriarchs. This remarkable event seems thoroughly Byzantine in its spirit, its form and the arguments adduced: no doubt the last public occasion of its kind in European history. Following the Byzantine canon-law book (*Nomokanon*) the council held 'Whosoever troubles the Emperor and disturbs his Empire has no defence', deposed Nikon and chose a successor. Nikon expected martyrdom, but was merely reduced to the status of a monk and sent off to the northern Ferapontov and Kirillov monasteries, where (still regarding himself as the true Patriarch) he proved a considerable embarrassment. He outlived the Tsar and died on his way back from exile (1681); a hagiographic *Life* was written of him by a disciple, Shusherin, and some considered him a miracle-worker.

Hopes rose among the traditionalists in the run-up to the Council. Avvakum returned and seemed to find favour with the tsar. But the Council, while condemning Nikon's actions, upheld the reforms (behind which Aleksey had thrown his weight). Some traditionalists were persuaded into compromise. But the majority realized there was no alternative, now the Schism was formalized, but to go into opposition – the more so since the Council anathematized them, as well as condemning as ignorant the councils convened a century before under Ivan IV, and which had been a cornerstone of Muscovite belief. The 'Old Believers' or 'Old Ritualists' (*starovery, staroobryadtsy*) as the Orthodox called them (in their own eyes, 'true believers') risked, sometimes provoked, social discrimination, legal disabilities, exile, punishment, even death: the great Solovki monastery on an island in the White Sea, an 'oppositional' bastion even before the Schism proper, was reduced only by a lengthy military operation, while Avvakum and his most intransigent colleagues were executed by fire at Pustozyorsk in 1682 (after Aleksey's death, when measures against the dissenters became more severe). Many Old Believer congregations immolated themselves in their wooden churches rather than submit to the authorities: such a scene forms a climax of Musorgsky's *Khovanshchina* (a gallant if unfinished and maybe

[35]   Cf. P. Longworth *Alexis Tsar of All the Russias* (London, 1984) Chapters V-VI.

unsuccessful attempt to encompass this dramatic age of Russian history in operatic form).[36] More frequently Old Believers took refuge in remoteness, and played a leading part in the colonization of Siberia, Central Asia and the steppe country (where Old Belief played its part in Stepan Razin's great Cossack rebellion, 1671–2, and also in Yemelyan Pugachov's a century later). Old Believers, like 'Pilgrim Fathers', proved tremendously hardy, resourceful and industrious. Peter the Great, recognizing and approving this, stopped persecution, but with characteristic pragmatism made the Old Believers pay double taxes. Only under Catherine II, probably at the instigation of her far-sighted and statesmanlike consort Grigoriy Potyomkin, were disabilities lifted and an attempt made at reconciliation. But the Schism represented a cultural gulf too deep to be overcome, and persists to this day. No tsarist census statistics ever truly revealed its extent, since the authorities were concerned to minimize its impact; but it is likely that at least in the early decades of the Schism a third to a half of the population was alienated from the official Church and hence largely from the State and society.

It has often been pointed out that the Old Belief was nostalgic and pessimistic in its essence, hence very different in spirit from sectarianism with its apocalyptic hopefulness and inspirationalism (though schismatics and sectarians, as 'fellow-outsiders', sometimes forged close links). In Georgiy Florovsky's words 'the Schism, consumed by memories and premonitions, possessed a past and a future but no present . . . [it] marks the first paroxysm of Russia's rootlessness, rupture of conciliarity (*sobornost*), and exodus from history . . . sacred history had come to an end; it had ceased to be sacred and had become without Grace.'[37] With the apostasy of the Tsar himself, the reign of Antichrist (whether in the form of an actual person or a malign invisible spirit) had arrived. All that was left for believers was a yearning for the 'lost city of Kitezh' and for the previous organic society of a Muscovy of the imagination, before the catastrophe (of the Schism? the Time of Troubles? Ivan IV's 'terror'?). The extreme of denial was reached by the schismatic movement of *netovshchina*, 'negativism', rejecting as polluted not just authority and the Church, but the sacraments, religious rituals, even prayer, and

---

[36]   On Musorgsky's original concept of the role of Old Believers in the opera, see R. Taruskin 'Christian Themes in Russian Opera', in Brumfield and Velimirović *Christianity and the Arts in Russia*. Self-immolation has been related to the ancient Slavic tradition of the 'fine death' (voluntarily sought): see T. Bernshtam 'Russian Folk Culture and Folk Religion' in Balzer *Russian Traditional Culture*.
[37]   Florovsky *Ways of Russian Theology* vol. I p. 98ff.

naturally the things of the world – nothing was left appropriate for the believer save lamentation (by curious coincidence – or was there any influence? – there was a similar 'rejectionist' movement in the arts during the 1920s: the *nichevoki* or 'nothingists'). The Schism, too, had its own internal schisms, thus complicating its situation for the worse. The 'Priestists' (*popovtsy*) continued to believe in the need for a priesthood. Unfortunately there were no surviving bishops who rejected the Nikonian reforms (the only one who did so had died in 1656, long before the Schism was formalized), and the Priestists had to rely on renegade Orthodox priests despite their having been ordained by reformers. Priestists continued to nurture hopes that somewhere in the world – maybe in the invisible city of Kitezh, in the mythical land (somewhere in or beyond Central Asia) which they called 'Belovodye', or even in Japan – there existed a true, unreformed Church with which they might make common cause some day.[38] They were always open to the lure of reintegration or reconciliation with the official Church, and many so-called 'Single-Believers', *yedinovertsy*, moved in this direction.

The heart of the Schism, however, lay with the more numerous – and, from the authorities' point of view, more elusive – *bespopovtsy*, the 'Priestless'. For them the apostasy of the Tsar and Church hierarchy annulled holy orders and all save the most fundamental, often self-administered sacraments (over which there was considerable dispute). It is worth mentioning that such 'minimalized' ritual life was not wholly novel in the context of the vast northern Russian forests, where a parish could cover hundreds of square kilometres and where isolated communities might seldom even set eyes on a priest; where, moreover, priests were by old tradition elected by, and responsible to, their parishioners. The Priestless subdivided further, with their more extreme offshoots moving ever further both from worldly society and from any kind of ritual; for the Quaker-like 'Prayerless' all visible objects and institutions of religion (church buildings, the Scriptures, the Cross, fasts, relics, marriage and funeral ceremonies, prayer itself) were rejected save insofar as they had a purely inward, spiritual meaning, while the 'Wanderers' (*stranniki*) led a totally fugitive life, living in hideaways, agonizing whether they could even carry coins (bearing the portrait or symbols of Antichrist) on their persons, adopting a worldly alias if they were obliged to apply for the internal passport the tsarist (and Soviet) government demanded.[39] Nonetheless it would be wrong to assume that the values of the Priestless Old Believers were entirely 'rejectionistic' and nostalgic. Many – particularly those prepared to make the minimum

[38]   F. Conybeare *Russian Dissenters* (London, 1962 edn) p. 111.
[39]   Ibid. p. 167ff; see too Veletskaya (note 15) p. 60–1.

compromises with the regime that permitted them to form part of settled society, and specially the 'Shore Dwellers' (*pomortsy*) of the northern-most regions near the White Sea and Arctic coasts – organized themselves into efficient communes of traders, fishermen, craftspeople, hunters and explorers. The most famous and successful such enterprise, organized in the 1690s by a family of genius, the Denisovs, included a string of villages, religious houses and farms along the course of the remote and agriculturally unpromising river Vyg; it was run on strictly communistic and in part monastic lines, and became not only a prosperous trading settlement but a democratic seat of learning, culture and religious enlightenment until suppressed by Nicholas I (no friend of the Schism, or of any dissent) in the mid-nineteenth century.[40] It was the chief centre of what became virtually the 'parallel society' of the Old Belief, whose members all over Russia decided not just religious questions but matters of economics, discipline and justice among themselves. By the late tsarist period there was even an all-Russian postal service, better than that of the state, within the Old Believer community; it used private codes and networks of sympathizers and informants.

It is remarkable how the various strands of faith within the Old Belief were able in a short time to encompass, at one extreme, the formalistic and retrospective ritualism of its originators, and at the other a self-sufficient inwardness whereby the only 'temple of the Lord', the only Church, was the person of the individual believer. Modern historians have not come anywhere near agreeing what to make of the whole phenomenon, even if the extraordinary durability, communality and steadfastness of the schismatics have always commanded respect. To one historian, the Schism marks the 'dead end' of Muscovite culture; to another, Avvakum and Nikon were essentially similar 'Muscovite prophets'; to some commentators the Old Believers were the best elements in Russian society, or held within them some precious and intangible essence of Russianness or Russian holiness; to another, they were the unwitting conservers of many archaic aspects of folk belief; to others the whole experience was 'Protestantism through the looking-glass'. Both sides involved in the Schism would have fiercely resisted the validity of any Western comparisons, but it is hard to deny that a juxtaposition of its history with that of the European Reformation and seventeenth-century sects provides one of the most fascinating examples of Russian culture as a parallel 'other case' to the Western experience. The Schism put Russian popular unintellectualizing resourcefulness to

---

[40]   See R. Crummey *The Old Believers and the World of Antichrist* (Madison, 1970) on the Vyg community.

the severest test, and it came through; having created for themselves – under what harsh conditions! – new patterns of communal and religious life, Old Believers in the next two centuries provided Russia with many of its hardiest colonists, traders, and free peasants (as well as many rebels). By the mid-nineteenth century there was a prosperous Old Believer urban class of merchants, and they were among the first to encourage the serious and widespread study of the culture and artefacts of Old Russia, thereby putting the very concept of 'Russianness' in a new light.

### Beyond the Schism

The Great Schism is self-evidently a defining moment in the history of Russian belief systems and culture generally. It would be far beyond the scope of this book to attempt any detailed account of the subsequent history of belief (and unbelief) in Russia; but in the same way as it has been necessary to reach forward into the eighteenth century and beyond to indicate the Schism's significance, we can look at least cursorily at the subsequent fate of Orthodoxy and belief generally in more recent times.

It has sometimes been said that the death of Avvakum and his colleagues on Good Friday 1682 marks the end of Old Russia. If so, we might be equally precise in pinpointing the origin of the new Russia, at least from an ideological point of view, to 26 August 1698, the first day after Tsar Peter (eventually to be styled, at his own instigation, Father of the Fatherland, the Emperor Peter the Great) returned to his capital after well over a year's absence in Western Europe on the 'Great Embassy'. The years between had been a confused time: the Schism was establishing itself, the often violent methods of the authorities to suppress it were not working, the Russian economy and army were dominated by several thousand hired foreigners largely concentrated in the 'German Suburb' on the outskirts of Moscow, there was uncertainty over the succession to the throne after Tsar Fyodor, Aleksey's eldest surviving son, died (resolved only in 1696 when the 24-year-old Peter became sole ruler), the musketeers (*streltsy*: an old-fashioned force of part-time soldiers who felt their position threatened by foreign mercenaries) staged a couple of revolts of which the first gave them considerable power in Moscow, while the second was quickly defeated shortly before Peter's return.

On his first day back in Moscow, Peter was ceremoniously greeted by members of the aristocracy, on whom he played what seems to be a comic trick: he produced a dry razor and began to shave off

*Plate 11* Lubok *(popular print) of Barber and Old Believer, referring to Peter the Great's directive that the upper class must shave, and to the Great Schism of half a century earlier (woodcut, c.1770).*

their beards.[41] This no doubt painful gesture was not so funny to those involved, nor indeed to the population at large. It is often interpreted as an act symbolic of the policy of 'Westernization' Peter was thenceforward to pursue, and it was certainly that: but it also represented an incredible humiliation (if not emasculation) of his own elite servitors and a scandalous, reckless assault on the authority of the

---

[41] See L. Hughes 'A Close Shave: a Pogonic History of Petrine Russia' in *Study Group on Eighteenth-Century Russia, Newsletter* 23 (1995) for a concise and perceptive account of this episode and its significance.

Church. For many centuries Orthodoxy had held that natural beard growth was a God-granted symbol of man's divinity, serving to differentiate beasts, demons and heretic foreigners from God-fearing men. Shaving was not unknown in late Muscovy, and must have been general in the German suburb; Peter of course shaved (though kept a moustache). But by ordering his entire male elite and urban class to go cleanshaven, while peasants and priests were to retain beards, and by linking this with the concomitant obligation to wear Western European or Russian clothing respectively, Peter opened up an instantly visible and unbridgeable gap between classes, brutally symbolizing the end of what in retrospect seemed the organic society of Rus, which anyhow was being transformed into 'Rossiya' (see p. 1–2). A week later Peter ordered another such mass shaving, this time with a court jester handling the razor. It was 1 September, by the old Byzantine calendar the first day of the new year of 1699. For Russian traditionalists the times were full of alarming millenarian signs and portents. The year 1666, a sinister number, had witnessed the council that formalized the Schism. In 1676 Tsar Aleksey had died suddenly within a week of his troops' final assault on the redoubt of the Old Belief – the Solovki monastery – when they massacred its defenders. The year 1699 was expected by many to witness the start of the reign of Antichrist. How far Peter knowingly played up to this image is uncertain. But he immediately instigated an action that struck terror into Muscovite hearts: the interrogation and punishment of the rebellious musketeers who had been captives since the defeat of their ineffectual mutiny outside Moscow. Around 1200 were executed, many brutally and publicly in the holiest location of Moscow, Red Square; their families were sent to beg in the countryside. The Tsar's disproportionate revenge seemed like a war on his own people. Soon afterwards (1700) he refused to permit the election of a new Patriarch, and the Church became in effect an arm of the state, run by civil servants; Peter himself was sometimes regarded as 'surrogate Patriarch'.

Peter's behaviour scarcely seems modern or 'Westernized', though it is fair to say that tolerance in matters of religion or clemency in the exercise of authority generally were not yet deep-rooted concepts in most parts of Europe. Rather it was 'antibehaviour', designedly outrageous,[42] of a piece with the blasphemous jocularity and hooliganism of his

---

[42]  On the semiotic significance of Peter's 'antibehaviour', see B. Uspensky 'Historia sub specie semioticae' in B. Khrapchenko et al. (eds) *Kulturnoye nasledie drevney Rusi* (Moscow, 1976): English translation in D. Lucid (ed.) *Soviet Semiotics* (Baltimore, 1977).

'All-Drunken Synod' (which meant far more to Peter than even a 'Hell Fire Club', let alone the 'jolly company' into which some historians have softened it). This 'Synod' was headed by the sinister figure of Fyodor Romodanovsky, Peter's secret police boss and virtually his *alter ego*, a 'parody Tsar' to whom Peter feigned deference and whom he left as regent during his year-and-a-half's absence on the Great Embassy. The sinister 'carnivalism' (in Mikhail Bakhtin's sense) of Peter's disorientating behaviour irresistibly suggests Ivan the Terrible, whom Peter admired (he also admired and learnt from his father, Aleksey Mikhailovich, probably too from Nikon – for all his Western ways, Peter knew his Russian history and absorbed lessons from it). In fact Peter was not as irreligious or even anti-Orthodox as he seemed (he founded a great monastery and several churches, loved singing in church, had many religious books), and Westerners who hoped to interest him in some other state Church, or even Quakerism, were disappointed. But he applied to church people the same harsh criterion of 'usefulness' as he applied to everyone else in his realm, and was fearful of religion as yet another possible focus of the oppositional elements that he cracked down on so ruthlessly. He was an authentic 'blasphemer' for both State and – so far as we can judge – personal psychological reasons. To many of his people he was, if not the embodiment of Antichrist, then a German changeling who had been substituted for the true tsar while abroad (as it happens, from Peter's second marriage onwards the dynasty rapidly 'Germanized' itself through marriage with non-Russians). The Tsar's new capital of St Petersburg, on the inclement edge of the realm, seemed un-Russian, a German or Dutch parody city that would one day disappear as suddenly as it had arisen – an unholy place, constructed by forced labour with much suffering, that Old Believers refused to enter, but which Peter called his 'paradise'. For Peter, the city represented not just the proverbial 'window onto Europe', but a revival of ancient Novgorodian traditions on recaptured Novgorod territory: to the mass of the population however it was scarcely 'real' at all, with its stage-set buildings, crowds of foreigners and bureaucrats in foreign costumes, its lack of hinterland and the difficulty of its location. It took another century for this strange, ambiguous, masquerade quality of the city to be adequately reflected in the imaginative writing of Pushkin (*The Bronze Horseman*) and Nikolay Gogol (*The Overcoat, Nevsky Prospect*) and a century more till its definitive expression in Andrey Beliy's *Petersburg* (see Chapter 5, pp. 221–3).

Belief was as disorientated as was political life in the Petrine epoch. The Orthodox church had apparently weathered the storm of the Schism, but it had become evident, in the words of a cultural historian, that 'the real loser amidst all this religious conflict in Russia was – as it had been in the West – the vitality of surviving Christian commitment'.[43] Effectively in captivity, deprived of its head, its hierarchs little more than State propagandists, threatened on several different fronts, its more dynamic elements drained off into Schism or sectarianism, the Russian Church not surprisingly seemed exhausted for most of the eighteenth century. The upper-class males, all in compulsory State service, had little choice but to ally themselves with the Petrine reforms (their womenfolk however were less likely to share this orientation).

After the mid-century, Enlightenment ideals, Freemasonry and eventually varieties of pan-Christian mysticism came to fill the void in faith among many members of the educated classes; from the mid-nineteenth century, of course, fervent materialism, scientific positivism (cf. Ivan Turgenev's *Fathers and Children*) and various types of socio-political activism were to supplant them. Meanwhile Orthodoxy itself began to stir and revive in the later eighteenth century. Under its most intelligent official leader, Platon Levshin (Metropolitan of Moscow from 1775 to 1812) the Church moved seriously into the field of elementary education, providing a counterweight to the Enlightenment-inspired freethinking of the universities: in the early nineteenth century these were to come under a militant Christian counterattack from Mikhail Magnitsky and others (mostly inspired by Joseph de Maistre) who discerned the form of Antichrist in Western Enlightenment ideas generally. A revived Orthodox church naturally interested the government. Under the Empresses Elizabeth (Peter the Great's daughter, 1741–61) and Catherine II (1762–96) the church was regarded benignly, as a force for social stability, but to be kept in its subordinate place (monastic lands were confiscated under Catherine).

By the early nineteenth century things were different. Alexander I, full of unfocused piety, saw religion as the cornerstone of the 'Holy Alliance' set up in the wake of the French revolutionary wars to keep Europe safe for monarchs. His own prestige was enormously boosted by the seemingly miraculous victory over Napoleon in 1812; he was awarded the title *blazhenniy*, 'The Blessed', implying an almost divine status (not surprisingly, it rather went to his head).[44] But 1812 was also seen as a victory for the spirit of Russianness, in which Russia's age-old

---

[43]    J. Billington *The Icon and the Axe* (New York, 1966) pp. 158–9. Note in this context the famous *Letter* addressed to Gogol (who had just published a would-be pious work) in 1847 by the progressive thinker V. Belinsky: 'According to you the Russian people is the most pious in the world . . . Take a closer look and you will see that it is by nature a profoundly Godless people . . . Religiosity among us appeared only in the schismatic sects.'

[44]    M. Cherniavsky *Tsar and People* (New Haven, 1961), Chapter 5.

belief system was a crucial component: soon ideologists and writers alike would refer to the 'Russian God'. It interested the rationalistic and politically progressive 'Decembrist' revolutionaries of 1825, and far more so the so-called Slavophiles of the mid-century. The State tried to muscle in on the religious revival to further its own interests (as had happened on several occasions in Russian history since the fourteenth century – maybe even as far back as the Conversion!); in Nicholas I's reign an ideology of 'official nationality' under the slogan of 'Orthodoxy, autocracy, national spirit (*narodnost*)' was promoted officially – this trilogy was strangely parodied under Stalin when Socialist Realism, the official 'method' for all the arts, was defined by the triple slogan 'party-spiritedness (*partiynost*), ideological content (*ideynost*), national spirit (*narodnost*, again).' Apparently unable to tolerate a 'belief vacuum', or perhaps because their mindsets worked in binary oppositions, even the Marxist revolutionaries of the late nineteenth and twentieth centuries had to indulge in their own religion-making, whether in the form of 'God-building' – that so infuriated Lenin – or the more acceptable militant atheism, promoted to a real religionless belief system. The latter's effective collapse in the Second World War (when Stalin made a semi-secret compact with the Orthodox Church) heralds, in retrospect, the beginning of the long-drawn-out decline of Soviet Communism itself.

The authentic revival of Orthodoxy from the last third of the eighteenth century onwards, however, is not really connected with its public status but with its spirit of conciliarity (*sobornost*), a communalism that so fascinated the Slavophiles, and, on the other hand, with the revival of the *starets* tradition of individual spiritual discipleship (whose much cited literary example is Dostoyevsky's Father Zosima in *Brothers Karamazov*). The revival of personal (and indeed, monastic) spirituality was given impetus by the translation of the *Philokalia* from Greek into Russian (as the *Dobrotolyubie*) by Paisiy Velichkovsky (d. 1794). This work became highly influential and marks the re-establishment of links between the new Russia and the traditions of Mount Athos, where Paisiy spent seventeen years, and the Trans-Volgans, in particular Nil Sorsky, whom he specially admired. An associated phenomenon highly characteristic of Russian spirituality – and particularly significant, it seems to me, since it stretches far beyond Orthodoxy, and even involves figures who would have repudiated any religious allegiance – is that of the individual sage, teacher or (in modern times) artist who rejects worldly success and rewards to live an eccentric, self-motivated, more-or-less ascetic life as one who seeks and shows the right path, and so performs difficult feats (the old religious tradition of the *podvig*, 'deed'). The eighteenth-century figure from whom this tradition (in modern times) seems to originate is Grigoriy Skovoroda

(1722–94). A brilliant student and teacher in Kiev and elsewhere, he was also a singer in the St Petersburg court choir and took part in a diplomatic mission to Hungary; he was versed in classical and early Christian Latin literature. All doors were open to him, but in 1766 he gave up his beckoning career, and for the last three decades of his life wandered through Russia and his native Ukraine as a mendicant village teacher and writer of poems, philosophical dialogues and varied religious works, seeing himself as the 'Russian Socrates'. Orthodoxy was too narrow for him (he helped the Dukhobor sectarians to draft their declarations), though he did not abandon it; he was at heart a freedom lover, a pantheist and a seeker after Sophia, Divine Wisdom, to whom the Bible was not to be read literally, but as 'a world of symbols'. When death was near he dug his own grave and left his own memorable epitaph '*Mir lovil menya i ne poymal*', 'The world hunted me and did not catch me.'

If in the nineteenth century no-one could quite match Skovoroda's legendary life and self-denial, several important figures operated in the same spirit: the philosopher Vladimir Solovyov, his opponent Lev Tolstoy in later years, the painter Alexander Ivanov, above all the humble librarian Nikolay Fyodorov, whose strange philosophical teachings of 'brotherliness' and the conquest of death influenced both Tolstoy and Dostoyevsky, not to mention several twentieth-century writers (Mayakovsky, Boris Pasternak and Nikolay Zabolotsky among them). In the twentieth century such ascetic sages include the visionary scientist Konstantin Tsiolkovsky, the poet and thinker Velimir Khlebnikov, the artists Vladimir Tatlin and in particular Pavel Filonov (1883–1941). Alexander Solzhenitsyn in his Soviet days must have felt kinship with this tradition, and the proverb he adapts near the end of his story 'Matryona's House' – 'that righteous one, without whom no village can stand. Nor any city. Nor our whole land' – can serve to conclude this account of some elements and roots of belief in Russia.

# 4

## 'Let Us Join Word to Word'

### Russian Traditional Literature

In the eyes of the world Russian literature is perhaps the chief glory of Russian culture. What the world knows, above all, is the classic Russian novel, whose great age was amazingly brief – a mere quarter century, all within the reign of Alexander II (1855–81), witnessed the publication of the best works of Tolstoy, Dostoyevsky, Turgenev and Ivan Goncharov. Those with a deeper interest might extend their knowledge back to the time of Pushkin and Lermontov in the early nineteenth century, and forward to Chekhov and the modernist 'silver age' – around a century, altogether – so becoming aware that Russian literature has more to it than blockbuster narratives: in particular an intensely developed poetic tradition. Few outsiders (and not all Russians) understand, however, how deeply *literaturnost* ('literariness') has been ingrained in Russian cultural consciousness over the thousand years since the Conversion, or realize that what is usually called Old Russian literature forms part of a distinctive tradition whose effects are far from being exhausted yet. Of course the forms of sophisticated literature, like the forms of upper-class behaviour, were changed radically and forcibly after Peter the Great's 'Westernizing' measures, but many underlying older principles remained intact, to be revealed in numerous ways as time went on.

Analogous situations are obviously to be seen in the other sophisticated art forms: painting, sculpture, architecture, music. In each, wholesale innovations of form, genre and purpose apparently (though *only* apparently) swept away 'medieval' artistic systems. It may be, however, that literature, embedded as it must be in practices of language, is less susceptible than the other arts to the sudden and complete imposition of new methods. Whatever the reasons, mid-eighteenth century writers such as Vasiliy Tredyakovsky and Mikhail Lomonosov, themselves propagators of Western literary forms, had considerable interest in the literary tradition they were engaged in remodelling, an interest redoubled at the turn of the century with the generation of Radishchev, the Decembrists and subsequently of Pushkin and his contemporaries, when the issue of 'Russianness' in literature came into sharp focus. It was then, too, that a growing antiquarian and historical interest in the manuscript heritage of Old Russia was galvanized by the sensational discovery (*c.*1795) of a complex, subtle and highly original work thought to date from the twelfth century, the *Igor Tale*, or properly speaking *The Discourse about Igor's Armament* (*Slovo o Polku Igoreve*), raising questions about the nature and aesthetic qualities of Old Russian literature that have been with us ever since.

To discuss this literature in any detail would take a volume or several volumes. The purpose of treating it here is to fit it into the larger picture of Russian cultural history: so, though I shall give a quick characterization of a few of the main works, I intend chiefly to make some general, and I hope in some cases original, points about the diachronic nature of the literary experience in Russia.

First, some preliminary observations have to be made. The term 'Old Russian Literature', which is near-universal in scholarly usage, needs to be employed with caution. It (with its variants 'Early' or 'Medieval' Russian literature) is a temporal designation, tying literary development to historical periodization. Taken as implying that literature of the Old Russian period (i.e. up to Peter the Great's reforms) is qualitatively separate from what came afterwards, it is misleading. 'Modern' literary forms (i.e. like those of the Baroque elsewhere) are observable in Russian literature at least from the early seventeenth century (even if they do not lead then to masterpieces of European quality), within a still largely-medieval literary system, whose after-effects, as has been suggested above, in turn long outlive the end of 'Old Russia' itself. I propose instead the coinage 'Russian Traditional Literature' as a conceptual rather than periodic term.

There is far more 'traditional' (or 'old') Russian literature than is usually thought – plenty of it still unpublished. Two compendious works from the time of Ivan IV have over 20,000 pages each in manuscript. More significantly, there are literally thousands of chronicles from the early twelfth to the eighteenth century originating from a large number of local centres, often small or remote; hundreds

*Plate 12   Manuscript initials in the form of* skomorokhi *(minstrels): the 'teratological' interlaced style is characteristic of the late fourteenth to early fifteenth centuries, cf. pp. 156, 173.*

of versions of oral epic poems have been transcribed; we must not forget the hundreds or thousands of translated religious and learned works, mostly of Byzantine origin, that were the bedrock of sophisticated traditional literature. Despite the large quantity of works that remain, we also know for certain of some that have not survived, and can postulate the former existence of many other lost works. There are probably still significant rediscoveries to be made. Several important early works have been discovered in modern times, some in only one copy. As for the durability of traditional Russian literature, one may mention as a curiosity – but more than just that – the fact that there are still so-called Old Believer communities in out-of-the-way areas where a manuscript tradition of religious polemics in an essentially seventeenth century vein has been prolonged to the present.[1] More significantly, the guru of modernist Russian poetics, Velimir Khlebnikov (1885–1922), could claim to be the culminating 'Old' Russian writer (to the extent that he purged from his work all vocabulary of Western European origin). The poet Osip Mandelshtam (admiringly) wrote of him that 'he cannot distinguish which is nearer, the railway bridge or the *Tale of Igor's Campaign*.'[2] His followers up to the present generation (e.g. Viktor Sosnora) have shown the continuing vitality of his example, and it has rippled outwards to affect much modern Russian writing. And even had Khlebnikov never lived, through Aleksey Remizov and other writers the older Russian traditions of 'literariness' would have been revived and given credibility for the twentieth century, and doubtless beyond.

The next general point that must be made about traditional Russian literature is that it existed in two great complementary spheres: the 'visible' and the 'invisible', in other words the written and the oral. Historians, for obvious reasons, concentrate on the former, admitting the latter only when (as with oral epics – the so-called *byliny*) it achieved permanent 'visible' embodiment by being written down – often in confusing multiple variants and probably several centuries after the work first arose. Early Russians perceived, it seems, the distinctiveness, but also the complementary nature of each of these spheres, allotting them separate roles (so that, for example, lyric

[1]   See N. N. Pokrovsky 'O drevnerusskoy rukopisnoy traditsii u staroverov Sibiri', in *Trudy otdela drevnerusskoy literatury*, XXIV, 1969, describing and illustrating the results of expeditions in 1966–7 to Old Believer communities on the upper Yenisey.

[2]   O. Mandelshtam *Burya i natisk*, in *Sobranie sochinenii* vol. II (New York, 1966) p. 390. In another article (*O poezii*) he wrote that Khlebnikov's language is 'as profane and vulgar as if neither monks, nor Byzantium, nor intellectual writing had ever existed' (ibid., p. 305).

poetry is absent from written literature until the seventeenth century, though evidently abundant in the Russian experience in the form of folksong). It would be tempting, but wrong, to equate these two spheres, written and oral, with the 'sacred' and 'profane' respectively. The written word indeed often carried overtones of sacredness, and this is a point to which we shall return. But of course it was used for entirely humdrum practical purposes too (and the boundary between the literary and the non-literary is particularly hard to draw in a pre-modern age). Unwritten, oral literary creativity, by contrast, derives in direct descent from pre-Christian Rus, and never ceased to carry undertones of 'pagan' folk belief – though it also acquired a multitude of Christian motifs as the centuries passed, often strangely metamorphosed and 'folkified'; the most remarkable products of such creativity are the 'spiritual songs' (*dukhovnye stikhi*) sung by wandering pilgrims (*kaliki*). So while to some extent a sacred/profane, or more profoundly, a Christian/pagan dichotomy can be observed in Russian traditional literariness, it cannot wholly or permanently be equated with the written/unwritten spheres. In fact the conceptual world of oral literature subtly and significantly penetrated that of writing in Christianized Rus, and lent a specifically Russian coloration to some of its best monuments: whether, for example, through turns of speech, proverbs or epic fragments in the early chronicles, through the stylized evocation of pagan divinities in the *Igor Tale*, through the wit and wordplay of *The Petition of Daniil the Exile*, the ecstatic transformation of peasant lamentation in Yepifaniy's *Life of Stephen of Perm*, the overtones of heroic epos in various military tales, the 'folkishness' of many aspects of Avvakum's *Life, written by himself*, the chilling evocation and personification of the popular conception of human destiny in *The Tale of Misery-Luckless-Plight*, or the fairytale motifs of *The Tale of Peter and Fevronia of Murom*. More generally many stylistic features – types of antithesis and parallelisms, paratactic structures, riddling formulations, stock epithets – come into even sophisticated traditional literature from the folk sphere. The question of a reverse influence, from the written to the oral, is harder to assess: but such influence was probably to some degree felt at least in the last century of Old Russia and indeed the first after Peter the Great: as Čiževskij writes, in the Baroque age 'The novel turns into a fairy-tale in short-story form, the love poem into a popular song, the religious lyric into a 'spiritual song'.'[3]

A corollary to my suggested way of perceiving traditional Russian

[3]   D. Čiževskij *A History of Russian Literature from the 11th Century to the end of the Baroque* (The Hague, 1960), p. 433.

Plate 13    Manuscript illumination (seventeenth century) to the
Tale of Peter and Fevroniya of Murom: ostensibly a work of
hagiography, the Tale (probably dating from the fifteenth century
if not earlier) has many folkloric, pre-Christian elements.

'literariness' is that literature is no longer to be regarded as simply the
business of the literate segment of society. Much scholarly ingenuity has
gone into trying to establish what proportion of the Old Russian
population could read and write (in sixteenth-century Muscovy it may

have been well below five per cent, in pre-Tatar Novgorod by contrast much higher).[4] But such figures, even if they could be reliably established, would not have any readily ascertainable cultural significance. The written sphere of literature – at least its dominant religious component – was suffused even among the illiterate through readings in churches, in monastic refectories and in princely courts; oral literature – whether through folk tales and songs, oral epos, the performance of itinerant minstrels (*skomorokhi*) – would have reached the entire population of pre-modern Russia without exception, however much it may have been frowned upon by the authorities and the church.

The last and largest of these general observations that I wish to make concerns the most fundamental and individual aspect of the world of Russian traditional literature, that of its language. It has already been mentioned that with the arrival of Christianity in Rus there was also imported the new religion's inseparable concomitant, a fully-fledged literary language known to us as Old Church Slavonic. The 'Apostles to the Slavs', Cyril and Methodius, together with their assistants, devised this as a written language designed to express the conceptual world of the Bible, the Church Fathers, theology and late-antique 'high culture' generally (i.e. with complex structures and a large abstract vocabulary), basing themselves on the South Slav speech of the hinterland of Thessaloniki, from which they came. At the time (mid-ninth century) the South, West and East Slav dialects, later each to give birth to several distinct languages, were sufficiently close to each other to be intercomprehensible, and the Apostles' translations (and, soon, original texts) were of equal use in Moravia – for which they were first commissioned – Bulgaria and, over a century later, Russia. Thus the written language for religious and translated literature generally was not exclusive to Rus: it constituted, in Likhachov's phrase, a 'Byzantine-Slav cultural milieu': 'a sort of common culture for the southern and eastern Orthodox Slav lands that evolved simultaneously as a single totality in various Slavonic countries as a result of the transplantation of Byzantine culture into them . . . a supranational cultural milieu.'[5] Riccardo Picchio

---

[4]   S. Franklin 'Literacy and Documentation in Early Medieval Russia', in *Speculum* 60:1 (1985) pp. 1–38; G. Marker 'Literacy and Literacy Texts in Muscovy: A Reconsideration', in *Slavic Review* 49 (1990) pp. 74–89, both partially reprinted in D. Kaiser and G. Marker (eds.) *Reinterpreting Russian History* (Oxford, 1994).

[5]   D. Likhachov 'Byzantium and the Emergence of an Independent Russian Literature', in D. Daiches and A. Thorlby (eds) *Literature and Western Civilization*, vol. II (London, 1973), pp. 173–4. Natalya Tronenko kindly points out to me that some recent scholars have also demonstrated a 'Scandobyzantine' or 'Scandoslavic' North–South cultural axis.

and others have called this community *Slavia Orthodoxa*, 'Orthodox Slavdom' – though it also included some non-Slavs, above all Romanians.

How did Church Slavonic (so-called by us) relate to the spoken and eventually written language of the East Slavs, progenitor of Russian, Ukrainian and Belorussian? At the time of the Conversion the two still had large areas of vocabulary, phonology and morphology in common, while such differences as existed were of a regular nature that was easily comprehended. Syntactically Old Church Slavonic was partly based on the Greek from which most of its literature derived. But while over the centuries Old Russian evolved in syntax and vocabulary, shedding some complexities of its grammar, Church Slavonic, fixed in the forms established in the canonical religious texts, underwent no significant changes. At the end of the Old Russian period, Heinrich Ludolf's pioneering grammar of Russian (*Grammatica Russica*, published in Oxford in 1696) could state in a famous formulation 'loquendum est Russice & scribendum est Slavonice' ('Russian is for speaking and Slavonic for writing'), going on to point out that nowhere in the world was Slavonic actually a spoken language.

Ludolf's dictum, together with the modern perception of Russian and Church Slavonic as separate languages, can lead to a serious misunderstanding of the subtle and idiosyncratic linguistic situation in Rus. In West European countries the early medieval language of religion and scholarship was the international medium of Latin; vernacular literatures emerged only slowly and haphazardly towards the end of the Middle Ages (save where, as in some Nordic lands, oral epos and similar folk works were transcribed or imitated in written versions). The role of Church Slavonic in Russia and other Orthodox Slav lands looks similar to that of Latin in the parts of Europe dominated by the patriarchate of Rome (the Papacy); but the resemblance is superficial. Latin carried with it from its pre-Christian past the weighty baggage of the largest and most diverse literature the world had ever seen (leaving aside the socio-political pretensions wrapped up in this baggage): it was a fully developed linguistic system usable in a multitude of registers from the poetic and rhetorical to the colloquial and legalistic. Church Slavonic, by contrast, was created to be a written language with the express purpose of transmitting the sacred Word to the Slavs. It proved in practice a flexible instrument for the creation of new works as well as the translation of pre-existing material, not all overtly religious. But it remained in its essence a sacred language, occasioning awe, respect and considerable pride among the Orthodox Slavs – seen as their main highway to salvation. Unlike Latin among West and Central Europeans, it was not sensed by its users as 'other'. Specialists often still write as if an 'Old Russian literary language' existed side-by-side with Church Slavonic, the two available for use as the writer's choice or the task to be fulfilled dictated. But this would have astonished an early Russian, who did not even have the term 'Church Slavonic' at his disposal. Far from being linguistically alien to him, what we call Church Slavonic was perceived as the time-hallowed, lofty register of Russian – its 'bookish' (without modern pejorative connotations) version.

The contemporary scholar Boris Uspensky has brilliantly analysed the fundamental 'diglossia' that characterized this linguistic situation, at any rate until the mid-seventeenth century when the modern attitude that gave rise to Ludolf's comment became widespread. Until then diglossia meant that translation (and parody) was impossible as between Russian and Church Slavonic: they fulfilled functionally different roles within what was felt to be a single language. That does not mean, however, that the distinction between them was not powerfully felt: after all, the 'bookish' language had to be learnt, had fixed and 'correct' forms, was a microcosm of the divine order, while Russian vernacular language forms were unstable, unregulated, 'undivine', and hence potentially pagan or devilish. As Uspensky puts it

The specific character of the Russian linguistic, and more broadly cultural consciousness consists for the most part in the fact that here – in the functioning of diglossia as a linguistic and cultural mechanism – there exists no zone that is semantically neutral and which does not make reference to the sacred sphere. Hence, an absence of a connection with the sacred, the Divine, basically signifies a connection with its opposite, with the world of the Devil.[6]

Uspensky gives some startling and thought-provoking examples (in Russian folk tradition, we learn, the Devil loves to be called *chort*, the Russian word for him, and dreads the Slavonic term *bes*). Nonetheless there were perfectly legitimate areas for the use of written vernacular Russian: for practical purposes (decrees, laws, letters, ambassadorial messages, etc.) and – from the point of view of literary development most interestingly – in contexts where it is mixed to a greater or lesser degree with Slavonicisms. Sometimes this mixing is well-demarcated: thus in Yepifaniy's *Life of Stephen of Perm*, basically written in Slavonic, the Permian sorcerer who figures in its climactic scene speaks colloquial Russian (Uspensky likewise cites Russophone Chaldeans in the 'mystery play', derived from the Book of Daniel, that was performed in cathedrals: there is a memorable recreation of this play in the second

---

[6]   B. Uspensky 'The Language Situation and Linguistic Consciousness in Muscovite Rus', in H. Birnbaum and M. Flier (eds) *Medieval Russian Culture*, vol. I (Berkeley, 1984), p. 376.

part of Eisenstein's *Ivan the Terrible*). Often though such stylistic mixing could be more complicated, with subtler purposes: thus stylistically marked Slavonicisms can achieve lofty effects or suggest biblical reminiscences in chronicles or military tales whose language is fundamentally the Russian vernacular; the author who calls himself Daniil the Exile deliberately combines popular and learned (Slavonic) language to dazzle his audience with his wit; many other instances could be adduced, involving some of the most interesting and idiosyncratic Old Russian works and genres.

In the later seventeenth century, as we have mentioned, the diglossia that has been described began to be questioned: vernacular Russian had moved far enough away from Church Slavonic for them to be perceived as distinct languages. Yet neither then, nor (astonishingly) in the eighteenth century, when in the wake of Peter the Great's reforms the entire Western European literary system was imported piecemeal to Russia, did the Russian language turn its back on its Church Slavonic heritage. The most influential mid-eighteenth century poet and theorist, Mikhail Lomonosov (following similar attempts in France, Germany and elsewhere) codified what to eighteenth-century taste seemed the chaotic literary language into three stylistic levels – 'high', 'middle' and 'low' – suitable for various genres. For Lomonosov the defining factor was to be the quantity and nature of the Slavonicisms in the vocabulary employed at each level (Church Slavonic elements that had become incomprehensible to Russians on the one hand, and crudely colloquial or dialect forms on the other, were excluded from the system altogether). Though Lomonosov's system was too fiddly and cumbersome to be a practical guide for long – and was alien to the spirit of simplicity and spontaneity that characterized the early Romantic age that followed that of the Baroque in Russia as elsewhere – its principles were not unsound. In Pushkin's age there were still 'archaists' for whom the Slavonic component was the truly literary element in Russian, and could be made a bulwark against the flood of Western Europeanisms (in vocabulary, syntax and style) that inundated Russia from Peter's time onwards; needless to say, questions of national identity were closely linked with the language question. The further history of the problematics of the literary language shows, very briefly, that the general nineteenth-century attempt to produce a neutral, middle-of-the-road, internationally based and homogenized all-purpose language was continually liable to be subverted by a Russian partiality for folk elements (including semi-literate speech) on the one hand, and the continuing vitality of its Slavonic component on the other. The latter was indeed strengthened by a great deal of new abstract vocabulary, Slavonic in form and derivation. The modern scholar Boris Unbegaun was tempted to speculate in print as to whether the Russian literary language is Russian or Slavonic in essence, coming down in favour of the latter.[7]

This problem is not really susceptible to resolution: all one can say is that modern written Russian is a hybrid, whose 'grandparents' are normalized Russian, folk and dialect Russian, Western European imports and Church Slavonic elements. Juggling the balance between them has given modern Russian literature an extraordinary richness of texture; the reader even of classic nineteenth-century writers such as Gogol and Dostoyevsky will miss much by not appreciating it – and in translation such things can all too easily be missed. In the twentieth century a host of writers, among whom Beliy, Remizov, Isaac Babel, Andrey Platonov and Zoshchenko are merely among the outstanding names, play brilliantly and wittily with linguistic possibilities that are, after all, rooted in the age-old Russian tradition of 'literariness'.

## Some Individual Works

Early Russia did not produce any of the select group of independently standing masterpieces which have entered the canon of 'great works' of medieval literature, accessible in theory to readers of all cultures, such as the *Divine Comedy*, the *Decameron*, the *Canterbury Tales*, the lyric poems of Dafydd ap Gwilym or Li Po, the Icelandic sagas or the *Niebelungenlied*. As far as Russia is concerned, only the *Igor Tale* seems to have been occasionally promoted to such status, and for reasons that will become apparent later, it fills the role rather awkwardly, despite its undeniable individuality and poetic richness. The failure of this literature to engage the world's consciousness would seem to have distinctive causes that are not really to do with intrinsic literary merit or the lack of it. The problem is that there is something curiously ungraspable about Russian traditional literature and about the individual works within it. The boundaries between 'literary' and 'unliterary' texts are even more blurred than is usual in early literatures. Many of them are extremely unstable, and in the versions that have come down to us are clearly the result of multiple editing or rewritings; they can appear in such different guises that even identifying them and naming them as separate works is a contentious business. This textual instability, incidentally, is a result of the purposes and methods of literary production in pre-modern Russia,

---

[7] B. Unbegaun 'Le russe littéraire est-il d'origine russe?' in *Revue des Etudes Slaves* XLIV, 1965, pp. 19–28; see also his 'The Russian Literary Language: a Comparative View', Presidential Address in *Modern Language Review* 68:4, 1973.

and not merely of scribal sloppiness: canonical religious works, whose wording carried divine authority, were copied and recopied through the centuries with few, if any, changes. When the ancient norms of Church Slavonic seemed in danger of being forgotten or ignored around the late fourteenth to fifteenth centuries a powerful (though not always well-informed) movement for the restoration of its correct orthographic form and other principles spread through the Orthodox Slavs, starting in the Balkans – hence cumbersomely known to Russian literary historians as the 'Second South Slavonic Influence' (the first having been in the aftermath of the Conversion) – which was really part of, paradoxically, a great movement of cultural renewal in the Orthodox lands, still poorly understood in its totality.[8] Likhachov has called it the 'Orthodox Pre-Renaissance'.

The biggest problem in the appreciation of traditional Russian literature is that of contextualizing the works in question. An out-and-out 'new critical' or indeed Formalist approach, concentrating exclusively on the text alone, can be of little help to our understanding. The latter will gain immeasurably if we have access to its extra-literary contexts, and the further the work is from us in time or space, the more this will be so. It takes a conscious effort for most Westerners to enter into the civilizational context of early Russia; for Russians themselves the difficulties are much less, and it may be noteworthy that Russians are often on terms of familiarity with their own pre-modern literature to a degree that seems to be matched in English only from the age of Shakespeare and the 'Authorized Version' of the Bible onwards.

After these preliminary remarks it may come as something of a surprise if I now maintain that however problematic traditional Russian literature may be in many respects, there seems to me to be no doubt whatever as to where one should begin the study of it, or what constitutes its central masterpiece. The modern name of this work will already be familiar to readers of this book as the 'Russian Primary Chronicle', but it is more picturesquely known to most educated Russians, from its opening words, as the *Tale of Bygone Years*. It is a unique work, but not unique in the manner of the *Igor Tale*, which is an exotic plant in the garden of Russian literature. It is unique in the sense that the trunk of a great tree is unique – the single support from which a multitude of branches spring: limbs which, different as they may look, are of the same substance, drawing nourishment from the one stem. The 'branches' of course are the hundreds, probably thousands of chronicle

---

[8]   Only D. Likhachov has investigated this comprehensively, in several works; see also R. Milner-Gulland 'Russia's Lost Renaissance' in D. Daiches and A. Thorlby (eds) *Literature and Western Civilization* vol. III (London, 1974).

redactions that emerged throughout the lands of Rus, in monasteries in the deep provinces as well as national and local capital cities, up to the eighteenth century (during which the first 'modern' historians arose – some of whom, notably the indispensable Vasiliy Tatishchev, were in spirit and often in method still Old Russian chroniclers). Most chronicles indeed take the Primary Chronicle, implicitly or explicitly, as their opening section, making it the canonical account of Russian history up

Plate 14   Manuscript illumination: the Monk Silvester writes the
Primary Chronicle (or Tale of Bygone Years, 1110s) in the
Vydubitsky Monastery, Kiev, with iconic representation of the
Archangel Michael over the church door (from the
sixteenth-century Illustrated Chronicle Compendium.)

to the 1110s when it was compiled. The ceaseless subsequent re-reading and recopying of this work over the centuries mean that it has become a fundamental component of Russian 'mythistory' – the fusion of history, supposed history and the tendentious interpretation of history that constitutes the bedrock of national self-awareness in any country (the Homeric poems played such a role in both Ancient and Byzantine Greece; the Pentateuch for the Israelites; maybe Shakespeare's history plays for the English).

At this point one must indicate a curious paradox. Though it is simple enough to make out the case for the centrality of the *Tale of Bygone Years* to Russian self-awareness, though it is full of good stories that make their way independently into anthologies, though its format of year-by-year entries (often evidently well-crafted into individual 'essays' sometimes with cross-references to other entries) sets interesting problems of narrative technique, it is usually ignored in its role as not just the foundation-stone of a specifically Russian literature but as its towering early monument (the current standard critical study of early Russian literature in English scarcely even mentions it).[9] I am not here concerned to argue the 'post-modern' case that *all* history writing is essentially a literary endeavour, though (unlike *bien-pensant* traditionalist historians) I think a valid case for this can easily be made. Rather, I wish to emphasize my belief that the *Tale of Bygone Years* is not just literary in some general way, but is a literary work of a specific and remarkable kind in other words, one with its own deliberately crafted structures, its own subtexts, its poetics, its ideology, its own stylistic armoury. The great scholar Čiževskij, one of the few to perceive this, rightly wrote 'The ancient chronicles are not only historical monuments but also literary works of high artistic value.'[10]

Why then is that 'value' not immediately obvious and universally acknowledged? First, I think, because commentators have tended to examine it primarily with regard to questions (significant ones, admittedly) of authorship, textual integrity, historical sources and factual reliability: they have begun by dissecting it rather than by taking a global view of its overarching form and purposes. Secondly, because, to quote Čiževskij again, the Primary Chronicle is a kind of literary encyclopedia . Dispersed among its often laconic year-by-year annalistic entries are all sorts of documents, public records, military tales, biographies, devotional texts – themselves of various kinds – sententious reflections, popular anecdotes (sometimes jocular), eyewitness reports, miniature epics, extracts from translations, anthropological observations,

---

[9]   J. Fennell and A. Stokes *Early Russian Literature* (London, 1974).
[10]   See Čiževskij, note 3 above, p. 52.

even at one (crucial) point a long supposed dialogue with a Greek philosopher. This 'collage' of different materials naturally also involves a wide range of appropriate styles. Even purely from the historian's viewpoint the *Tale of Bygone Years* is an interesting conglomerate: it represents the welding-together of the two characteristic medieval chronicle types – local annals and universal history. The 'annalistic' element gives us a record and a view of the specificity of Old Russia, its political problems and the various attempts to overcome them; the 'universal' aspect locks Russia into a world geography and history, thereby establishing its place in the divine scheme of things – a 'spiritual geography'. Together they supply the *Tale of Bygone Years* with its central climax – the long-drawn-out story of Vladimir's conversion to Christianity – and its provisional endpoint (no historical ending can ever be better than temporary and provisional), the reign and personal example of his great-grandson Vladimir II Monomakh (as it happens – though the chronicler of the 1110s could not have known this – almost the last great ruler capable of asserting the all-Russian authority of Kiev, repelling its enemies and bringing concord to the fractious, violent and shortsighted rulers of the various principalities of Rus).

This then is the 'religious' strand of a triple-stranded thread that binds the disparate, fortuitous elements of the Primary Chronicle together, furnishing its 'grand narrative'. The other strands – closely woven, often hardly distinguishable from each other – are, I believe, political and cultural in nature. The political element is signalled by the opening words of the Primary Chronicle, when the writer announces his quest for the origins and first rulers of Kievan Rus; the restoration of Kiev's primacy under Vladimir II Monomakh (the people of Kiev's choice for ruler) is a suitable end-point. The political strand of the chronicle has two climactic moments. One is the reign of Svyatoslav, the archetypal warrior-hero ruler, with his bluntly direct challenge to his opponents 'I intend to march on you' (*khochu na vy iti*), his disregard of personal comfort, his establishment of a huge steppe-country empire that proved his undoing; the other is the reign of his son Vladimir I, focused on Kiev itself, bringing harmony and glory internally and internationally, a ruler who 'loved his retinue (*druzhina*), consulted with them about the good order of the country, about warfare, about the laws of the land', and lived at peace with the neighbouring rulers of the Poles, Hungarians and Czechs.

The cultural strand relates to the enlightenment of the Russian land. Its climactic moment is the reign of Vladimir's son and eventual successor, Yaroslav. It had passed through Vladimir's baptized grandmother, Olga, then through the efforts of Vladimir himself to institute systematic book-learning, thus fulfilling Isaiah's prophecy that 'the deaf shall hear the words of the Scripture and the voice of the stammerers shall be made plain' in Rus. In Yaroslav's reign, under the year 1037, we read first the account of the foundation of the great church of Kiev, Santa Sophia ('Holy Wisdom'), and that is designedly followed by a description of Yaroslav's activities on behalf of learning, and by praise of books – and wisdom – in general. The words of books (writes the chronicler, in a noble metaphor) 'are rivers, watering the universe; they are fountains of wisdom; in books there are measureless depths'. Likhachov makes the fine observation that this is an appropriate metaphor for the chronicle itself: its 'epic narration of Russian history can be compared to the mighty flow of a vast river', joining together many tributaries.[11] The chronicler recounts how Yaroslav has numerous books copied out and deposits them in Santa Sophia (which has ample galleries and side-chambers for the purpose), suggesting that the foundation of his 'Holy Wisdom' church is closely associated with these educating and enlightening endeavours. It is likely too (though the documents themselves do not survive) that part of this programme of enlightenment was in fact the origination of systematic chronicle writing in Russia, producing some of the stock of material on which the author of the *Tale of Bygone Years* drew – together with, for example, Biblical and Byzantine Greek writings (he cites the historian George Hamartolos by name), epic tales both Russian and Viking, legal documents, formalized speeches, hagiographic and military tales, local traditions about people and places, and the accounts of eyewitness participants in events (he cites two in particular, the high Kievan official Vyshata and his son Yan Vyshatych).

The grand narrative of the *Tale of Bygone Years* seems upbeat in character: the illustration of divine benevolence working itself out in respect of a favoured people. In another metaphor from nature for Russia's enlightenment, the chronicler envisages Vladimir I ploughing and improving the soil of Rus, Yaroslav 'the Wise' sowing the seed of learning in the hearts of the Russian faithful and 'ourselves' as reaping the harvest. Yet seen from the perspective of the early twelfth century the Russian historical process never quite seemed to be yielding up its promised bounty of peace, prosperity and enlightenment. On the contrary, things were always going wrong: externally from the frequent successes of the enemies of Rus, notably the damaging and alarming raids of nomad Pechenegs and Polovtsians, internally from internecine rivalries and strife between the component parts of the loose-knit Rus federation (as well as occasional popular uprisings of pagan inspiration in a still incompletely Christianized country). There is a dark subtext to the apparent triumphalism of the chronicler. The Devil and his wiles

[11]  D. Likhachov *The Great Heritage: the Classical Literature of Old Rus* (Moscow, 1981), p. 44.

were far from defeated, while God must be sending the steppe pagans to ravage Rus in punishment for its sins (this characteristic medieval fatalism is implicitly contradicted by the praise of great, voluntaristic leaders when they occasionally appear).

To illustrate this, and indeed several facets of the chronicler's viewpoint and verbal art, it is worth quoting at length from the final section of the notable chronicle entry for 1093. Half-a-dozen pages long, this entry (one is tempted to call it a chronicle microcosm) begins with an interestingly even-handed obituary of the Kievan ruler Vsevolod (Vladimir II's father). The political manoeuvrings and rivalries that follow lead to incursions by the Polovtsians that culminate in a circumstantially described battle and the siege, disastrous for the Russians, of the frontier town of Torchesk. The chronicler breaks off his tense and eventful narrative to search for scriptural quotations and consoling maxims that will permit a justification in the divine scheme of things for such disasters, magnified in 1093 by their coinciding with major feastdays – even the new, specifically Russian feast of Sts Boris and Gleb: 'After all it was God who let loose the pagans upon us – not because he favoured them, but to punish us, so that we might restrain ourselves from wicked deeds.'

Lamentation and self-questioning follow, then an unforgettable picture of the consequences of defeat:

For when used there to be such emotion among us? And now all is full of tears. When was there misery among us? And now in every street there is lamentation for those whom the lawless ones have killed. The Polovtsians harried us much and returned to Torchesk; the people were weakened by hunger and gave themselves up to the besiegers. The Polovtsians took the town and set fire to it, meanwhile dividing up the inhabitants and carrying off a multitude of Christian folk to their strongholds, for their families and relatives. Suffering, sorrowful, tormented, in bitter cold, in hunger, thirst and misery, their faces sunken and their bodies blackened, tongues inflamed, barefoot and unclothed, feet cut to ribbons by thorns, they tearfully answered each others' questions: 'I used to live in such-and-such a town' or 'I am from this-or-that village'. Thus they enquired of each other through tears, naming their origins, sighing and turning up their eyes to Heaven and to the Most High who knows all secrets. And yet let no-one say we are hated by God! May that never happen! For whom does God love as he has loved us? Whom has he honoured as he has glorified us and raised us up? No-one else! He has all the more unleashed his anger upon us insofar as, being more favoured than any, we have sinned worse than others. For being more enlightened than the rest, knowing the Lord's will, we have scorned it and all that is beautiful, and we have been punished harder than others. Indeed I myself, sinner that I am, incur God's anger greatly and frequently, and often commit sins daily.

In the same year there died Rostislav son of Mstislav, grandson of Izyaslav Yaroslavich, on 1st October and was interred on 16th November in the Tithe Church of the Holy Mother of God.

Thus at the end of a single year's entry during which the chronicler has run through a remarkable gamut of narrative and emotional effects, with even a first-person digression, he resumes the role of deadpan recorder of events. I speak of 'the chronicler', and doubtless the compiler of the *Tale of Bygone Years* in the early 1110s remembered the eventful year 1093 well. One must stress again that Old Russian chronicles, deriving from many disparate sources and ultimately the work of many hands, did not arise simply as the sum total of year-by-year notes (though such notes must somehow have been kept). Rather they were written to mark special events and are thus 'shaped' works. Often they have a polemical axe to grind: in favour of one or another city, prince or ecclesiastical figure, against others – possibly a whole group such as the local boyars. Some fifteenth-century chronicle compendia (e.g. the Trinity Chronicle) try to adopt a balanced all-Russian perspective: by the sixteenth century they become vehicles of Muscovite propaganda. An objective picture of Old Russian history can emerge only from a conspectus of available chronicles and any other documents available, though in Russia the latter have survived in much lesser quantities than in most Western European countries.[12]

So that this discussion of chronicles as literature should stay within reasonable bounds, it has concentrated on the *Tale Of Bygone Years*, which is in any case the defining work of the genre. Yet it must not be imagined that all the many other chronicles are identical in style or in the sort of information they give. In particular the Novgorod First Chronicle has a quite distinctive tone: down-to-earth in the most literal way, full of information on weather conditions, the environment and geographical circumstances that gave the city its peculiarly marginal existence. In complete contrast the Galician Chronicle, that is found as a continuation into the thirteenth century of the *Tale Of Bygone Years* in the Hypatian manuscript, is a continuous narrative, remarkable in its consistent high tone of emotionalized rhetoric. A haunting episode given under the year 1201 recounts the return of two over-adventurous Polovtsian chiefs (khans), Syrchan and Otrok, to their native land, and shows a novel degree of empathy with the enemies of Rus:

Grand Prince Roman . . . equalled his grandfather Monomakh, who drove Otrok into Abkhazia beyond the Caucasus. But Syrchan remained by the Don, living on fish; that was when Vladimir Monomakh drank from the Don out of his golden helmet, and captured all their land, and drove out the cursed Hagarenes [i.e. Muslims]. At Vladimir's death, when only one minstrel, Orevi, remained with Syrchan, Otrok sent him to Abkhazia with the message: 'Vladimir is dead, so come back, brother, to your own land: repeat my words to him, and in addition

---

[12]   J. Fennell 'Textology as a Key to the Study of Old Russian Literature and History', in *Text* 1981 vol. 1, describes this situation concisely and forcefully.

sing him Polovtsian songs; but if he still remains unwilling, give him some of the herb we call wormwood to smell.' Syrchan however did not wish either to return or to listen to the songs, so he was given the wormwood. He sniffed it and burst into tears, saying: 'Indeed it is better to lay down one's bones on one's native soil than to win glory in foreign parts.' And he came back to his own country. From him was born Konchak, who scooped water from the River Sula, going on foot and carrying his cooking vessels over his shoulder.

The reference to Konchak leads us on to the other major literary work of pre-Tatar Russia, in which he also happens to play a role, the *Igor Tale (Slovo o polku Igoreve)*. This anonymous work, some 15–20 pages long, in what seems to be highly poeticized prose, tells the story of a rash expedition instigated by a minor prince, Igor the son of Svyatoslav, against the nomad Polovtsians, of its defeat in the steppe country on the (unidentified) Kayala river, of Igor's capture by the khans Konchak and Gzak, of his escape and return home. Chronicle accounts of the same raid date it to 1185; the *Tale* itself is normally thought to have been composed shortly afterwards, though the only MS of it known to have survived into modern times was probably made in Pskov *c*.1500 and included in a compendium. This MS, discovered *c*.1795, was twice copied out, was consulted by several historians, but then perished with the rest of the antiquarian Count Musin-Pushkin's library in the 1812 fire of Moscow.

These bare facts give little inkling of the role the *Igor Tale* has played in Russian culture. Every educated Russian has read it and would no doubt recognize many quotations from it. It is taken as a political plea for all-Russian co-operation and unity. Its simple plot has formed the basis for one of the classic Russian operas, Borodin's sprawling and magnificent four-hour work *Prince Igor* (source of the all-too-famous 'Polovtsian Dances'). Hundreds of scholarly articles have been written about it. Why all this attention? The poet Nikolay Zabolotsky (1903–58), who – largely when a political exile in the 1940s – made a splendid translation of it into modern Russian verse, characterized it hyperbolically but memorably in a letter to his friend N. L. Stepanov:

Now that I've entered into the spirit of the work I'm totally awestruck, amazed and grateful to fate for preserving this miracle for us from the depths of the past. In the wilderness of our bygone centuries, where wars, fires and savage destruction have left not one stone standing upon another, this isolated temple of our ancient glory, resembling nothing else, still stands . . . Everything about it is filled with a special tender savagery – the writer's measure is not the same as ours. How moving to see it stand, this mysterious edifice, its corners battered, the haunt of ravens and wolves, for as long as Russian culture stands, knowing no equals![13]

[13] N. Zabolotsky (trans. and ed. R. Milner-Gulland) *The Life of Zabolotsky* (Cardiff, 1994), p. 222.'

*Figure 10   V. Favorsky (1886–1964, the leading Russian graphic
artist of the first half of the twentieth century): frontispiece to
the 1950 edition of the* Igor Tale *(wood-engraving).*

This sense of a 'miraculous' quality in the *Igor Tale* stems partly from
the strange fate of its manuscript, partly from its heaven-sent appearance
at a moment when the Russian cultural self-consciousness (still largely

unaware of its medieval artistic heritage) needed a major early monument to demonstrate its international credentials, partly of course from the work's inherent poetic qualities. The enthusiasm it has engendered is understandable (as perhaps is also a certain venom among the small band of its detractors). But its uniqueness has been less emphasized by modern researchers: its text reveals a web of interconnexions with other works of early written literature, with the oral epic and lyric traditions and with folklore.

The work itself is very strange and may well at points baffle the Russian as well as non-Russian reader. The outlines of the plot (presumably known already to the original readers or listeners) are given allusively; there are innumerable references to contemporary or historical personages, particularly to members of the far-flung princely family, and a geographical compass that includes all Rus and indeed many places beyond. The work's texture is replete with elaborate metaphors chiefly from the natural world, with sound-effects (Dean Worth calls it a 'very noisy poem'),[14] and with rhetorical figures such as apostrophe and negative parallelism ('But Boyan, brethren, did not let loose ten falcons upon a flock of swans, but laid his prophetic fingers upon living strings: and they themselves spoke forth praise to the princes'). In a curious but impressive opening section the poet evokes the figure of this Boyan, a bard from an earlier generation, in the course of self-questioning as to the manner in which he should recount his heroic tale, 'from Vladimir of old to Igor of the present, who girded his mind with strength and sharpened his heart with courage: filled with warlike spirit, he led his brave forces to the Polovtsian land for the sake of the land of Rus.' At the end, the poet's agenda reaches its fulfilment: 'Having sung a song for the ancient princes, we should then sing to the young; glory to Igor Svyatoslavich!' But the irony is that Igor's 'heroic' action has gone completely awry: though his opening words are 'Brethren and retainers! (*druzhina*) Better to be slain than taken prisoner', he himself is indeed imprisoned, his retainers and own brother are lost, his impetuous expedition has brought only sorrow to the Grand Prince Svyatoslav in Kiev, he has 'sunk his wealth at the bottom of the Polovtsian river Kayala and dissipated the Russian gold'. The rulers of the other principalities will not come to Igor's or Kiev's aid, for the 'time is out of joint' (*naniche sya godiny obratisha*) and the princes 'forge strife against each other' rather than resisting the common enemy. The irony and tragedy of this political situation (and of the bard's duty to respond to it) give the work its driving tension and lasting impact.

It is densely-textured, full of rhetorical addresses and questionings (to natural objects – rivers, winds – as well as to humans present or absent)

[14]   In V. Terras (ed.) *Handbook of Russian Literature* (Yale, 1985) p. 427.

with some notable set-pieces: the 'golden word' spoken by the Grand Prince Svyatoslav, his 'turbulent dream', the famous lament for the missing Igor by his wife Yaroslavna on the walls of Putivl. Many supernatural beings from folk belief are evoked, some in obscure contexts, and there is correspondingly an almost total absence of Christian references – to a unique extent in early Russian literature – until the very end of the *Tale* (where it is quite perfunctory: 'Long live the princes and the retinue, doing battle for Christians against the infidel hosts: glory to the princes and to the retinue! Amen').

What sort of a work can this possibly be? Most scholars have considered that it originated as a written text, though heavily influenced by an oral epic tradition of courtly poetry probably represented in the figure of Boyan. Surviving examples of Russian oral epos – not transcribed until modern times, and surviving in village milieux far from where they originated – known as *byliny* (singular *bylina*), 'things that happened' or *stariny*, 'ancient things', are not very close in manner, though they share the background in folk-belief: the *Igor Tale* by comparison is a deliberately dazzling, close-textured and difficult work. Likhachov compares it to Western medieval poems such as the *Song of Roland*. One of the most recent investigators, Robert Mann, basing his views on a close study of its formulaic structures and folkloric motifs in his book *Lances Sing*, has made a strong case that it was an orally composed and transmitted work (though that still leaves open the problem of when, how and with what modifications it was eventually written down). In any event one may be left with the sense that this is an intentionally riddling work, that there are unstated (and probably irrecoverable) subtexts to it. From early in the nineteenth century onwards there were sceptics who felt the whole thing was too good to be true, that it must be a forgery on Ossianic lines – though such forgeries are usually easily detectable when modern scholarly methods are applied, and it is scarcely credible that in the eighteenth century anyone had the vast knowledge of Old Russian language, folklore and even of certain unpublished texts that would have been necessary to carry out such a project (or indeed the motive: why select what came to be seen as a minor historical incident, discreditable to Rus, as the subject for such an endeavour?).

So the situation might have remained, had not a series of manuscript discoveries from the mid-nineteenth century onwards put things in a new and unexpected light. They revealed the existence, in several disparate and defective versions, of a late medieval work generally known as *Zadonshchina*, 'that which happened beyond the Don'. It tells the tale of the events surrounding the great battle of Kulikovo Field in 1380, when a Russian force led by Dmitriy Ivanovich (later surnamed 'Donskoy'), Grand Prince of Moscow, defeated the large army of the Tatar prince

Mamay. No-one doubts that *Zadonshchina*, in all redactions, has many verbal and structural correspondences with the *Igor Tale*. Sceptics have argued tenaciously that a falsified *Igor Tale* might have been based on *Zadonshchina* rather than the other way round – but such an idea occasions many more difficulties than it would resolve. The *Igor Tale* motifs in question seem to be handled more clumsily, sometimes inappropriately, when adapted for the purposes of *Zadonshchina* (one example: in the *Igor Tale* the River Dnieper is said to have 'broken through the strong hills in the land of the Polovtsians', a clear reference to the famous series of rapids where the Dnieper traverses a band of hard metamorphic rocks; in *Zadonshchina*, the image is inappropriately transferred to the River Don, which as everybody knows 'flows quiet' throughout its course).

*Zadonshchina* is anyhow an effective and poetic literary work, even if it lacks the rhetorical panache and metaphoric density of the *Igor Tale*. Unlike the latter, however, it is consistently Christian in tone, seeing the struggle with the steppe peoples (by now Tatars) as that of Christians and infidels. It seems the author (according to the manuscript, Sofoniy of Ryazan) had the stylistic mastery and imagination to create a fully independent literary work had he so wished, but chose to introduce motifs from the *Igor Tale* into a parallel but different story: not, it would appear, because these were mere literary commonplaces (evidently not the case), nor yet as a mechanically appropriated set of adornments, but as a self-conscious device to draw attention to the two works' intrinsic kinship. The defeat of the infidel army, in other words, was presented as a redressing of the historical balance, the restoration of the divine mercy to the suffering Russian people – for this purpose, no particular distinction between the Polovtsians and the Tatars who succeeded them more than a generation after Igor's raid was necessary. The *Igor Tale*'s pre-Christian frame of reference is counterbalanced by the Christian orientation of *Zadonshchina*. Roman Jakobson, one of the most perceptive scholars to examine both works closely, considered that they must have been presented to readers jointly, as a diptych – and pointed to the passage near the beginning of *Zadonshchina* where the author writes 'Let us set word next to word', taking 'word' (*slovo*) in its sense (used in the very title of the *Igor Tale*) of 'discourse'. The relationship between the two works is remarkably indicative of what must have been a network of intertextuality (that cannot now be fully reconstructed) within early Russian literature, characterized as it is by its 'open tradition' (Riccardo Picchio's phrase)[15] of unfinalized works, always

---

[15]   See R. Picchio 'The Impact of Ecclesiastic Culture on Old Russian Literary Techniques' in Birnbaum and Flier *Medieval Russian Culture*, vol. I.

subject to modification and recombination: hence the title of this chapter.

The *Igor Tale* is the only written work surviving from Old Russia that reflects a predominantly non-Christian world-view (this feature, indeed, has been taken as a prime reason for questioning its authenticity). We should not however doubt that a mass of literature based on pre-Christian folk belief existed: the point is that it belonged to the vast realm of oral literature, necessarily evanescent save where (as with cycles of Kiev and Novgorod byliny, some folk lyrics and tales) it has survived in an unlettered and remote environment – to be transcribed in the post-Petrine age. Such literature was composed and perpetuated in various environments, but above all in the remarkable fraternities of professional minstrels called *skomorokhi* (singular *skomorokh*). They go back to the dawn of recorded Russian history, and the last of them seem to have died out as late as the mid-eighteenth century. The only contemporary scholar to give them much serious attention, Russell Zguta, considers they represented successors to the old pagan priesthood.[16] This daring conjecture is plausible, though hard evidence is lacking (we are not even sure if there *was* such a priesthood); but in any case it is clear that the Church leaders associated *skomorokhi* with non-Christian religious practices, were alarmed by them and did their best, particularly in the later centuries of Rus, to suppress them: in the mid-seventeenth century, under the pious Tsar Aleksey, they were indeed officially banned. It is surprising, to say the least, that they survived for seven hundred years or more in Christianized Rus, and this testifies to the vastness of the country, the difficulty in imposing centralized order on it, the protection the *skomorokhi* must at least sometimes have enjoyed from people in authority (even from the Tsar, at least in the case of Ivan the Terrible) and above all to the fact that they provided something that was needed in the country's life and culture. Though they are quite often dismissed as crude buffoons, all the contemporary evidence – including the testimony of the Western European visitor Adam Olearius in the early seventeenth century – shows that they were, or could be, highly skilled and varied performers. They kept alive a series of forms of non-written literature whose intricacy, subtlety and aesthetic worth we have no reason to doubt. They were keepers of the record of 'folk history' through historical songs, which it is known they could also compose *ad hoc*, songs to praise the deeds of living rulers (compare the *Igor Tale*), and they were sometimes hired to perform these to inspire the army of Rus to battle. They were probably the chief conservers and transmitters of the ancient *bylina* tradition (migrating to Novgorod after the breakdown of

[16]   R. Zguta *Russian Minstrels* (Oxford, 1978), p. 8ff.

Kiev in the thirteenth century, and thence to the northern forests). They told folktales, anecdotes, proverbs and riddles. Above all they were bearers of a theatrical tradition that included song and dance, playlets involving performing bears, and puppet shows (there is a unique and extraordinary contemporary illustration of a puppeteer in Olearius).

What seems to have happened (how, and how consciously, we cannot tell) was a carve-up of the various possibilities within literature in its broad sense between the written and the oral spheres, with little subsequent trespassing on each other's territory. Most Christian-inspired and edificatory literature (all that had Church approval), translations, chronicles, military tales, travel-accounts, politico-historical works and a very few sophisticated but indefinable pieces (*The Petition of Daniil the Exile* from before the Tatar period, the strange parable *Tale of Misery-Luckless-Plight* from late Muscovy) fell within the written sphere, that which is ordinarily considered 'literature'. Works based on folk belief and myth, including wedding and similar rituals, Christian apocryphal tales and 'sacred poems' (*dukhovnye stikhi*, of folk inspiration), lyric poems, stories, epics remained unwritten until transcribed, usually from the eighteenth century onward (a few lyric poems were written down by

*Plate 15    Adam Olearius (early seventeenth century):*
skomorokhi *(minstrels), including the unique representation of an*
*otherwise unknown type of puppet show.*

an English visitor to Russia, Richard James, as early as the beginning of the seventeenth century). This generic distinction was of course also reflected in subject matter: the great range of erotic material found in Western European late medieval literature, to take an obvious example, has no equivalent in the Old Russian written record until the clumsy picaresque tales that begin to appear in the mid-seventeenth century (*Savva Grudtsyn, Frol Skobeyev*). As for poetry, it has been suggested more than once (first by Tredyakovsky in the mid-eighteenth century) that the early Church deliberately avoided it because of its pagan-oral connotations: thus we have great quantities of poeticized prose, approximately though never exactly falling into rhythmically regular patterns, but no precise written verse-forms – a situation that could hardly have arisen in countries with a Greco-Latin literary background. Theatre (despite the existence of Church mystery plays) must have been kept out of written literature for similar reasons. In the circumstances of this clear demarcation – at least until the mid-seventeenth century – it is rather astonishing that 'seepage' of folk patterns of thought and wording into 'high', written literature unobtrusively took place from early Kievan times onward, and give it much of its unmistakably Russian coloration. Occasionally we may even feel we are in the presence of a real literary equivalent to *dvoyeverie*, 'double belief', the unforced synthesis of Christian and pre-Christian belief-systems: nowhere is this more consistently to be sensed than in the *Tale of Misery-Luckless-Plight* (*Povest o Gore-Zloshchastii*), the laconic and scalp-tingling parable of a life haunted by the monstrous personification of Misery (extant in a single seventeenth-century copy).

Within the 'high culture' of pre-Petrine Russia, Christian literature clearly and for obvious reasons carried greatest prestige. The Russo-Slavonic linguistic medium made Old Russia part of the major civilizational unit often called 'Orthodox Slavdom' which was discussed earlier (see p. 139ff.); the Slavonic written language was considered of its nature sacred, maybe holier even than the ancient religious languages (Hebrew, Syriac, Greek, Latin) since it alone was designed specifically to bear the messages of the sacred texts. One can distinguish various levels of 'sacredness' in Christian Slav literature. The highest level is represented by works of specifically divine inspiration (the Bible, liturgical hymns, writings of the Church Fathers), the common heritage of all Orthodox peoples, not subject to any textual alteration. At the opposite extreme are works such as chronicles, biographies, letters, polemical works and military tales that in a post-medieval society might be regarded as wholly secular but in Old Russia have a specifically Christian coloration. In between comes a mass of variously devotional and edificatory writing of great importance to the early Russian reader:

saints' lives of varied kinds, spiritual instructions, epistles, sermons, commentaries, etc. Sometimes polished and high-flown works, entirely Byzantine in spirit, resulted (e.g. the sermons of Bishop Kirill of Turov), sometimes styleless and mechanical conveyor-belt products (the large quantity of sixteenth-century saints' lives), but at nearly all periods certain writings in this category can be found that – even for a modern reader remote from the thought-world that produced them – have the spark of individuality and the power to move one emotionally. 'Individuality' however should not be taken in a modern sense of exalting unique perceptions: medieval literature (and art) tend to seek the general rather than the particular, and make calculated – not always unsubtle – use of *topoi*, 'commonplaces'.

Such literature begins, so far as we know, in the reign of Yaroslav (d. 1054) with the joint *Life* of Princes Boris and Gleb (martyred in 1015) and the *Discourse on the Law and the Grace*, composed as a sermon to be delivered in the newly built cathedral of St Sophia in Kiev by Ilarion, apparently the first Metropolitan of the Russian Church to be a native-born Russian rather than a Greek. The *Discourse* is a work of impressive rhetorical power: Law (given to Moses) represents the Old Testament, Grace (through Christ's baptism) the New, and the 'newness' of Russia's Conversion is implicitly endorsed and celebrated. The most remarkable part of the work is its final section, a self-contained paean of praise to Vladimir I, who (though not yet canonized) is presented as equal to the Apostles – and, in what sounds more like a folk formulation than a Christian sentiment, calls on the great Kagan (a Khazar title!) Vladimir 'to arise and shake off [his] sleep', returning to behold the glory of Kiev under his son's rule. This is clearly a work in which religious and national-political considerations are inseparable, a feature to be encountered over and over again in early (and, indeed, subsequent) centuries. So, differently, are the various writings dealing with the martyrdom of Boris and Gleb. To unravel the interconnections of the three main such works and their numerous later redactions would be a specialized and contentious endeavour. What seems clear is that a very early text, dating back to soon after the brothers' deaths and the decision to promote them as the first Russian saints, must have been written in a laconic, eventful, 'saga-like' manner and (though it has not survived) remained a main component of the known subsequent redactions that variously prolonged, ornamented, emotionalized, variegated, politi-cized, homogenized, even eventually re-simplified the narrative. One early version was turned into the vivid Primary Chronicle account. Despite its tormented textual history the story of the deaths of Boris and Gleb – in whichever version – remains a gripping and affecting work, that had a cultural role beyond the mere legitimization of Yaroslav and his successors: the brothers were taken as exemplars of martyrdom in the cause of the 'non-resistance to violence' (yet they were also depicted in icons as warrior-saints, defenders of the Russian land).[17]

Saints' lives (hagiography) remain, for the modern reader, probably the most interesting area of Old Russian devotional literature: the form never ceased to throw up problems, often political, that different writers had to resolve anew, despite the evident fact that there were numerous stereotypes available to depict sanctity and commonplaces to represent a given saint's life events (thus in childhood a future saint might either be described as highly precocious in book-learning – e.g. Stephen of Perm – or backward and illiterate until enlightened miraculously – e.g. Sergius of Radonezh). Every new saint had to have an iconic 'type': indeed, the writing of hagiography tended to move away from narrative, to our taste 'realistic' and detailed biography into the realm of a carefully wrought, if often rather abstract 'icon in words'. Such are the two *Lives* just mentioned, of Stephen and Sergius, composed *c.*1400 by Yepifaniy Premudriy (Epiphanius the Wise), probably the finest Russian writer whose name is known to us between the thirteenth and the seventeenth centuries. Both are long (each over 100 pages in standard editions) and feature a highly ornate literary style nowadays usually known as 'word-weaving' (*pletenie sloves*, a term Yepifaniy himself employs). This is the ultimate development of a rhetorical mode whose roots reach far back in the literature of Orthodox Slavdom – to Ilarion's *Discourse on the Law and the Grace* in some respects, to the highly wrought biographies (in hagiographic manner) of Serbian kings in others, and of course has Byzantine analogues. Trying to account for such 'word-weaving' in Russia, literary historians until quite recently attributed it to a supposed 'second Slav influence' on Russian culture (the 'first' was at the time of the Conversion). This was at the period during which the Ottoman Turks overran the Balkans, and indeed a few South Slav (Bulgarian and Serbian) intellectuals – notably the Metropolitan Kiprian – migrated to Russia and played a part in Russian public life. But there is no evidence that they brought Yepifaniy's word-weaving in their baggage: in its variegation, daring and 'emotional extremism', Yepifaniy's stylistic brio leaves his South Slav predecessors (most often cited is Bishop Euthymius of Trnovo) sounding pallid and vacuous rhetoricians.

Piling up epithets, near-synonyms and rhetorical questions till it would seem impossible to find yet more, parading compound abstract nouns

---

[17]   G. Lenhoff *The Martyred Princes Boris and Gleb* (Columbus, 1987) not only examines the texts in detail, but has an interesting opening chapter proposing a methodology through which to approach Old Russian literature generally.

and adjectives of his own devising, making mosaics of Biblical quotations (sometimes adapted to context), playing on words, meanings, phrase-rhythms and sound-repetitions, Yepifaniy, in his most idiosyncratic, virtuoso passages builds fairytale castles of language. Probably his most consistently striking and poetically saturated effects are to be found towards the end of the *Life* of Bishop Stephen, missionary to the pagan nation of Perm. Here, after Stephen's death, when an account of some posthumous miracles might have been expected, Yepifaniy in a bold stroke gives us instead a threefold lament (influenced partly by the folk tradition of lamentation): the lament of the Permian people (as of a child for a father), of the Permian church (as of a widow for a husband), and finally 'of the monk who wrote this work', Yepifaniy himself, merging into panegyric. The flavour of these sections can only inadequately be conveyed in translation:

And I too, much-sinful and unlearned, following the words of your praises, weaving the word and fructifying the word, and with the word hoping to honour you, and out of words gathering praises together, and taking them in and weaving them in, am saying again: What then should I name you?

Leader of the strayed, finder of the lost, instructor of the tempted, guide of those inwardly blind, cleaner of the defiled, seeker of the dispersed, guard of the warriors, comforter of the sorrowing, nourisher of the hungering, provider of the needy, punisher of the thoughtless, helper of the offended, ardent intercessor, loyal intermediary, for the pagans a saviour, for devils a curser, for idols a destroyer, for images a breaker, of God a servant, of wisdom a guardian, of philosophy a lover, of purity an upholder, of truth an agent, of books an author, of Permian writing the creator!

Many are your names, o bishop! Manynamedness have you earned, of many gifts have you been worthy, with many virtues have you grown rich!

Stephen's great feat had been not only to convert the heathen Permians, suspicious of Muscovite intentions, to Christianity, at the latest moment (the end of the seventh millennium – 1492 in our calendar – was expected to herald the Last Judgement), after an eyeball-to-eyeball confrontation with their chief shaman, but to devise for them an appropriate alphabet and to translate Slavonic and Greek texts into Permian, making him the equal of Cyril and Methodius: hence Yepifaniy's insistent stress on 'word' and 'naming' in all their ramifications. Needless to say, this was all too good to last – uncompromising Muscovite centralization in the next century wiped out not only the independent Permian church but also its alphabet and literature, leaving to the modern world a single icon carrying Permian script as testimony to Stephen's endeavours.

The highly-wrought, emotionalized tone of Yepifaniy's word-weaving does not in fact interfere with its clear narrative progress, and much factual information is given in his two great *Lives* (that of Sergius has however suffered in all its extant versions from rewriting soon after Yepifaniy's death, probably in the interests of Muscovite propaganda). Both contain an unprecedented mixture of varied generic materials: biographical narrative, impassioned emotional word-weaving, encomium, oration, sermon, prayer, lament, personal reminiscence, hymn, scriptural quotation, dialogue both dramatic and undramatic, possibly folk-elements. Yepifaniy was clearly using unusual means to commemorate very unusual people, both of whom (most exceptionally among hagiographers) he had known personally. Neither had been canonized when Yepifaniy wrote the *Lives*, which thus represent a personally involved testimony to their sanctity and an urgent, indeed daring, plea for its public recognition through canonization.

A few other works of around 1400 share some of Yepifaniy's baroque linguistic verve (notably the *Tale of the Life and Death of the Grand Prince of Moscow, Dimitriy Donskoy*, where a dry military biography is strangely enhanced by virtuoso passages of word-weaving). But this was a summit, or maybe a dead end, of medieval literature; the literature of what Likhachov calls the Orthodox 'Pre-Renaissance'. No full Renaissance followed, and Yepifaniy's dynamic example was reduced within a couple of generations to a set of vapid and uninvolving rhetorical formulae (a prime instigator of this process was an industrious immigrant hagiographer-to-order, Pakhomiy the Serb). The most affecting *Life* from some time in the century following Yepifaniy is of a quite different, unassuming kind: that of the semi-legendary princely couple Peter and Fevroniya of Murom, with many fantastical and characteristic folkloric elements and an etherealized, yet most moving love interest. A note of involvement and individuality re-enters such literature only after the turn of the seventeenth century: new types of saint emerge, standing in close relationship to writer and to reader. Early in the century the biography of Iulianiya Lazarevskaya (or Osoryina) was written in terms of a saint's life by her own son: hers is a completely domestic piety within the orbit of a minor landowner's household, full of down-to-earth detail, and brings to mind nothing so much as the lines of Iulianiya's contemporary George Herbert: 'Who sweeps a room, as for thy laws, makes that and the action fine'. Yet more strong-minded women, and more vivid details from daily life, are the subject of a triple *Life* of the earliest Old Believer heroines: the high aristocrats Morozova, Urusova and Danilova, who became 'modern martyrs' in the eyes of their co-religionists for their unwillingness to compromise with the Nikonian innovators in the face of harsh persecution. An even more stubborn and extraordinary pillar of the Old Belief, the archpriest Avvakum Petrovich (1620–82), is both hero and author of the famous and, in Russia, unprecedented *Life Written by Himself*, which has justly become one of the few works of Old Russian literature widely known outside Russia. Indeed it demonstrates the artificiality of the very category of 'old' or 'medieval' Russian writing (as was argued earlier in this chapter): while its author was the staunchest of upholders of old cultural ways (elsewhere he defended the traditional forms of icon-painting against innovators), the *Life* itself opens up a world of inner feeling and a handling of diction – from the loftiest rhetoric to the coarsest speech – that seems more 'modern' than anything to be produced in the wake of Peter's reforms.

Avvakum – towards the end of his life, when incarcerated in the remote northern outpost of Mezen – wrote and rewrote his autobiography over many years at the behest of his spiritual elder; how else to justify not just the appropriation of the form and panoply of a saint's life as a statement in one's own defence, but make insistent hints that one actually deserved sainthood? Avvakum is visited by angels, survives unimaginable hardships and seems to perform miracles. No reader though would find the work only, or mostly, an exercise in self-aggrandisement. What takes over from any such self-serving project is Avvakum's acute observation and narrative sense, coupled with a tremendous instinctive human sympathy extending to his bitter enemies and tormentors, swamping (or justifying) his egotism, which is anyhow mixed with frank self-criticism. He can write as he speaks or thinks, with breathtaking spontaneity, but structures and variegates his story cunningly. Its dominant theme is a great enforced journey lasting several years, together with his unfortunate family, to Eastern Siberia as chaplain to a military expedition: his prime antagonist Pashkov, the commanding officer, holds all the cards, would dearly love to see the last of Avvakum, but cannot ultimately bully or outwit his tough victim into submission. By comparison with this epic theme the confrontations with real political movers, the Tsar Aleksey and Patriarch Nikon, take second place. One characteristic passage (in what has become the classic Harrison-Mirrlees translation, published at the Hogarth Press by Virginia and Leonard Woolf) will give the flavour of his narration:

In other rapids – called the long rapids – he [Pashkov] set about driving me from the raft. 'You bring bad luck', says he, 'to the raft. You're a heretic', says he, 'off with you to the mountains! It is not for such as you to keep company with Cossacks.' Alackaday! The mountains were high, the ravines impassable, there was a stone crag that stood there like a wall – you'd crick your neck before you saw its top. In these mountains great serpents were to be found, and in them dwelt geese and ducks with red feathers, and black crows, and grey jackdaws; in these mountains also were eagles, and hawks, and gyrfalcons and guinea fowl and pelicans, and swans and other wild things in plenty; every variety of bird.

Moreover, on these mountains many wild beasts wandered at liberty; wild goats, and deer and bison, and elk and boars, and wolves, and wild sheep – clearly to be seen but not to be caught.

Pashkov was of a mind to turn me out into these mountains to live with beasts and birds, and I wrote him a letter that began thus: 'O man! Fear God who sits on the Cherubim and gazes into the abyss; before him tremble the celestial powers and every creature including man; thou alone despisest him and doest things that are not seemly', and so forth. It was a long letter; and I sent it to him. And some fifty men rushed on me; they seized my raft and hastened towards him, who was distant some three versts; and I stood there, boiling some porridge for the Cossacks and I fed them with it; and they, poor souls, ate of it and trembled, and some of them, looking at me, began to weep for me.

It turns into a truly epic duel: 'For ten years he had tormented me, or I him – I know not which. God will decide on the Day of Judgement.'[18]

Avvakum had lamented the end of Rus, and maybe Old Russia breathed its last on Good Friday 1682 when he and three equally intransigent colleagues were burnt by the government they had goaded to breaking-point. But the culture of Rus had long been in transition, as its seventeenth-century literature makes clear: new forms (rhymed poetry, picaresque stories, verse dramas, various kinds of parody and satire) were making their appearance; there was much unsystematic translation activity; Ukrainians, products of what was essentially a Latin-based Jesuit education system in Kiev dominated written literature in the latter part of the century. But the old literature died hard, and for many decades in the eighteenth century nothing remotely as powerful came to take its place.

### Traditional and Modern Russian Literature

Our cursory survey of the traditions of Russian literature would be incomplete without a brief attempt (even if only in note form) to indicate how some of its characteristics have lived on to become determinants within the apparently very different circumstances of post-Petrine – and in particular twentieth-century – Russian literary culture. I make no claim, of course, that the points listed represent all the significant features of Russia's specific 'literariness', or indeed that they are exclusive to Russia, or add up to some fully integrated picture, or are very profound. But in each case they seem to me to relate both to pre- and post-Petrine literature; if we take them all together (and there are no doubt others that could be added) we may find that collectively they help

[18] *The Life of Archpriest Avvakum by Himself*, trans. J. Harrison and H. Mirlees (London, 1924) pp. 64–5 and 90–1.

us to map out a phenomenology or 'conceptosphere' of Russian literature in its *longue durée*: something that seems seldom if ever to have been attempted. I start from rather large, perhaps banal points and move on first to others that have a more specific connexion with literariness and its embodiments, then to some underlying 'psycholiterary' factors.

(1) Geographic' interests: implicit in much early and subsequent Russian literature is the creation of landscapes that are really mental maps or chronotopes of Rus (and of its boundaries, physical or mental, with outsiders). Note, too, the many 'idealized landscapes' of Russian literature, whether in the anonymous *Tale of the Ruin of the Russian Land*, Avvakum's *Life* or Goncharvo's 'Oblomovka'.

(2) Complementing this, there has been a pervasive historical concern that is really rooted in 'mythistoricism' – the creation, often spontaneous, of (not necessarily glorious) national myth: but by the nineteenth century, often involving its ironic or tragic juxtaposition with 'real life'. Just as characteristic is a sort of dialogue between the competing claims of history and literature for the source material (no reader of *War and Peace* can be unaware of this, but it is equally pervasive in Pushkin, Solzhenitsyn and much other literature, and is found as far back as early saints' lives and the *Tale of Bygone Years*).[19]

(3) The ideological saturation of much Russian literature ('ideology' is to be taken in the broad, Bakhtinian sense of a world-view; patriotic and political as much as religious) is particularly obvious in the pre-Petrine and Soviet periods, but is scarcely less apparent in the 18th and 19th centuries. This may not be unsubtle or monological: Bakhtin, for example, powerfully argued a view of Dostoyevsky's mature novels (and more generally of the post-Dostoyevskian novel) as a polyphony of incompatible ideologized voices.[20]

(4) Related to this point is a frequent concern with 'great questions' (in Russian often termed *proklyatye*, 'accursed' questions!) that may be of a moral or existential kind but are, perhaps, at their most interesting when they concern identity ('who/where/what are we?': cf. the first lines of the *Table of Bygone Years*). Of course there has been a reaction, explicit or implicit, against this all-too-obvious trait of Russian literature among some twentieth century writers (cf. Pasternak's remarks through the mouth of Doctor Zhivago on Pushkin and Chekhov as opposed to Gogol, Tolstoy and Dostoyevsky) – but it shows no signs of abating.

[19] See A. B. Wachtel *An Obsession with History* (Stanford, 1994).
[20] M. Bahktin *Problems of Dostoevsky's Poetics* (Ann Arbor, 1975, etc.) Chapter 4.

(5) Perhaps unexpectedly, Russian literature has at all stages of its history been remarkably open to outside influences – or anyhow ready to absorb large numbers of translated works into itself: whether from Byzantium and the South Slavs (predominantly) after Christianization and again in the fourteenth to fifteenth centuries, or from various Western European sources in the eighteenth to twentieth centuries. This absorption has not been indiscriminate however, and the 'life' led by translated texts (whether, for example, the Byzantine Greek history of George Hamartolos, the Orthodox *Philokalia*, Pope's *Essay on Man*, the long poems of Byron or the stories of H. G. Wells) can have a very different significance in a Russian context, where they fulfil new cultural needs, from their original existence.

(6) The diglossia mentioned earlier (p. 141) between the Old Russian and the Slavonic elements within the written Russian language has led to tensions, uncertainties (particularly in the eighteenth century) and great expressive possibilities for Russian writers, a peculiarly Russian situation that readers of Russian literature in other countries have not always understood. The consequent omnipresent awareness of the very materials of literature has often led to a sense of 'the word' itself being the real hero of the literary work (whether, to take a few examples, the pre-Tartar *Petition of Daniil the Exile*, in large medieval rhetorical works, in Gogol, the Futurists, Khlebnikov or Platonov).

(7) A strong awareness of what Likhachov calls 'literary etiquette', of the 'behaviour' of literature vis-à-vis the reader, is perhaps related to the above. It is not quite the same as conventionality, though (particularly in Old Russia) it can manifest itself through commonplaces or stereotypes, and it can for instance make the forms of twentieth century Russian poetry look curiously conventional to the Western eye. Not surprisingly, disruption of literary etiquette, especially among some twentieth century writers, can seem highly subversive – just as using not quite the right diction and phraseology in Soviet speech could do.

(8) By contrast there has always been instability and mixing of *genre* in Russian writing. Much Old Russian literature, specially where influenced by oral folkloric models, hovers tantalizingly on the boundary between prose and poetry (this is notoriously evident in the *Igor Tale*, irreducible to poetic metres yet sometimes included in anthologies of verse). Literature of the nineteenth to twentieth century is ostensibly well-defined generically, yet such definition is often skin-deep (even Gogol's *Dead Souls*, his only 'novel', is subtitled an 'epic poem'! – while by contrast Pushkin's *Eugene Onegin* is a 'novel in verse'; twentieth-century writers such as Khlebnikov and Daniil Kharms no longer try to conceal their freedom from generic constraints). Indeed this erasure of boundaries operates on a larger scale still: Russian writing has always had difficulty coping with the notion that clear distinctions can be made between the literary and non-literary use of

language, and many of its most characteristic works seem (by Western standards) awkwardly poised between 'literature' and 'non-literature' (the Chronicles, Avvakum's *Life*, Radishchev's *Journey from St. Petersburgh to Moscow*, Tolstoy's *War and Peace*, Alexander Herzen's *My Past and Thoughts* are just a few examples: the 'practical' orientation of much Russian literature has a distinctly medieval feel).

(9) Literature has always been open to cross-fertilization and co-operation with the other arts: the remarkable development of Russian opera from the early nineteenth century, to take one example, is neither 'literature-led' nor 'music-led' but a real partnership of music, text and spectacle. In the pre-Petrine period, sacred literature, art, architecture and music tended towards a single totalizing iconic vision.

(10) Narrative structure in Russian literature of all periods is often weak, or at least as seen from the viewpoint of the Western preference for neat plot structures and the rigorous operation of causality. Originality of plot seems often to have been regarded as less important than the realization of mythic or archetypal situations (Katerina Clark has compared the 'quest' motif of the typical Soviet novel to folk-tales and saints' lives).[21] The structural tendency is for *nanizivanie*, the stringing-together of plot elements – the very language, particularly in the early period, favours paratactic structures (that can cause insuperable problems for translators of Old Russian literature). Comparisons can again be made with Russian music: even such sophisticated nineteenth-century composers as Musorgsky and Tchaikovsky avoided the sonata form, preferring the 'stringing-together' of thematic variations.

(11) Agglomerative works tend to result from this. It is significant that the first major 'novel' in Russia, Lermontov's *Hero of our Time*, is called by its narrator 'my chain of tales'; it also happens to be a remarkable generic mixture. Again we can cite Radishchev's *Journey* and Herzen's *Past and Thoughts*, together with one of the biggest and most memorable of all 'agglomerative' works, Dostoyevsky's *Brothers Karamazov*, a ragbag of tales and tales-within-tales. Pre-Petrine folk and sophisticated literature (not only chronicle writing) is essentially episodic and agglutinative.

(12) A further consequence is the 'open-endedness' of much Russian literature, with its admission of apparently extraneous material and an 'unfinalized', even existentialist feel. Chekhov, in his mature plays and some late stories, is the obvious examplar here. One recalls with astonishment in this context an historical novel to which the author, Solzhenitsyn, appends a note inviting readers to send him material that might serve to correct the text.

[21]   In R. Freeborn and R. Milner-Gulland (eds) *Russian and Slavic Literature* (Cambridge, Mass., 1976) pp. 364ff.

The reader is a direct participant in the literary process (again, *Hero of our Time* with its two Prefaces is relevant here); Bakhtin's principle of 'dialogism' in the best modern literature appears nakedly. This characteristic may well be a necessary corrective to the 'ideological saturation' mentioned earlier (which anyhow is not always as monologistic as it may seem). In Old Russian literature, 'unfinishedness' is a normal feature of the text: new material can always be added to it.

(13) There has always been in Russian literature a tendency towards large forms, greater than the individual work as commonly perceived. At its simplest this may be a story (or lyric) cycle. More innovatively, it can mean the *sverkhpovest*, ('supertale', a term devised by Khlebnikov) whose building-blocks are diverse ordinary poems or tales, 'like a sculpture made from different coloured blocks of different stone'. Again the novels of Dostoyevsky and Tolstoy ('great baggy monsters', in Henry James's well-known formulation) can be cited. In Old Russian literature, the Primary Chronicle is an evident predecessor of the 'supertale', but it should also be noted that virtually every early Russian literary work that we consider independent came down to us as a component part of a larger manuscript, a miscellany comprising other texts; little scholarly work on the principles of compilation of such miscellanies appears yet to have been done.

(14) Certain literary modes and forms have acquired a special coloration in Russia from early times onwards (lyric forms have tended towards lamentation, epic towards celebration). Particularly significant has been the role of literary humour, the 'laughter world' of Rus as Likhachov and Panchenko called it in a famous study.[22] Laughter can be threatening, a form of 'anti-behaviour', associated with, for example, carnivalistic excesses and topsy-turveydom, with the 'unmasking' absurdities of holy fools, with Ivan the Terrible's corrosive and theatrical sarcasm. This dangerous aspect of laughter is never far away in Gogol, Dostoyevsky or their successors in the twentieth century such as Beliy (in his novel *Petersburg*), and once again was analysed by Bakhtin, who saw it as deriving from the ancient genre of 'Menippean Satire' – though in Russia it clearly also has folkloric roots.[23] As a milder phenomenon, laughter is often a mixed emotion in Russian literature (the characteristic 'laughter through tears' of Chekhov's plays, of Gogol, and Goncharov's *Oblomov*); but the most typical vein of humour, going back to Old Russian, is inventive paronomasia and similar word-play, assisted by the varied and unstable registers and the notorious diglossia of the Russian language.

(15) Self-consciousness about the literary process has often led Russian authors to 'metafiction', the examination of the literary process itself within the literary work: we may cite as examples the self-questioning of the bard of

---

[22] D. Likhachov and A. Panchenko '*Smekhovoy mir*' *drevney Rusi* (Leningrad, 1976).
[23] M. Bakhtin *Problems of Dostoevsky's Poetics* (Ann Arbor, 1973).

the *Igor Tale* as to the best mode in which to recount his story; the obsessive interest of the narrator of *Hero of our Time* in his position vis-à-vis his readers; Viktor Shklovsky's remarkable pseudo-eighteenth-century (but very 'modern') novel *Zoo, or Letters not about Love*.

(16) 'Publication' of literature in Russia has never meant exclusively the printing and dissemination of books through commercial channels. Naturally in Old Russia (even after printing was introduced in the mid-sixteenth century) written literature existed almost exclusively in the form of manuscripts that were copied *ad hoc* and usually collected into miscellanies; texts other than those considered sacred would be revised, shortened, conflated with others, modernized for whatever reasons patrons and copyists thought fit. This kind of manuscript tradition has actually continued to modern times, for polemical purposes, among some remote Old Believer communities. But *samizdat* ('self-publishing') for a limited circle of readers, in manuscript or (later) typescript form remained a characteristic aspect of Russian literary production through the eighteenth, nineteenth and twentieth centuries: in fact, copyings and recopyings could quite soon reach almost the entire educated public (as happened in the nineteenth century with Alexander Griboyedov's play *Woe from Wit*, and in the later Soviet period with many works). While clearly such 'self-publishing' in post-Petrine times was primarily a means of bypassing censorship, it is also a signal of a Russian view of literature less as the production of a commodity, more as the intense dialogue of a literate class (sometimes disaffected from authority) with itself.

(17) Perhaps because of this quality of literature as dialogue, an autonomous realm of debate, there is a powerful element of intertextuality – implicit or explicit reference to other writings the reader can be assumed to recognize – in modern Russian literature; after all, as Vladimir Nabokov used to point out, the whole of classic Russian literature can be housed on a few bookshelves and be familiar to the average reader. But intertextuality was a vitally important feature of Old Russian literature too. The frequent quotations from the Bible (particularly the Psalms) and writings of the Church Fathers, even in works that we might consider primarily secular in orientation, do not represent mere padding or general edification, but are generally carefully chosen to provide an eternal context to counterpoint transitory events. Within the field of Old Russian writing itself there are intertextual echoes of, for example, Ilarion's *Discourse on the Law and the Grace* in many subsequent works; while an astonishing example is of course the dependence of the various works known collectively as *Zadonshchina* (about Dmitriy Donskoy's defeat of the Tatar Mamay, 1380) on the pre-Tatar *Igor Tale*.

(18) There is equally a reliance on subtextuality, as much in Old Russian as in twentieth-century Russian writing. Modern scholars such as Picchio have shown how hidden, as well as explicit Biblical references constitute

'thematic clues' that may determine the proper reading of early texts (such clues are normally placed near the text's opening).[24] Late medieval literature particularly is fond of intricate puzzles, allegories, codes, of the riddling method (so well known too from folksong) of periphrasis, of not naming the object directly: features that readers of 'difficult' modern writers such as Khlebnikov will readily recognize.

(19) A deep and widespread subtext to all Russian literature is that of Russian folk belief, manifest even in explicitly Christian writers such as Gogol, Dostoyevsky, Kharms or Soviet writers such as Zabolotsky and Platonov:[25] particularly the concern with the connected concepts of *dolya* (fate, lot) and *volya* (free will, liberty), with *onniy svet*, the realm of the dead and its relation to that of the living.

(20) Finally, an enduringly persistent tradition in Russian literature, whether ancient or modern, written or oral, is that of the word as magical – note that in Old Russia 'word', *slovo*, had a broader reference than in English, implying also 'discourse' or 'piece of literature'. The opening of St John's gospel, supposedly the first item to be translated in the missionary project of Sts Cyril and Methodius (see p. 139), is of course 'In the beginning was the Word', immediately equating the Word with the divinity and divine order. Church Slavonic, which as we have seen was an inalienable element in the diglossia of Old Russian writing, was regarded as sacred in itself, and Russia as having been made holy after its adoption. But before Christianity (and persisting after it) there were the *zagovory*, magical spells or prayer equivalents within folk belief: note also the magical significance of the Scandinavian runes known to Russia's early Viking rulers. Silence, too, had a sacred significance (particularly after Hesychasm, 'quietism', was adopted as Orthodox church doctrine in the fourteenth century) – cf. Dostoyevsky's 'Legend of the Grand Inquisitor' in *Brothers Karamazov*. It is striking how modernists such as the Russian Futurists gave 'the word' (often the 'self-valid' or 'self-sufficient word', *samotsennoye/samovitoye slovo*) an almost supernatural significance: Mayakovsky's last poem, opening 'I know the power of words, I know the tocsin of words' is an extraordinary example, while Kharms noted in the 1930s 'I know four kinds of word-machines: poems, prayers, songs and spells.' It is not too much to suggest that the obsessive attention paid by the Soviet authorities to verbal expression was derived from a deep-seated fear of the word's magic power.

---

[24] Picchio 'The Impact of Ecclesiastic Culture', pp. 277–8.

[25] Cf. O. Sedakova *The Slavonic Mythology of Death*, paper to Neo-Formalist conference, Cambridge, 25 March 1994, to appear in *Essays in Poetics* (forthcoming): see pp. 88–91 above.

# 5

## Iconic Russia

### Folk Creativity

Among the major cultural 'transplantations' into Rus from the Byzantine world at its adoption of Christianity were carefully worked-out pictorial, architectural and musical systems. These interrelated with the written and spoken word and with each other to constitute an artistic cultural totality of great power and integrity. More obviously than in literature, the art and music of Rus invigorated their modern equivalents in the last century and a quarter, helping to give them not only a distinctive tonality but a rare sense of intellectual and spiritual purpose. This wave of artistic influence from the nation's past, however, included not only elements from the 'high culture' of Christianity but from folk creativity; not infrequently (probably more often than in the realm of literature) they could blend without strain.

The art of pre-Christian Rus that Christian forms superseded has left few relics. In southern Russia stone pillars, simply carved with human features and thought to represent divinities, have survived in some numbers into modern times and are picturesquely known as 'stone women' (*kamennye baby*). A very few pre-Christian carved wooden heads have been found in Novgorod. Little survives to help us reconstruct the appearance of pre-Christian buildings, though it is thought that at least the prince's residence in immediately pre-Conversion Kiev was of masonry construction, and there must have been a tradition of skilful wooden building not only to permit urban centres at Ladoga, Novgorod and so on to be habitable in northern Russian climatic conditions, but to make it possible for a 'thirteen-headed' wood cathedral (at whose appearance we can only guess) to be built in Novgorod shortly after the Conversion, as chronicles record. But these few hints and traces of ancient creativity are eclipsed by the vast heritage of Russian folk art and building that, though dating from much more recent centuries in its surviving examples, may well reflect extremely archaic ornamental motifs and constructional techniques respectively. It is not too much to say that the human environment of the entire Russian countryside was until recently (in places, to the present) an anthology of visual motifs of pre-Christian origin – some geometrical, but most figurative, even if in many cases so highly abstracted as to be not readily recognizable as such. Sun, moon and star symbols, stylizations of many animals, flowers and trees, of other elemental objects of the natural world, architectural elements, riders, humans – including female figures usually considered to represent a 'great goddess' – this 'common stock of images and abstract designs' seem nearly all to have 'derived from symbols of power and protection found on ancient Slavic ornaments'.[1] But we should be wrong to speak exclusively in terms of an ancient East Slav folk art, since it is by no means clear to what extent ethnic boundaries are represented in the common heritage of northern European (or Eurasian) design motifs that spread from people to people, continually variegated but always bearing familial traits. As with the society of Rus itself, the East Slavonic, Scandinavian and Finnic input is hard to separate out, and there may be influences from further afield too.

Encountering the all-embracing decorative environment of villages in the remoter, eastern parts of the Vologda province on an ethnographic expedition in 1889, Vasiliy Kandinsky – then a young doctoral student of anthropology and law, later one of the most self-consciously revolutionary initiators of twentieth-century artistic innovation – found it an 'amazing spectacle': 'The table, the benches, the stove so imperious and huge, the closets, the sideboards – everything had been painted with multicoloured and bold ornaments.' the impact on his aesthetic development seems to have been great: 'here was where I learnt to live within it' [i.e. within the picture].[2] By an interesting coincidence one of the most widely admired Russian illustrators (and more than just an illustrator), Ivan Bilibin (1876–1942), seems to have developed his stylized folk manner

---

[1]    A. Hilton 'Piety and Pragmatism' in W. Brumfield and M. Velimirović *Christianity and the Arts in Russia*, (Cambridge, 1991) p. 55.

[2]    Kandinsky's fragmentary memoir has been published several times, first in Russian in *Tekst khudozhnika* (Moscow, 1918); see K. Lindsay and P. Vergo (eds) *Kandinsky: Complete Writings on Art* (Boston, 1982). Kandinsky's subsequent debt to the pre-Christian, shamanistic art-world of the Komi and of the Siberian indigenous peoples has been highlighted in P. Weiss *Kandinsky and Old Russia* (London, 1995).

after taking part in two similar expeditions – on which he too wrote scholarly articles – a little later, to just the same region. From Kandinsky's memoirs it would be easy to imagine that such villagers simply slapped a totally undifferentiated decoration on the objects that surrounded them with some sort of primitive enthusiasm. Yet it is clear that the elusive code of folk design makes – is based on – considerable hierarchical distinctions. It is concentrated upon objects, and areas within those objects, of high significance: the borders of ceremonial towels (including those that drape the house's main icon), festive clothing, the window-surrounds (*nalichniki*) and bargeboards of houses, lace objects, the distaffs that are inseparably connected with one of the great female activities of the household – teasing and spinning flax (that often took place at ceremonious 'sit-downs', *posidelki*, that are linked with courtship and marriage). These distaffs are often decorated with surprising intricacy and intensity, with a host of motifs from geometric patterns to scenes from life, maybe representing the very occasions on which they would appear.

As with traditional literature – more so, indeed – there was seepage between the apparently self-sufficient, water-tight worlds of folk art and 'high' or sophisticated art (first Byzantine in origin, later Western European). The popular saints and the symbols of Christianity made their appearance in folk guise. Pseudo-classical pediments around windows make an odd but effective contribution to elaborate traditional houses. Wooden church and domestic architecture (much argued over – the pre-1600 evidence has largely disappeared) seems to be essentially of folk derivation. An interesting instance of folk influence on Christian art is the appearance during the fourteenth and fifteenth centuries of northern European interlace and teratological ('monstrous') animal or human motifs in Russian manuscript illumination. The folk craft of low-relief carving (occasionally even wooden sculpture in the round) makes itself felt in icons and on churches at various times from the twelfth to the eighteenth centuries. Where there was no readily available Byzantine model, in fact, or where (say) ornamental motifs in masonry or paintwork were not perceived as carrying overt pagan meaning, folk creativity would step in even at a sophisticated level to fill a need (of course it is hard for us now to reconstruct which motifs of ancient origin *were* perceived as 'pagan' or un-Christian).

These are merely a few examples of the many certain or probable interactions between sophisticated and folk art, and we shall touch on them again later. But it remains to mention what became the most characteristic and widespread field for such interaction, indeed hybridization: the type of popular print known as *lubok* (plural *lubki*). Arising towards the end of the seventeenth century (German prints circulated earlier), when inexpensive techniques of reproduction became available and there began to be a public for cultural novelties, the *lubki* treated at first Biblical, then soon proverbial, satirical, politico-social, everyday, folkloric and fairytale subject-matter with an intriguing combination of words and boldly coloured illustration, going beyond Epinal prints and similar work from other European countries in their variegation of manner and (often) fantasticality. Developing over a period of at least 200 years, they give an insight into the mind set, preoccupations, pleasures, fears and fantasies of ordinary people not readily available from any other source.

*Plate 16* Lubok *(popular print) of the Great Cat of Kazan, in origin probably a comment or satire on the Tsar's authority (woodcut, 1800s).*

## The Iconic World

When Rus accepted Christianity on the Byzantine pattern in the tenth century it entered a cultural sphere whose visual component was of the highest significance. How this came to be the case is by no means obvious, given the general (if not always consistent) hostility to religious representations in Judaism – most obviously expressed in the Second Commandment, against graven images – and the hesitant, unsystematic use of them by the early Christians. The vast heritage of Greco-Roman imagery played its part, particularly after Constantine the Great gave Christianity official status; the classical element in the forms and aesthetic of Byzantine and Old Russian art should never be forgotten. When in the ninth and tenth centuries various Slav nations, including eventually Rus, joined the Christian 'family of nations' centred on Constantinople, Orthodoxy had emerged from the protracted period of crisis associated with 'Iconoclasm' (the years 721–843; see p. 108) and had hammered out a set of principles concerning visual representation that have had the greatest artistic and theological importance for the Orthodox world – to some extent, beyond – ever since. Rus, then, accepted as a major item in the cultural package that accompanied Conversion a sophisticated sacred art and architecture centred on the concept of the 'icon'.

The Greek word *eikon* is a non-specific term for any image; in its Russian form (*ikona*, though sometimes *obraz* is used), and in Orthodox usage generally, it means the representation, according to various canons of correctness, of holy persons and events. The further frequent narrowing of meaning to refer only to panel-paintings of religious subjects is understandable – these objects (that ultimately stand at the origins of the whole European tradition of easel-painting) are highly characteristic of the Orthodox world, were made in vast numbers and are portable, thus often encountered in the West – but it is also regrettable: the concept of 'icon' reaches far beyond them. It includes devotional objects of metal (often enamelled) and fabrics (usually embroideries), carved wood, ivory or stone; the wall-paintings or mosaics that covered the interior, occasionally finding their way onto the exterior, of all churches; more broadly still, a building, a monastery, a city – notably the 'Great City' of Constantinople – may be viewed as an icon; so can written texts and musical compositions; so even is Christ, the 'the image of the invisible God' (Colossians 1:15). The limits of iconicity were probably reached by the ambitious twelfth-century Cypriot holy man Neophytos, who arranged for himself to be viewed as a 'living icon'.[3] But the Russian

[3]  R. Cormack *Writing in Gold* (London, 1985) Chapter 6.

*Plate 17 Praise the Lord: a sixteenth-century carved walrus-ivory icon whose complex iconography represents a hymn.*

Avvakum (see pp. 122, 162ff.), writing his autobiography in the manner of a saint's life, is not far behind.

For the Orthodox, seeing was believing (the great ninth-century Patriarch Photios put it almost in those words in a sermon commemorating the installation of the Virgin and Child mosaic in Santa Sophia in 867). Words, they well knew, were inferior to visual images in conveying the truths of religion; such images or icons were indeed central to Christian practice and understanding of the cosmic order, just as the Incarnation was to the message of the Bible. They mediated between the temporal and the eternal as a two-way channel for worship and prayer: the company of sacred portraits adorning a church participated in the rituals, thus constituting a 'society of the dead and the living'. In Robin Cormack's words, 'art was essential to the functioning of Byzantium' – and the rest of the Orthodox world – 'it would have been a different culture without icons'.[4] This art, accessible to all classes of largely illiterate society, was an enormous force for social cohesion, and played a part in its long survival. It helped to legitimize the hierarchical structure of empire; yet it was held in popular esteem – Iconoclasm, the destruction of icons, was a policy upheld by the political and ecclesiastical elite, while it was on the whole resisted by the unprivileged: by ordinary people, monks (the 'proletariat' of the Church), women and provincials. In the end the iconoclast elite had to capitulate, and the restoration of the images (843) was significantly commemorated as the 'Feast of Orthodoxy'.

Thus sacred images played a profounder role in the Eastern Church than that of decoration or instruction ('Bibles of the poor') to which, since Charlemagne if not Gregory the Great, they were often consigned in the West. Naturally it presupposed a pre-modern (ultimately neo-Platonic) sense of correspondence – going much deeper than mere metaphor or depiction – between the object of representation and the image.[5] Icons were given a pedigree going back to Gospel times: St Luke supposedly painted the Mother of God (and won her approval), while even more significantly, Christ was said to have impressed his face on a cloth which he sent to heal King Abgar of Edessa in Syria, producing an image famously 'not made by hands' – the first and greatest icon, reproduced countless times thereafter. But despite this miraculous origin for the whole tradition, and all the many miracles connected with icons thereafter, the Orthodox formulation of doctrine in the wake of Iconoclasm was properly concerned that they should not be taken as magical objects, that they should not be idolatrously worshipped, but rather venerated as the channel of communication between the prototype (the person or event imaged) and the worshipper, between invisible and visible worlds, the timeless and the temporal. The icon-painter was not thought of as a 'creator' or even an 'artist', but as one who 'reveals' (*raskryvayet*) an already extant image and the truths it embodies. Icons

---

[4]  Cormack *Writing in Gold* p. 11.
[5]  See for example P. Burke *The Fabrication of Louis XIV* (Yale, 1992) 127ff., with further refs.

of holy persons return the gaze of the viewer (though the head is often slightly inclined, the eyes make direct contact), so setting up a 'dialogue'. They are like gateways (a better metaphor, I think, than 'windows') to the other world, something well symbolized by the icon-covered 'royal doors' standing between the sacred altar-space and the nave of every Orthodox church.

A certain etiquette attended people's behaviour towards icons. In traditional Russian houses an icon, draped with a cloth, hangs in the further right corner from the entrance of the main room (the *izba* proper: see p. 30–1), often high up, to be reverentially greeted by visitors (who will then be entertained in that part of the room, the 'fine corner', *krasny ugol*). Merchants would take folding icons with them on their travels, to set up where they stayed (these were generally of metal). Icons that were no longer needed were not to be thrown away or burnt: they were often buried (though they were not meant to be interred with their owner) or floated off down a river, and in each case might make apparently miraculous reappearances. Panel-icons whose varnish had blackened with age or the effects of candle-smoke might be scraped down and reused, but were more generally overpainted (to preserve their power, as Uspensky has suggested in *The Semiotics of the Russian Icon*). Of course iconic images were in fact often treated superstitiously: the plaster beneath representations of faces in wall-paintings (particularly eyes) might be hacked out to provide folk medicine, while eyes of icons considered un-Orthodox might be attacked to discredit them (Patriarch Nikon – see p. 120ff. – did this) – such things testify to a belief in the extraordinary power of sight and the eye. An ineffectual icon might be thought to have been endowed with malign power through having had a demonic figure painted underneath the sacred one; Orthodox wall-paintings in a house to be occupied by non-Orthodox foreigners in Muscovy were removed.[6] Icons were encountered (and saluted with the sign of the Cross) everywhere: in each house, inside and outside churches, and installed in wayside shrines; while portable icons could be pretty mobile – they were given, sold, brought from holy places as souvenirs, relocated, repaired, repainted, carried in processions, paraded with armies or displayed on the walls of besieged cities. Through this mobility stylistic innovations could make themselves felt quickly throughout the Orthodox lands (manuscript miniatures could play a similar role, but were much fewer and far costlier). This mobility, both of objects and, doubtless, of the personnel who produced them, meant that – incredibly – over 600 years ago a basically Mediterranean art penetrated to

[6]   B. Uspensky *The Semiotics of the Russian Icon* (Lisse, 1976) p. 28, discussing an observation by Olearius: having scraped the walls, the Russians 'carried off the powder with them'.

the very shores of the Arctic Ocean, its artefacts the fundamental links between the remotest villages or hermitages and universal history and culture. Since in the southerly direction the world of icon-orientated Christianity reached Nubia and Ethiopia, it stretched virtually from the Equator to beyond the Arctic Circle.

At the center of the 'iconic world' stands, of course, the church building itself. The 'middle Byzantine' church, that Russia inherited after the Conversion, is a remarkably harmonious, uncomplicated yet subtle and multivalent vehicle for sacred messages, and location for sacred action. The old basilican form developed by the Romans – an elongated structure of several bays with side-aisles (which became standard in the West) – had been superseded largely by the centralized 'cross-in-square' plan, with a central dome on a drum over the crossing, sometimes subsidiary domes usually over corner compartments, three apses to the east and normally a narthex (vestibule) to the west. Four piers or columns would support the drum of the main dome, and the transition from the square they formed to the circular element above would be achieved through the elegant geometry of pendentives – spherical triangles (that had first been applied, at least on a major scale, in the Santa Sophia of Constantinople).[7] There would be plain semicircular

1 Sanctuary (bema)   2 Altar   3 Main apse   4 Prothesis   5 Altar of Offerings   6 Diakonikon   7 Royal or Paradise Door, in the iconostasis   8 Solea   9 Ambo   10 Position taken by the choirs   11 Crossing in the body of the church (naos), beneath the main dome   12 Vestibule (narthex)

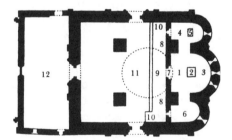

*Figure 11   Ground plan and cross-section of characteristic small cross-in-square Russian church: Trinity Monastery of St Sergius, (early fifteenth century).*

[7]   To make spherical triangles, cut an orange through its diameter, with three cuts along planes at right angles to each other: the peel of the eight resulting pieces will resemble pendentives (the Russian for 'pendentive' is *parus*, 'sail'). A less satisfactory transition could be made through the 'squinch' (made up of little bridging-arches, plastered over).

arches and simple barrel or groin vaults. Grand churches might have a
gallery above the interior arcade; in Russia, because of the climate and
the social uses to which parish churches were put, there was often an
external ground-level gallery. Such buildings would be small compared
with most Romanesque or Gothic churches, but through their verticality
and proportions would often achieve a remarkable feeling of monumentality. Windows round the drum could flood the central space with
light while corners remained in obscurity. There was an evident
progression in sacredness from the relatively profane narthex, a liminal
area with respect to the outside world, to the 'holy of holies' of the space
at the east, around the altar ('throne', *prestol,* in Russian), beyond a
screen; also an upward progression in sacredness from floor to dome.
There are no pews; the congregation stands, comes and goes during the
lengthy services, has to move round the building to follow its decorative
scheme. Such a church is a cosmic symbol, its dome, like domes
everywhere, representing the heavens, and as such is the House of God; it
also functions as a sort of three-dimensional calendar both of human life
and of the church year; on a more down-to-earth and touching level it is
felt to be a living being itself – hence the anthropomorphic Russian terms
for its various parts: 'head' for dome, 'neck' for drum, 'brows' over the
windows, 'shoulders' for exterior roof-line, 'belt' for mid-wall frieze,
'footing' at the foundation level, *kokoshniki* (an elaborate women's
head-dress) for the massed gables so characteristic of Muscovite
architecture.

Wall-paintings or mosaics, panel paintings and sometimes other
objects of iconic art adorn the church in a way that is far from random.
At the highest interior point, the central dome, is the half-figure of Christ
the Ruler of all (*Pantokrator*), often considered 'stern' but to the
Orthodox comforting and protecting. Apostles, evangelists, seraphim
occupy the drum and pendentives. The middle wall zone displays the
Major Feasts of the Church (which also of course articulate the people's
lives through the calendar year): crucial events, usually twelve in
number, selected from the Gospel narrative, representing the intersection
of the timeless with the human history of Christ's ministry. Usually a
representation of the Virgin and Child in the central east apse will face a
large and multifigured scene of the Dormition (i.e. Assumption) on the
West wall, wherein the soul of the Mother of God is shown as an infant
being received by Christ – thought-provoking complementary images. In
the lowest zone, and on the columns or piers, there will be figures of
saints, nicely symbolizing their role of 'upholding' the earthly Church.
The scheme, though soon after Iconoclasm it became traditional, was
never formally laid down and was always flexible. There was scope for
many more images, for example Nativity or various Old Testament

*Plate 18   Church of St Demetrius, Vladimir (1194) from the north-east: a royal chapel, it is sumptuously carved in low relief with a multitude of ornamental and figurative motifs presided over by King David as psalmist.*

cycles, and in narthex and galleries one may encounter such figures as ancient philosophers considered to foreshadow Christ, or the family tree of a royal donor who financed the church.

In late Byzantine and Muscovite painting rather complex scenes such as representations of Councils of the Church or hymns to the Mother of God became popular – the latter reminding us that music had as essential an iconic role as visual images in the great multisensory drama that the Liturgy constituted. Russian ecclesiastical music, at first monophonic, then polyphonic but solely vocal, is an elusive subject for study: the notation used before the sixteenth century has not been deciphered. Iconically the music of the Liturgy represents – corresponds with – the unheard singing of the heavenly choirs of angels. Only recently have systematic attempts begun to analyse what, if any, interrelationships there might be between Orthodox chant and the ubiquitous folk music of the Russian village – in which of course instruments, notably the stringed *gusli* and bagpipes, were used – though there was plenty of unaccompanied singing too.[8] One clearly worthwhile point of comparison between the two musical systems is the tendency in each to develop long melismatic phrases sung to redundant syllables: a practice the official church, but not the Old Believers, eventually terminated. The only 'instruments' sanctioned by the Church were of course peals of bells (for which a *semandron* or sounding-board was sometimes substituted), symbolizing the Hebrew Old Testament *shofar* or trumpet (see, for example, Numbers 10:1–2),[9] not to mention the Last Trump of the Day of Judgement. Bells, too, were anthropomorphized in Rus. The 'totalizing' aspect of Orthodox culture is manifest in the interdependence of text, spoken word, music and painting, each capable of deriving from, evoking or inspiring the others, all dependent on architecture and on human action of a dramatic kind (prayer, blessing, chanting, the opening and shutting of doors, processions etc.). How naturally synaesthesia came to the Orthodox iconic world can be illustrated by a phrase from Simeon the New Theologian (*c*.949–1022) 'Light resounded as a loud voice.'

Icons indeed often represent other icons – visible, verbal, aural – and icons of icons of icons are not infrequent, particularly when one remembers that a church building is itself iconic. An interestingly complex example is the 'Voloshanka Shroud' now in the Moscow Historical Museum. It was commissioned in 1498 by Yelena Voloshanka, the widowed daughter-in-law of Ivan III.[10] At its centre is represented a processional icon of the Virgin 'Hodigitria' ('She-who-shows-the-way'). The composition is crowded with figures, and includes a double choir singing. Two groups of figures are holding branches, showing the event in progress to be the great Palm Sunday procession. The central

[8]   See Brumfield and Velimirović *Christianity and the Arts in Russia*, articles by Vladishevskaya and Mazo.
[9]   E.V. Williams 'Aural Icons of Orthodoxy', in Brumfield and Velimirović *Christianity and the Arts in Russia*.
[10]   M. Flier 'Breaking the Code' in M. Flier and D. Rowland (eds) *Medieval Russian Culture* vol. II (Berkeley, 1994) discusses this.

rank of figures includes the high dignitaries of Muscovy: the Metropolitan, the Grand Prince himself and members of his first and second families. Some are haloed – surprising perhaps in living figures who have no claim to sainthood, yet reminding us of Kantorowicz's subtle observation that 'the "halo" always indicated, in some way or another, a change in the nature of Time' (*tempus* becomes *aevum*).[11] The nimbed figures are in fact Yelena's son Dmitriy, his grandfather Ivan III, and the Metropolitan Simon who in 1498 carried out the first Byzantine-style coronation ceremony in Rus, to anoint Dmitriy as Ivan's successor. Clearly the whole embroidery is drawing our attention to the solemn, transcendental implications of this great iconic event, as well as to Yelena's short-lived triumph in what was evidently a sharp family conflict (Ivan subsequently withdrew his favour from Dmitriy, who was imprisoned; his uncle, by Ivan's second marriage, Vasiliy in fact succeeded to the throne). Not only is this an iconic object representing several distinct iconic events, themselves featuring a significant icon; it is a particularly vivid illustration of the fact that, otherworldly as we may think them, icons were closely linked to the circumstances and history of their society, as well as to people's personal lives. This was always the case, both in Byzantium and early Rus, though to reconstruct contexts may be difficult for us nowadays: in later Rus it becomes more blatant, and there are famous polemic examples such as Novgorodian representations of their army defeating the men of Suzdal (with the help of the icon of the 'Virgin of the Sign'), and the huge panel of the 'Church Militant', deriving from Revelation 19 but 'iconizing' and commemorating Ivan IV's victorious campaign against Kazan (1552), with the Tsar himself as the 'righteous one' leading his host on a white horse.

## Art and Architecture in Rus

For some time now the rumble of low-level warfare has been detectable in the literature on icons. The combatants have been representatives of what might loosely be called the 'theological' or 'devotional', and the 'art-historical' or 'aesthetic', approaches to the subject. 'Devotionalists' disdain what they perceive as the aesthetes' complete failure to understand the most important thing about icons, which is that they are not 'works of art' in the post-Renaissance Western sense, rather focal points of a whole religiously-orientated way of life; art historians have little time for the intellectual fuzziness and self-referentiality they see in a devotional approach. Both positions are understandable, though one

---

[11]   E. Kantorowicz *The King's Two Bodies* (Princeton, 1957) p. 94.

may fear that the sniping has rather discouraged disinterested scholars from venturing into the field. Anyhow, as the best minds in each camp realize, there is no need for hostilities any more: art history has changed, a strictly formalist approach is no longer viable (still less is pure connoisseurship), and any history of the arts that does not pay close attention to ideological and social factors would nowadays be seen as a waste of time. The images of the Orthodox world, specifically Rus, timeless and supramundane as they may be (or may have been intended to be), turn out to have a history and a distinct aesthetic. A full treatment of these would obviously take a whole volume or volumes, but it is worthwhile at the risk of superficiality to sketch in the main outlines.

The aesthetic is to many Western eyes alluring yet disorientating, familiar and unfamiliar. Compared with the writhing contortions and sheer savagery (as it must have seemed to Orthodox eyes – we tend to appreciate its expressivity) of much Romanesque Western art, the wall-paintings and panel-icons of Byzantium and Rus look, as intended, decorous and serene. The classical Greco-Roman impulse is seldom far away in figure-types, postures, gestures and above all garments, with their often carefully modelled drapery folds. Iconographic types (strikingly, John the Baptist) seem to derive in many cases rather directly from Hellenistic models. Yet nothing is quite what it should be by classical or naturalistic canons of taste, and this is not just because of the artists' need to portray the supernatural, though that does come into it. Bodies are generally a little too elongated, their disposition conventionalized anti-realistically; their feet never quite seem to rest on the ground; emblematic objects and inscriptions obtrude; landscape (often, from the fourteenth century on, full of picturesque details) could never for a moment be taken as observed landscape. Colours (clear and harmonious compared with the Romanesque) are suffused with a light that has no logical source: 'sky' is often gold (in mosaics, almost always) or dark blue. Of course there can be no hint of Renaissance perspective (at least until the pictorial system begins to break down in the seventeenth century), but what is particularly strange, often captivating, is the use of what is usually called 'reverse perspective', where lines seem to converge on a vanishing-point in front of the picture space rather than in the far distance. This is particularly evident where stylized architectural elements in the background indicate that the action is taking place in a building or a city. Leonid Ouspensky, one of the wisest and most knowledgeable specialists from the 'theological' party, has an ingenious explanation for this:

If we compare the manner in which an icon represents a human figure with the manner in which it represents a building, we shall see a great difference between them. With rare exceptions, the human figure is always constructed correctly – everything is in its right place. The same applies to the clothes . . . But architecture, both in form and grouping, is often contrary to human logic and in separate details is completely illogical . . . The meaning of this phenomenon is that architecture is the only element in the icon with the help of which it is possible to show clearly that the action taking place before our eyes is outside the laws of human logic, outside the laws of earthly existence.'[12]

There has been much argument as to whether there was a conscious system of 'reverse perspective' – characteristically, the early sources are completely silent on such matters – but the viewer, particularly in an Orthodox church where painting is applied to alternately flat and curved surfaces, soon realizes how effectively the curiously constructed picture space pulls him or her into the world of the image.

In this connection there is a further point that should be emphasized. We perceive this art, quite justifiably, as symbolic, stylized and spiritual in its essence: we marvel at the power of its expressive distortions. But to its practitioners and early viewers (judging by the sources – we must realize that art theory struggled with an inappropriate classical vocabulary in Byzantium, and scarcely existed in Rus) its merits were largely those we associate with realism: images are generally praised for being lifelike. Indeed, its supposed realism and its traditionalism went hand-in-hand, since the tradition was seen to have handed down faithful representations of people and events from the time of the Gospels that were not to be altered at whim. People would often dream of saints, and would recognize them by their likeness to their iconic types. The artistic code of the Orthodox world might seem to us, after all that has happened in art since, a curiously inappropriate vehicle for naturalistic effects – but we are in no position to say if anyone felt this at the time. Incidentally we can be sure there were wall-paintings, fabric hangings and mosaics in early secular buildings too; though virtually nothing survives, our sparse information would indicate they shared a similar artistic language.

A last observation on the aesthetic of iconic art concerns its dynamic qualities. Icons may seem to us redolent of stillness, but if we look closer we begin to see that they are full of implicit movement: garments flutter in an unseen wind, highlights flash on silk robes, choirs sing, prophets read from scrolls. The static image of a saint on a panel-painting is likely to be surrounded by vivid scenes from his or her life, full of agitated action. Most of the Major Feasts are moments of dramatic, transformative activity – the Raising of Lazarus, the Entry into Jerusalem, the Anastasis (Descent into Hell) and others. Their ostensible tranquillity is full of potential energy (at least until the tradition becomes rather vapid during the sixteenth century): it is an art whose purpose, honourably

---

[12]  L. Ouspensky and V. Lossky *The Meaning of Icons* (Olten, 1952) p. 42.

*Plate 19    Andrey Rublyov, Daniil Chorny and others: detail of*
*The Last Judgement fresco executed at the restoration of the*
*Dormition Cathedral in Vladimir (1408).*

achieved, is to fix the moment of transfiguration, of change of state.

Does this artistic system, transplanted into Rus with the Conversion, show any subsequent growth or change – does it have a history as well as a theology? Indeed it does, and its evolution in defiance of all the pressures to keep it as it was is not only a remarkable case history of

*Figure 12   Santa Sophia, Kiev: conjectural elevation of the church in the eleventh century.*

what the art historian Henri Focillon memorably called 'la vie des formes' but an illustration of art's interaction with social and spiritual developments. Such evolution is as marked in the buildings of churches (one hesitates to use the anachronistic term 'architecture') as in the imagery housed in them, and we may begin with the former. With Christianization Rus inherited the middle Byzantine domed cross-in-square church type that has already been described. Techniques of masonry construction, of brick and plaster making (even, in one or two grand buildings, of the incredibly costly business of mosaic-making) must have been taught by Byzantine or South Slav masters very early – maybe even before 988; the characteristic manner of the period is *opus mixtum*, alternating courses of brick, pinkish mortar and stonework, giving such buildings their characteristic and decorative 'striped' appearance.[13] Vladimir's great Dormition Cathedral (or 'Tithe Church' – destroyed at the Tatar invasion) was of middle-Byzantine type. By the

---

[13]   Brick did not disappear in Eastern Europe as a constructional material as it did for example in England from Roman times till the late Middle Ages. Byzantine and early Russian bricks were thin, flat and square; alternate courses were recessed and hidden by plaster in *opus mixtum*.

time of Yaroslav, for whatever reason (his own self-assertiveness?) local idiosyncrasies are appearing. His personal foundation, Santa Sophia of Kiev, is an ambitious structure, not quite like anything in the Byzantine lands: with seven naves and side-arcades that make it broader than long, the unprecedented number of 13 domes, stout staircase-towers originally giving access to a walkway to the palace, and above all a massing of elements to give a striking pyramidal outline. This quite un-Byzantine emphasis on verticality is more marked still in the craggy Santa Sophia of Novgorod (1045) and the Yuryev (St George) Monastery (1119) nearby. The more refined approach to verticality inherent in the building-up of architectural elements, usually gable-ends rounded or pointed, into an elegant pyramid continues in the twelfth century with distinctly original buildings in Chernigov (Pyatnitskaya church), Polotsk and Smolensk. Later, when Moscow was recovering from – and profiting by – Tatar conquest, the so-called 'early Muscovite' style of the late fourteenth to early fifteenth centuries makes great play with such decorative gables, above all in the Andronikov Monastery (possibly designed, and undoubtedly painted, by Andrey Rublyov, 1427).

Meanwhile the smaller churches of Novgorod develop to a different pattern: a more-or-less cuboid block, the façades articulated with pilaster-strips into three round-headed bays (later a cheaper, flat pitched roof was usually substituted, masking the elegant original form, until the twentieth-century restoration of many of them). Some time before the Tatar period the Byzantine semi-circular dome becomes 'helmet-shaped' and then develops into the familiar Russian 'onion' – for uncertain reasons, though probably because it throws off the weight of northern snow more effectively. Such cuboid churches, humble and almost without decorative elements at their origins, are transformed into something remarkably different from the middle of the twelfth century in the north-eastern 'land beyond the forest', under the bullish Prince Andrey Bogolyubsky (1158–74) and his successors, who established their capital, and the effective capital of Rus, at Vladimir. There was a fine-grained white limestone available in the locality, and the Vladimir masons – perhaps influenced by building methods in the southwestern principality of Galicia (Galich), and beyond that maybe from Romanesque Central Europe, though this is speculative – used this carefully dressed 'white stone' to adorn their new capital with buildings as perfect as ivory caskets. Their most astonishing, and for Rus innovatory, feature is a wealth of external decorative and figurative sculpture in low relief. Its apogee is reached in the palace church of St Dmitriy (1194), part of whose complex and carefully worked-out iconographic programme is centred on the figure of King David, singer of Psalms – again, a 'musical icon'. Historians have been at a loss to explain the appearance and development of this phenomenon; influences have been sought in the Caucasus, Byzantium and the Balkans, the German lands – but the native tradition of wood-carving and the ordering of decoration may well have had their part to play. In any case, the technique developed over the course of some seventy years, so we cannot attribute it entirely to external influences or immigrants. 'White stone' was also used in early Muscovite building, but largely gave way to brick in the sixteenth century, when the 'cuboid' manner became the vehicle for many large official buildings (the cathedral of the Novodevichiy Convent, Moscow; St Sophia in Vologda, maybe intended by Ivan IV to be the centrepiece of a new capital for his *oprichnina*, the 'realm apart', etc.). Near Vladimir there stands the earliest surviving relic of Russian domestic building: a tower of Andrey Bogolyubsky's palace (where he was assassinated by his servitors in 1174), also in dressed 'white stone'.

The vast majority of Russian churches (as of houses and even palaces) till the nineteenth century were of wood; but all the early ones are gone, victims of fire, decay or modernization, with one exception: a little chapel (now at Kizhi) from the St Lazarus monastery, datable to the late fourteenth century. Its three-cell structure – low narthex, larger nave, smaller chancel – mimics that of grander churches; but here and elsewhere the entirely different constructional techniques of wood impose their own forms. Can the tall spires that we know existed in early wooden buildings have influenced masonry architecture? There has been much inconclusive argument, but it does seem likely. Perhaps the striving towards pyramidal forms observable even in pre-Tatar buildings is in a general way influenced by the wooden tradition. We are on firmer ground when we reach early sixteenth-century Muscovy. A new conception of church architecture, unrelated to Byzantine proto-types, appears in the so-called 'tent' (*shatyor*) church plan. At first such buildings seem to have been commemorative churches (the most famous early example, at Kolomenskoye near Moscow, probably celebrated the birth in 1530 of the future Ivan the Terrible). The greatest of them is of course St Basil's on Red Square, celebrating the victory over Kazan (see below, p. 212ff.), the first clear example of the plethora of unfunctional exterior decoration that results in the calculatedly picturesque, colour-ful, rather enervating mannerism of the later sixteenth to seventeenth centuries. Patriarch Nikon tried to ban the type as uncanonical, though his own 'New Jerusalem' monastery church of the Resurrection in some ways derived from it (see p. 219ff.). The pyramidal impulse was subsumed into the transitional Moscow Baroque style of the late seventeenth century; yet even in the Westernized Petrine period it never wholly disappears, and receives a boost with the reaction in favour of

*Plate 20   Krutitsky Teremok, Moscow (late seventeenth century).
The main buildings of the residence of the Bishops of Krutitsa – where
Avvakum was imprisoned – still survive: the small gatehouse chamber
(teremok), faced with decorative ceramic tiles, is a notable example of
domestic 'Moscow Baroque' architecture (nineteenth-century drawing).*

Orthodox traditions – admittedly in a new, European Baroque
architectural language – under Empress Elizabeth (1741–61), when
among other things the Russian gilded dome makes a comeback.
Curiously, in some ways the succeeding age of neo-classicism (*c*.1760–
1840), ostensibly a great pan-European style (or 'absence of style')
returns Russian church architecture to the purity of its late-antique,
Byzantine roots, before mid-nineteenth century eclecticism sets in.

The images within these buildings also evolve and have a stylistic
history, even if their iconography remains more-or-less constant. The
middle-Byzantine style that Rus inherited was monumental, linear,
uncluttered and virtually expressionless: it is represented in the earliest
Kievan wall-paintings and mosaics, and lingers on as an archaism
particularly in Novgorod (it is to be seen in a few great panel-icons,
though none that survive can be proved to predate the twelfth century).
Gradually during the twelfth century changes take place – throughout
the Orthodox world, including Rus – that add up to little less than an
artistic revolution, though its course and causes are rather obscure.
First, emotion enters the representational system: through faces and
postures, painters make an impressive attempt to convey grief, ecstasy,

*Plate 21  Icon known as the Vladimir Mother of God (Tretyakov Gallery, Moscow). A Byzantine work of the early twelfth century (only the faces and hands are original paintwork), it was considered the palladium of the city of Vladimir and later of Moscow, and progenitor of the various 'tenderness' (umilenie) icon types.*

tenderness. The last of these emotions was particularly associated in Rus with an imported early twelfth century icon of the Virgin and Child (later overpainted, though the faces and hands are original), known as the 'Vladimir Mother of God', and treated as the palladium of Vladimir and subsequently Moscow. A richer, darker palette, less dependent on line, more on modelling, is slowly adopted, together with a return (such 'renascences' were frequent in Byzantium) to more classically based postures and facial types. Finally, in the latter part of the century there begins to be a systematic – and sometimes very strange and mannered – attempt to portray movement, usually through swirls of flying drapery, sometimes, for example, with windblown hair.

Thus far Rus has largely shared the destinies of Orthodox art in Byzantium, the Balkans, the Caucasus (and is not wholly remote from early medieval art in Western Europe, though there the twelfth century developments are more attenuated). In the early thirteenth century all was to change, partly as a result of catastrophes that overcame the Orthodox lands – the fall of Constantinople to the Fourth Crusade (1204), the Tatar conquest of Rus – partly as a result of further artistic evolution (while the path of most Western European art diverged towards the Gothic). Those areas of the Orthodox world that remained free, where large-scale projects continued to be commissioned (Serbia, Trebizond), took an important further step: towards mass, weightiness, corporeity of figure-style, together with a 'painterly' manner, strongly contrasting with the old linearity. This manner (remote from the Gothic) was to have considerable impact on Giotto (who from the Byzantine viewpoint looks like a rather eccentric provincial), and percolated eventually – in the fourteenth century – to Rus. Meanwhile, and more significantly, Rus was forced back on its own resources. The few panel-icons dateable to the first century of Tatar rule (there are no known wall-paintings) have a pronounced 'folkish' quality that never wholly leaves Russian icon painting thereafter: clear, unnaturalistic patches of colour; a free play of line; expressive, often naïve-seeming distortions; an uncluttered immediacy.

After closer contacts with the Balkan and Byzantine south have been restored again by the late fourteenth century, the mingling of the revived sense of Byzantine-classical poise and *gravitas* with a folkified spontaneity gives Rus its greatest age of painting in the fifteenth century. There is a renewed spiritual input into iconic art, too: this is the age of St Sergius's eremitic movement, of the first Trans-Volga Elders, of St Stephen of Perm's mission; of new political developments that, as we have seen, were to shape the future of Rus and Rossiya; above all of Hesychasm (see p. 108) throughout the Orthodox world. Its influence on Orthodox art is elusive, has never been systematically investigated, but is, I believe, pervasive. It leads above all to the development of a close painterly interest in effects of light and shining, whether exemplified – very differently, it must be said – in the harsh and sometimes alarming chiaroscuro of the industrious immigrant Greek Theophanes (late fourteenth-century frescoes by him survive in the Church of the Transfiguration in Novgorod) or in the airy, light-flooded work of younger colleagues, notably Andrey Rublyov (d. 1430). Rublyov's work – though question-marks of attribution hang over most of it – is justly seen by Russians as the climax of their whole art before the twentieth century. When almost miraculously it was rediscovered at the beginning of this century, it proved indeed enormously influential – see below, p. 199. Too much has been written about Rublyov (by Russians – Western scholarship has hardly touched on him) to attempt a summary here:[14] but of all his characteristic qualities, one that demands to be mentioned is their rhythmic effect, so often tending towards a circularity of overall composition, and of individual details – particularly faces – within. Rublyov is one of art's great instinctive classicists, seeing, one might say, the classical behind the Byzantine, stripping away all inessentials, avoiding all that is mannered. His central work, painted in memory of St Sergius a short time after Sergius's Trinity monastery had been destroyed in the Tatar raid of 1408, depicts the Holy Trinity in the symbolic Old Testament guise of the 'Hospitality of Abraham' (according to the brief and strange episode recounted in Genesis 18:1–8) – a scene that since early Christian art had been taken as representative of the Trinity itself, but is here painted with a suavity, simplicity and gravity unmatched before. Abraham and Sarah are out of the picture; so is the feast they set before the three mysterious angel-travellers; all attention is focused on the single central cup, symbol both of communion and of suffering, being blessed by the central angel. Behind them and rhythmically echoing them are three emblematic constants of worldly existence: a house (Abraham's), a tree (the oak of Mamre), a rock (standing for the wilderness). Unobtrusive use of reverse perspective draws the viewer into the picture-space; brilliant lapis-lazuli blue on each of the angelic garments contrasts forebodingly with the central splash of dark blood-red on sleeve and chalice.

Rublyov's Rus saw, rather briefly, an age of creative diversity in the still autonomous principalities before first civil war, then centralization ushered in a new political era. There were many opportunities for painters, and several recognizable provincial schools. A significant

---

[14] For an appreciation in English, see M. Alpatov *Art Treasures of Russia* (London, 1968) pp. 107–32.

*Plate 22   Andrey Rublyov: Hospitality of Abraham or Old Testament Trinity
icon, his most famous and most securely attributed work, painted for the
cathedral of the Trinity Monastery of St Sergius, north-east of Moscow (early
fifteenth century, now in the Tretyakov Gallery).*

development of the church interior opened up great possibilities for the
icon: the appearance of the 'high' iconostasis, from floor to ceiling a
gallery of images comparable only, perhaps, to the west fronts of the
Romanesque and Gothic cathedrals. The central and mightiest tier is
known as the Deisis, 'intercession': a series of holy figures, led by the
Mother of God and the Baptist, process towards a centrally located
figure of Christ in Majesty to intercede on behalf of the worshippers. It
seems that this kind of iconostasis, which became general in the
Orthodox lands, may have arisen on Russian soil: the earliest known
complete example, and doubtless the finest, was done by Rublyov and
his team of associates for the Trinity Monastery in the 1420s, and still

stands there.[15] Rublyov's manner of painting still dominates the rest of the fifteenth century (though not in Novgorod), and as late as the 1550s he is cited as an example to be followed at the *Stoglav* church council; but he gradually became a figure of myth. His last creative followers were Dionisiy and his sons, who *c.*1500 painted the Ferapontov monastery with a complete (and surviving) set of frescoes that include virtuoso Hymns to the Mother of God. But the style becomes curiously dematerialized, bloodless though still elegant, in Muscovy: local schools fade away, formulae are repeated. In the later sixteenth to seventeenth centuries new inspiration comes only (again) from folk motifs, whether in the far north or in the so-called Stroganov icons associated at first with the patronage of the merchant family of the same name that did much to open up Siberia. The characteristic manner of these icons is small-scale, finicky, jewel-like: objects intended to be personal prized possessions (their ultimate modern descendants are the well-known lacquered boxes produced at Palekh and some other old icon-specializing villages, maybe also the intricate book illustrations of Ivan Bilibin – see above p. 172–3). But finickiness also enters into wall-painting, particularly of the seventeenth century Yaroslavl school: these works are often most picturesque in detail, but in overall effect are remote from the great totalizing schemes of earlier periods. From mid-century they were much influenced by iconographic details borrowed from Northern European woodcuts – in particular, from those in the widely disseminated Dutch 'Piscator Bible' of the early seventeenth century.

By the second half of the seventeenth century Western European painterly techniques, perspective effects and slickness of execution were beginning to invade traditional panel-painting. Both Nikon and Avvakum inveighed against this, but ineffectively. The painter Simon Ushakov (1626–86), head of the workshop at the Moscow Armoury Chamber that set the tone for artistic production, developed a skilful hybrid art that occasionally (notably in a large 'political' icon, The Planting of the Tree of the Muscovite State)[16] had interesting and original results. But from Peter the Great's time icon-painting sinks into a provincial torpor – the best talents were headed in a Westerly direction,

[15]  Most accounts of Russian art give primacy to the iconostasis of the Kremlin Annunciation Cathedral (1405), but it is now generally agreed that, though containing some early icons, it was put together after a fire in the sixteenth century. Many of the icons from the huge iconostasis put up by Rublyov's team in the Vladimir Dormition Cathedral (1408) survive, but the screen itself has been dismantled.

[16]  L. Hughes 'The Age of Transition: 17th Century Icon Painting' in S. Smythe and S. Kingston (eds) *Icons 88* (Dublin, 1988) p. 66.

*Figure 13  Sketch of characteristic design of a 'high' iconostasis as developed in late medieval Russia (based on the Annunciation Cathedral in the Moscow Kremlin): the central tier represents the Deisis (Intercession); above it are the Major Feasts.*

and icon-producers were scornfully dubbed *bogomazy*, 'God-daubers'. In the later nineteenth century the imperial authorities, anxious to revive icon painting as a socially cohesive factor and raise its standards, were aghast to find that icon production was almost entirely in the hands of foreign firms producing millions of cheap prints.[17] Yet some deeper effects from the world of the icon lingered on in Russian art of the eighteenth to nineteenth centuries, determining its orientation towards portraiture and even some of the personal attitudes of the painters to their task, and were to be reinvigorated with remarkable effect at the turn of the nineteenth and twentieth centuries.

## Icons and the 'Modern Movement'

The question of the influence of the traditional art of the icon on the leading artists of the period of 'Modernism' (*c*.1890–1930) in Russia is highly interesting and problematic. Perhaps it is *the* fundamental question of the history of Russian art: and given the importance of the Russian contribution to the Modern Movement as a whole it has a global art-historical dimension. It is commonly mentioned in general accounts of modern Russian art; yet, save in a few specialized contexts, it seldom gets more than superficial attention. Quite detailed studies of, for example, Malevich have been published in which the role of icons goes unmentioned. The entire bibliography of the topic in English boils down to a couple of short articles and sections of a few relevant monographs, while in the Soviet Union both the religious component of culture and the modern movement in the arts were sufficiently delicate topics to discourage the publication of any broad investigation. The specialization of art-historical studies has not helped: medievalists, folklorists, 'modernists' have been reluctant to enter each other's territory.

The artists themselves felt no such inhibitions: in particular the generation born in the last quarter of the nineteenth century took to this aspect of their heritage with such enthusiasm that it would be hard to find a major figure who was not affected by one aspect or another of 'iconicity', the ethos of icons. Yet pervasive as this was, it manifested itself in very various ways, formally or conceptually (after all the modern age has also been an age of assertive individualism in the arts), and often far from obviously. Clearly the full scale study of the topic would have to be a many-sided and lengthy undertaking. Yet such is the confusion and hesitancy that has characterized handling of the issue up to now that

[17] R. Nichols 'The Icon and the Machine in Russia's Religious Renaissance', in Brumfield and Velimirović *Christianity and the Arts in Russia*.

even a short account may be of some use. It will encourage us to consider not just the lives and work of some remarkable twentieth century artists, but the whole question of how, products as we are of another age and culture, we can or should respond to icons, what we can legitimately 'read into' them and how they may modify our own perceptions. I intend to divide my subject-matter into three parts: first, to give a very brief account of the historical circumstances; second, to list some qualities in icon painting that the modern artists (and contemporary critics) discovered and valued; third, to mention the main figures involved, particularly focussing on problems of 'iconicity' in the two most famous and radical figures in Russian art of the 1910s–20s, Kazimir Malevich and Vladimir Tatlin.

Icons as we have seen were ubiquitous in pre-revolutionary Russia; churches were full both of mural and panel paintings, they were on view in private homes (whether or not particularly pious) and were the centrepiece of numerous wayside shrines. Yet icon painting as an art form had to be 'rediscovered', and rather recently – largely within the twentieth century. To nineteenth-century progressive intellectual taste icons smacked of superstition: their aesthetic qualities and indeed their antiquity were in almost all cases concealed under layers of candle-grease, varnish that had darkened, applied metal casings and inferior over-painting. Only on a 'folk' level did icon painting by the late nineteenth century retain spontaneity and artistic appeal, and thus attracted the attention of those who propagated a Russian equivalent to the English Arts and Crafts movement, attempting to preserve or revive folk creativity (though in a context of sophistication). The building and furnishing of a small pastiche Old Russian church at Abramtsevo, on the Mamontov estate north of Moscow, in 1880 was a significant moment in preparing for the coming revaluation of Old Russian art, and it is equally no accident that many historians of modern Russian art take the Mamontov circle as the starting point of the 'Modern Movement' in Russia.[18]

Other forces were also at work. Old Believers – many of them rich merchants – made a point of collecting ancient icons dating from before the seventeenth century schism. A revival of interest among intellectuals in the Orthodox Church encouraged a reassessment of the art that was an essential part of it. The advent of Symbolism – the first great avantgarde movement (in all the arts) to become fully acculturated in Russia – immeasurably widened the spectrum of aesthetic appreciation among educated people. The art of the Byzantine Empire (cultural 'parent' to

[18]   See, for example, C. Gray *The Russian Experiment in Art* (London, 1988, 3rd edn).

Old Russia) was already being rediscovered, particularly in its Italian manifestations, before the turn of the century in Western Europe, affecting 'moderns' such as the French Symbolist Gustave Moreau and subsequently the *Jugendstil* painters: some Russian artists of the first Modernist generation – notably Mikhail Vrubel (1856–1910) – found their way towards the Old Russian heritage through the Byzantine.

After the turn of the century two events in particular signalled the major impact that their ancient religious art was to have on the Russians. The better known was the great exhibition of newly restored icons – "Ancient Russian Painting" – held in Moscow in 1913, the tercentenary year of the Romanov dynasty. Before this, in 1903–4, however, took place an even more significant event, from which the whole process acquired momentum: the first cleaning of the Old Testament Trinity icon by Andrey Rublyov. This work, whose provenance was attested by unbroken tradition from its time of origin, re-established the historicity of Rublyov (who had become a figure of myth) and permitted his heritage gradually to be ascertained and restored; furthermore, its outstanding artistic quality – 'classic' rather than 'vernacular' – ensured that henceforth the aesthetic qualities of the great icons had to be taken seriously. The Trinity itself acquired a mythic status and to this day is generally taken as *the* quintessential Russian icon. Strangely enough, for many years after 1904 it was known (and much written about) on the basis only of a single black and white photograph, since its later metal casing was put back onto it.

After 1904, restoration experts and art historians worked with great vigour to reinstate the Old Russian heritage of painting. Important private collections were formed, notably that of Ilya Ostroukhov, seen by Henri Matisse – whose reputation in Russia was already considerable – in 1911: his extravagant enthusiasm, though it annoyed some Russian intellectuals (such as the poet Blok), confirmed the new-found prestige of the Russian icons within Russia itself and beyond, lending them a more than merely Russian context of influence. After the exhibition of 1913 no Russian artist could reasonably remain in ignorance of the power and diversity of the icon tradition, while a critical literature of considerable sophistication, exemplified by writers such as Igor Grabar and Nikolai Punin, sprang up around them; it is significant that Grabar was not only an art historian but was active in restoration work and himself a painter of mildly 'modern' inclination; Punin became one of the great champions of the most innovative modernists, notably Tatlin.

What qualities then could Russian artists find, or believe they had found, in the icon tradition during the period of its rediscovery? Their reactions were of course conditioned not merely by the icons' intrinsic qualities (themselves very diverse) but by the historical circumstances in which the artists found themselves: at a generally acknowledged crisis point in the 400-year post-Renaissance development of art, but a moment too when the potential of artistic creativity for the deepening of human perceptions or even the reshaping of society seemed particularly propitious, when a new 'pictorial language' to supersede the slick realism of the nineteenth century was urgently sought.

A list of such qualities, even though based on programmatic statements or artistic practice of the time, will unavoidably seem rather arbitrary and schematic. In proposing such a list, I begin with a group of very general qualities and move to more specific ones. It will readily be seen that not all of them are consistent with each other, not all of course are exclusive to the art of the icon, and that even those artists most imbued with the sense of iconicity would emphasize some while ignoring others.

1 *Spirituality*   This obvious characteristic of icon painting needs little comment: it corresponded particularly with Symbolist strivings (note that one of the most influential aesthetic tracts of the period was Vasiliy Kandinsky's *On the Spiritual in Art* [1911])

2 *Transcendency*   The icon seemed to transcend the accidental phenomena of the material world, and, even more important, of temporality: it represented 'timeless', elevated existence, yet far from rejecting materiality it seemed to symbolize or presage the latter's transfiguration.

3 *Symbolism*   The world depicted in the icon was an allegorical, or, more broadly, a symbolic world; the first studies of Rublyov, in particular, revealed a multi-layered symbolic expressivity.

4 *Abstraction*   Before the birth of what we recognize as 'abstract art' in the 1910s – indeed throughout the history of painting – artists had been exercised by the competing pulls of mimesis and decorativeness; the abstract qualities of the icon seemed satisfactorily to reconcile the ornamental principle with the figurative.

5 *Impersonality*   As an art form of medieval origin the icon was generally anonymous, often 'collective', the direct expression of the needs of its society: its calm impersonality appealed particularly to the post-symbolist generation, reacting against the entire nineteenth-century cult of individualism.

6 *Musicality*   The 'harmonious' composition and 'rhythmic balance' of icons has attracted comment since the first cleaning of Rublyov's Trinity: musicality was of course considered in the late nineteenth century an ideal towards which the arts in general strove.

7 *Stylization*   The iconographic conventions and formalized gestures of Old Russian art seemed – specially to a generation sated with romantic and decadent individualism – to point a way towards a new classicism beyond the vagaries of 'style', just as had been the case in the late eighteenth century: 'stylization' could lead to 'stylessness' (Punin already recognized the 'Hellenic', classical origins of the Byzantine art that led to Rublyov's manner).

Here our list becomes more specific.

8 *Naiveté* A lack of refinement, fussiness and 'effect', a simple directness in the icon appealed to a generation that was rediscovering the primitive in art (not that, outside a purely folk context, icon painting was actually as 'primitive' as it was sometimes taken to be).

9 *Picture-space* An age that had tired of the rigidity of Renaissance laws of perspective found in Orthodox medieval art an alternative handling of picture-space, including a flexible yet sometimes quite sophisticated use of 'reverse perspective' (see above p. 184–5).

10 *Colour* The 'rhythmic' or 'harmonious' quality of many icons – see 6 above – was attained above all through the unnaturalistic use of clear, unmodulated patches of colour (derived of course from naturally obtained, rather than factory-made pigments).

11 *Materiality* The icon is not illusionistic, is no mere 'window into another world': its materials – wood, metal, sometimes jewels, pigment – are 'obvious', unashamed and unconcealed; in this context the common incorporation of calligraphy into the picture texture is significant (an effect of course much employed by modernists from the period of Cubism onwards).

12 *Utility* Icons, as depictions of sacred personages and events, were venerated, yet they were also simple objects of household utility: they were a necessary art, not produced for the disinterested gratification of connoisseurs; their location – in church, shrine, the corner of a room – was purposeful, not arbitrary or decorative.

13 *Humanism* Icon painting was fundamentally concerned with the representation of the human figure (as Russian painting indeed has been throughout history); it has been humanistic too in its quasi-classic idealization and generalization of human types and emotions, as too in its harmony and balance: see 6 above.

14 *'National' quality* For Russians the icon was incontrovertibly their own, alternative 'classical' artistic tradition, hallowed by its antiquity, ennobled by its classlessness and ideological purposefulness; at a period of Russian national self-definition and cultural self-assertion no quality was more widely appreciated by artists, critics and public.

Finally, beyond all such discrete points, there could be sensed a greater, all-suffusing quality that even in the context of a largely secular culture gave icons their exceptional significance and power that they were a essential rather than optional or peripheral part of their culture, that they were the object of veneration, some considered 'wonder working', some even of supernatural creation, 'not made by hand': they were indeed works of art, yet more importantly belonged in a realm of experience different from, and superior to the merely 'artistic'.

The artists who to a greater or lesser extent experienced the influence of these qualities formed no school, differed in their political and religious views, and in some cases disliked each other to the point of active hostility (Pavel Filonov despised and attacked Kuzma Petrov-Vodkin; Tatlin supposedly came to blows in public with Malevich; the latter ousted Marc Chagall from the Vitebsk art college in a '*coup d'état*'). They vary greatly too in the extent to which the 'iconic impulse' is visible in their work, whether it is an occasional or pervasive feature, how it blends into or differentiates itself from other stylistic idiosyncrasies or influences. The iconic impulse is not always predictable in its workings: two examples of Russian artists who, both springing from Symbolist roots, became enormously famous in the West, make this clear.

The first is Vasiliy Kandinsky (1866–1944). His commitment to spirituality in art, his adherence to the Orthodox Church, his intense interest in 'musicality' and in pure colour harmony at the best-known stage of his career, his nostalgia for Old Moscow, would all lead one to look for iconic influence – and probably to be disappointed: the billowing, unstructured forms of his abstract and near-abstract paintings of the 1910s can well be analysed in terms of Romanticism, Primitivism, Symbolism or Expressionism but scarcely of the icon tradition. It is noteworthy that the numerous illustrations he chose for the *Blue Rider* almanac (1912) include specimens of folk religious art from various lands and even Russian peasant woodcuts, but no icons: he left Russia for Munich before the turn of the century, and probably the rediscovery of ancient icon painting did not impinge on his consciousness.

The contrary example is provided by Chagall (1887–1985). It may seem amazing that the painter so well known for his vaguely surrealistic imagery of flying lovers, village fiddlers, donkeys, bouquets of flowers, who was so closely tied to his Hassidic Jewish small-town origins, should have produced any work with iconic associations, yet – particularly in the important period of the 1910s – such can be found not only in religiously inspired works such as *Golgotha* and its study *Calvary* (1912), but in one of the strangest and most commanding of all his paintings, *Homage to Apollinaire* (1911–13), glutted with imagery from many sources. An even more remarkable case is that of Naum Gabo (1890-1978), known as a rigorously abstract Constructivist sculptor from early in his career (*c*.1915); however, his work includes some dematerialized yet easily recognizable inclined heads, powerfully evoking icons of the Virgin, all the more so when framed by two planes meeting at a right angle, as if at the angle of a room (it is known that Gabo – from a well-off Orthodox Jewish family – had nonetheless a Christian nanny in childhood, who hung icons in his bedroom).

Picasso did not go to Africa to learn about the carving of masks, the Pre-Raphaelites were unable to step backwards through the centuries – but Russian artists who were affected by their tradition of icons and wall-paintings could, and in many cases did, get to know them in an entirely practical way. One of the first and greatest of Russian Modernists, Vrubel, was fundamentally influenced at the outset of his career by his work on the restoration of St Cyril's church in Kiev (he subsequently took part in the painting of the new St Vladimir's Cathedral). Kuzma Petrov-Vodkin (1878–1939) was commissioned to paint a set of icons in the 1910s. Pavel Filonov (1883–1941), from an impoverished background, turned his hand to all manner of workaday painting jobs, including the touching-up of religious paintings, and made copies of icons: his ascetic way of life had its own 'iconic' impulse. It is sometimes said that Vladimir Tatlin (1885–1953) first encountered icons at the 1913 exhibition, but it is now known that he, like Filonov, undertook humdrum religious painting tasks to earn money at an earlier stage in his life. This atmosphere of practical artisanship had considerable importance not just in the absorption into modern art of the iconic tradition but in the whole ethos of Russian modernism, which never retreated into hermetic aestheticism, despite what its later detractors were to claim.

In charting the impact of the icons on art during the first half of this century, we can note a general progression from pastiche echoes in easel-painting of the icons' characteristic forms, colours, spatial effects and human postures towards a more 'conceptual', less obvious but profounder influence – on the artists' attitudes as much as on the forms through which they realized their work. To this generalization perhaps Vrubel is the chief exception: his 'medieval' impulse has to be sought underneath his weirdly fragmented, apparently expressionistic or even proto-Cubist surface textures.

In the work of Petrov-Vodkin and of Natalya Goncharova (1881–1962), however, compositional influences from icon painting are far from concealed. Petrov-Vodkin's bold patches of even colour, his strangeness of perspective, his stylized figures in gravely rhythmic postures all proclaim the iconic source of their inspiration boldly. A more muted and delicate painting of 1920, even more evidently iconic in origin, was to prove his masterpiece: *Petrograd 1918*, generally known as *The Petrograd Mother of God*, one of the most widely admired paintings of the post-Revolutionary period.

Goncharova, who knew members of the Abramtsevo circle and herself dreamed of decorating a church, seems to have been experimenting with iconically based painting from soon after the turn of the century. Her close association with Mikhail Larionov and the general ethos of 'neo-Primitivism' that became a powerful force in modern Russian art from *c*.1907 led to the incorporation of evidently iconic forms into the most avant-garde painting in Russia of the time. Goncharova's early work is highly ornamental, with more than a lingering hint of art nouveau about it: her inspiration is eclectic, and such an 'icon' as *Flight into Egypt* (1908–9) seems to derive more from Coptic or Syrian than Russian models. She attained real monumentality – though still with pastiche effect – in the series of more than life-size *Evangelists* of a couple of years later (the Church hierarchy banned their display).

The 1910s, in fact, see an explosion of 'iconicity', affecting the most diverse artists: we can detect it, here rather improbably moderating an ostensibly Cubist approach, in Vladimir Burlyuk's portrait of Benedict Livshits (1911), equally in Larionov's serio-comic portrait of Tatlin (1913); differently in the early wood-engravings of Vladimir Favorsky (1886–1961). To close this section, however, we shall limit ourselves to a rather closer examination of the two artists who not only seem in retrospect two of the most adventurous and perhaps emblematic figures of their age, but who both, though very differently, absorbed the icon on a conceptual, not merely formal level into their deepest experience.

Kazimir Malevich (1878–1935) grew up among the West Russian peasantry, a background that conditioned his fierce populism and, though with some initial delay, his commitment to an iconic approach to art. From his earliest, eclectically Symbolist, work, the stylized human

Plate 23   K. Petrov-Vodkin Petrograd 1918
('The Petrograd Mother of God', 1920).

figure was his overwhelmingly dominant subject: often the bearded peasant face (the beard a traditional symbol of God-given dignity). By the early 1910s the crudity and simplification of his figures surpasses even the primitivism of Larionov and Goncharova: his *Chiropodist* (1908) has been interpreted as a parody of Rublev's Trinity icon, though this seems somewhat far-fetched. In 1911–14 there is an abrupt transition to cubism and 'alogistic' manners (in which disparate elements are jumbled apparently inconsequentially). The human presence, however, lurked behind all these paintings, though in some cases made evident only through their titles. Iconic elements can in fact be distinguished in several of these complex, baffling and rather alarming paintings, shot through with a characteristic dualism expressed particularly through light/dark contrasts. They hardly prepared the public, however, for the most spectacular stylistic disjunction of Malevich's career, embodied in the rigorously anti-figurative, geometric abstract manner that he called 'Suprematism' and unveiled at the *Zero-Ten* exhibition of 1915.

Tatlin, meanwhile, had developed as an artist under Larionov's tutelage: until his late twenties he earned his living primarily as a sailor, and there is a sense in which the sailing-ship remained an ideal of the work of art for him throughout his life (functional and beautiful, cooperating with nature to overcome natural limitations, effortlessly dynamic). His early paintings, like Malevich's, were almost exclusively concerned with the generalized human figure, and the iconic impulse was evident in their bold, but not garish colouration, their uncluttered and highly rhythmic composition based on the curvilinear forms that Tatlin cultivated throughout his life (he mistrusted the rigidity of straight lines and right angles preferred by the Constructivists who are often wrongly taken as his heirs).

Tatlin's lifelong interest in the 'culture of materials' (the realization and exploitation in life as in art of the inherent properties of wood, minerals, metals, etc.) led to an even more startling disjunction in his work when (after visiting Picasso) in 1914 he apparently abandoned painting for the abstract sculptural realm of 'reliefs' and 'counter-reliefs': works that, like Malevich's Suprematist paintings, first appeared in public at *Zero-Ten*; consequent rivalry here occasioned their notorious fight.

The genesis and summation of Malevich's Suprematism was represented by a single image (which, however, he painted more than once): the *Black Square* (more precisely 'quadrilateral', *chetyreugolnik*). To Malevich it represented the 'zero of form' through which art, ridding itself of its accidental baggage of figuration, had to pass to reach a superior, purer state. It was hung high up in a corner of the exhibition hall with other, mostly more complex and colourful Suprematist works grouped below and beside it. The artist and critic Alexander Benois immediately and with scorn identified it from its location as the 'icon that the Futurists prefer to Madonnas', a designation that Malevich proudly accepted. Devoid of figurative representation, it was for him all the more packed with meaning. Black signified intense energy (the uncreated but visible divine energy had for centuries been a concept of central importance to the Orthodox Church), the white ground cosmic space; but the black square was also a symbolic 'face', the iconic 'representation' of idealized humanity (hence a successor to the 'first icon', the *Holy Face* of Edessa: see p. 177). This and more is clear from Malevich's own frequent comments on the *Square*; the reading of other Suprematist works in the same spirit is a much harder task, yet perhaps should be attempted (the critic Norbert Lynton has pointed out that the black and red squares in a painting that hung close to the *Black Square* have a spatial relationship corresponding to the Virgin and Child in a well-known iconographic type).

It would seem impossible to discuss Tatlin's abstract constructions similarly in iconic terms: yet, though critics have generally drawn back from interpreting them, this may well be feasible (though most of them can only – with difficulty – nowadays be imagined or reconstructed from photographs). Some used the corner-space of the room (possibly thereby suggesting to Malevich the way to hang his *Black Square*). 'Found' and worked materials, wires, planes and curves were used, creating an alternative or potential world-structure. Most significant was Tatlin's use of wooden boards, the characteristic material of icons: it is interesting that as well as the three-dimensional constructions two remarkable paintings on wood from the same period (*c.*1916) have survived. Both, though completely non-figurative, have a strongly iconic 'feel', not least through their colour range which is (unlike Malevich's) entirely that of medieval icons; they can perhaps be read as 'answers' to Suprematism. But Tatlin's greatest icon is also his grandest 'construction'; his project (realized only as a maquette) for a Monument to the Third International (1919; previously it had been intended as a monument to the Revolution, and evidence has recently emerged that suggests the structure may have been conceived in general terms as early as 1916). This extraordinary concept, asymmetrical, mobile and functional, has multiple transcendental resonances drawing on a wide range of precedents and imagery from deepest antiquity to the modern age: it suggests a striding figure, superhuman yet at one with the earth from which it 'grows'.[19]

[19]   See J. Milner *Vladimir Tatlin and the Russian Avant-Garde* (London, 1983); also R. Milner-Gulland 'Khlebnikov, Tatlin and Khlebnikov's Poem to Tatlin' in *Essays in Poetics* 1987:2.

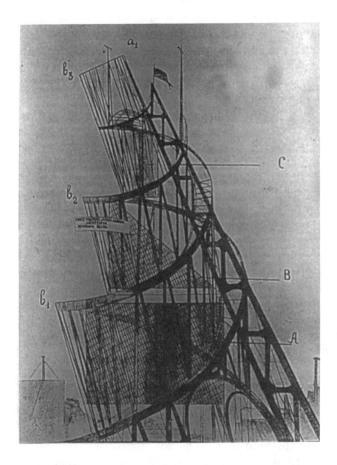

Figure 14 Vladimir Tatlin c. 1919: Diagram of projected Monument to the Third International known as 'Tatlin's Tower': a double skew spiral of steel girders, with internal revolving chambers of various cross-sections, intended to be 400 metres high.

A Russian scholar (N. Khardzhiev) envisaged Malevich and Tatlin as dividing up the heavens and the earth between themselves, each nonetheless having designs on the other's portion.[20] Malevich dematerialized his 'icon' in its lofty location, yet brought the 'non-objective world' of pure spirit into the range of human vision; for Tatlin the icon was of transcendent value precisely because of its materiality, its

[20]   N. Khardzhiev *K istorii russkogo avangarda* (Stockholm, 1976).

this-worldliness, yet his Monument was to be open-ended like a vast telescope, mingling with the sky. Subsequently he was to spend years in a stubborn effort to build on organic principles a glider that would give the power of flight to every individual. Malevich for his part returned to figuration, indeed to peasant images transfigured and simplified through the Suprematist experience to the point where facial features, all individuation, vanish. Many, though, incorporate into themselves the element of the cross – Malevich's final iconic emblem not only for the suffering of humanity, but for the intersection of the human with the more-than-human.

With Malevich's death in 1935, as was recognized at the time, a chapter closed in the history of modern Russian art, and also of its interiorization of the form and concepts of the icon. Those who have written about the culture of the young Soviet state have used the word 'icon' about posters, public statuary, even films – but this is a looser employment of the term than has been permitted in this chapter, and generally has little relationship to the 'modern movement', whose 'heroic' period was in the 1900s and 1910s. Obviously, though, the icon tradition itself has not ceased to have living force, and it cannot be doubted that whenever a Russian artist asks 'what am I doing in art?' the answers that this tradition supplies at least have still to be taken into account.

## Symbolic Landscapes

To identify certain landscapes or landscape features as having symbolic meaning, or to modify a landscape (or townscape) deliberately for symbolic purposes, is an ancient and widespread human impulse. It may involve construction-activity, it may be a matter of naming, but it will generally be intended to make the symbolic identification of a locality with some place or idea outside itself and usually greater than itself. This may be on a global or cosmic level – every walled monastery symbolizing an ideal city, every dome symbolizing the heavens (the greatest dome of antiquity, the Roman Pantheon, is insistent in such resonances: dedicated to the seven planetary deities, with a gap or *oculus* at the top that lets the elements in) – and anthropology has had much to say on such things. But it may be much more specific, and we shall be looking at some such examples. Though evidently not peculiar to Russia, it has special significance in a Russian context: I believe this is a phenomenon that marks a climax to the whole concept of iconicity, with which we have been dealing in this chapter. In so far as Rus was from early times perceived as a holy (or at least divinely favoured) land – note the Primary

Chronicler's rhetorical question (p. 149) 'Whom has [God] honoured as he has glorified us and raised us up?' – it could itself acquire iconic status.

The very boundlessness of Rus, its geographical and even ethnic indeterminacy, encouraged this. From a formless arena of disparate tribes, subsequently the place of transit described in the early pages of the *Tale of Bygone Years* (cf. fig. 4, p. 49), it – or rather its idealized image – could turn into an icon of paradise. A remarkably lyrical expression of this is a fragmentary work, extant in two manuscripts, that apparently dates from around the time of the Tatar invasion and is known as the 'Tale of the Ruin of the Russian Land' (*Slovo o pogibeli russkoy zemli*). It begins with an ecstatic evocation of Christian Rus and its features, then delineates it geographically and politically, and where it breaks off begins to lament its misfortunes:

O brightly brilliant and finely adorned land of Rus! thou art made marvellous by thy many beauties; marvellous art thou with thy many lakes, with rivers and with venerated springs, with steep mounts, with high hills, with pure oak-woods, with marvellous fields, with varied beasts, with innumerable birds, with great cities, with lovely villages, with monastic gardens, with church buildings; also with awesome princes, noble boyars, many men of might. Thou art filled with all this, land of Rus, land of Orthodox Christian faith!

Hence from the Hungarians to the Poles and Czechs, from Czechs to Yatvyags, from the Yatvyags to Lithuania, to the Germans, from Germans to Karelians, from the Karelians to Ustyug where the pagan people of the Toyma were, and past the Breathing Sea [the Arctic], from the sea to the Bulgars, from Bulgars to Burtas, from Burtas to Cheremnis, from Cheremnis to the Mordovians – all the pagan lands were placed by God under the dominion of the Christian people . . . And even the Constantinopolitan Emperor Manuel had forebodings, and sent fine gifts, lest the Great Prince Vladimir [Monomakh] should take the Imperial City from him.

But now evil has befallen the Christians . . .

An almost obsessive interest in the extent of Rus, its inviting spaciousness (*prostor* or *privolye*, favourite Russian concepts),[21] characterizes the *Igor Tale* (see Chapter 4), and reaches into the oral literature of the *byliny* recited by wandering minstrels (cf. p. 156); sometimes it is developed to fantastical and comic effect:

Oh, there is open country around Pskov,
And there are broad open spaces around Kiev,
And high hills at Sorochinsk,
And church buildings in Moscow, the city of stone,
And the ringing of the bells in Novgorod.

[21] Cf. D. Likhachov *Reflections on Russia* (Boulder, 1991) p. 6

Oh, there are cunning rogues in the Valdai Hills,
Oh, there are fine fellows and dandies in the city of Yaroslavl,
And easy kisses in the region of Beloozero ['White Lake'],
And sweet drinks in Petersburg,
And mosses and swamps by the blue sea,
And skirts with wide hems in Pudoga.
Oh, the sarafans are tanned with the wool inside along the Onega River,
And the women of Leshmozersk are fruitful,
And the women of Pozheresk have bulging eyes.
Oh, the Danube, the Danube, the Danube,
And beyond that I know of no more regions to sing.[22]

The common people's buoyant relish of the land's unconstrained
'spaciousness' has another side to it: the yearning to get away to
another, ideal, utopian or iconized Rus, parallel with the existing one but
free of oppression and want – somewhere in the 'blue distances', *sinie
dali*, where the subaqueous city of Kitezh or the land of Belovodye
('whitewater') beckon. Such utopian yearnings were still finding literary
form in the early Soviet period (the work of the economist and fantastical
writer A. Chayanov; Platonov; Zabolotsky's *Triumph of Agriculture*)
and maybe later still; in the eighteenth century they were a subtext to the
semi-literate, rather moving proclamations of the rebel Pugachov.

It has always been evident to historians that there was a demographic
shift in twelfth-century Rus from the south, around Kiev, to the north-
east, chiefly the 'land beyond the forest' or Suzdalia (its significance and
extent are more debatable). What gets little if any mention is the
extensive 'reinvention' of the northern townscape and landscape – both
through naming and through building operations – in such a way that
the widespread symbolic identification of its features with that of the old
Rus heartland around the 'mother of Russian cities', Kiev, must have
been intended – though how consciously or systematically we cannot
tell. Thus we find, in the south and north-east, two towns called Galich;
two Dmitrovs; two Vladimirs; at least two Zvenigorods; three Yuryevs;
three Pereyaslavls (four if we include the earlier Pereyaslavl founded by
Svyatoslav on the Danube), and so on. The authority on Russian
etymology, Max Vasmer, gives in his *Dictionary* a derivation of the
name 'Pereyaslavl' from Slavonic elements meaning 'the place to which
the glory has been transferred'. Each Pereyaslavl has a little river flowing
through it bearing the name Trubezh. The city of Vladimir on the
Klyazma, founded (or refounded) by Vladimir II Monomakh to be a new
capital of the 'land beyond the forest', clearly bears his name: but it is
rather odd that it is not an adjectival form (e.g. 'Yuryev' from Yuriy),

----

[22]   Translation by R. Zguta *Russian Minstrels* (Oxford, 1978) p. 91.

and one must suspect a conscious imitation of the major city of south-west Rus, Vladimir in Volhynia (both happen to have a great Dormition Cathedral – as also in Kiev – built at the same time in similar style). But Vladimir on the Klyazma was also given Kievan features: four city gates, one a 'Golden Gate' (which in Kiev was also a Constantinopolitan reminiscence), a tripartite division (with one area called 'The Caves'), a stream as in Kiev called Lybed; an out-of-town princely residence (Bogolyubovo) located along its river at the equivalent distance to Vyshgorod, the Kievan residence, as a chronicler pointed out. Its great Dormition Cathedral is the same height at its central dome as Santa Sophia of Kiev (95 ft), and when after a fire (1185) it was rebuilt and enlarged by Grand Prince Vsevolod 'it is clear Vsevolod had in mind the pyramidal silhouette of St Sophia in Kiev and encouraged his architect to reproduce it.'[23] There are also Kievan echoes in the last great city to be founded (1220s) before the Tatar onslaught, Nizhniy Novgorod – a river called Pochayna, a monastery of the Caves – but its name comes from Novgorod the Great, whose westerly trading potential it no doubt was seen to match in the east.[24]

The great nineteenth-century historian Klyuchevsky devoted an informative page to these phenomena, but explained them rather lamely by conjecturing that they 'can only have been the work of migrating settlers',[25] spontaneously reusing familiar names; however I detect a process more deliberately and ideologically motivated, an attempt to transfer the prestige and sacred character of early Rus to a destination 'beyond the forest', particularly since it does not seem to have been a random process associated with Russian colonization generally, but with a specific time and locality. Mikhail Tikhomirov was closer to the mark in writing 'The towns of Southern Rus served as prototypes for the princely towns of Zalessk Rus' (i.e. the north-east).[26] The whole matter deserves extensive investigation, the more so since cultural historians often make such assumptions as 'Any consideration of Old Russian culture invites one major division – which is both chronological and regional – between Kiev and Muscovy',[27] and since questions of continuities and dislocations in

---

[23]  H. Faensen and V. Ivanov *Early Russian Architecture* (Cambridge, 1975) p. 354.
[24]  N. Bondarenko and S. Shumilin 'Istoricheskiy put razvitiya Nizhnego Novgoroda' in *Arkhitekturnoye nasledstvo* XXXV (Moscow, 1987).
[25]  V. Kliuchevski (Klyuchevsky) *History of Russia* vol. I, trans. C. Hogarth, (London, 1911) p. 199.
[26]  M. Tikhomirov *The Towns of Ancient Rus* (Moscow, 1959) p. 439.
[27]  J. Billington 'Images of Muscovy', contribution to 'The Problem of Old Russian Culture', *Slavic Review* March 1962, pp. 24–7; also his *The Icon and the Axe* (London, 1966) p. 634.

Russian history have led to often acrimonious debate between Great
Russian- and Ukrainian-inclined historians. There can in any case be no
doubt that the rulers and ideologists of early Muscovy saw themselves as
direct inheritors of the authority and territory of pre-Tatar Vladimir: any
number of symbolic acts (the appropriation of the 'Virgin of Vladimir'
icon, the restoration of ruined Vladimir buildings, the adornment of
the Moscow Kremlin with a large Dormition Cathedral designed – by
Aristotele Fioravanti, an Italian! – on the Vladimir model, the
dissemination of the 'Legend of the Princes of Vladimir', the embellish-
ment of Ivan the Terrible's wooden prayer-throne with scenes depicting
the exploits of Vladimir Monomakh) testify to this. Hence the recent
attempt of the historian Edward Keenan to claim that Muscovite political
elites 'were only dimly aware of the history of the Kievan period, and even
less interested in claiming it as their inheritance . . . there is not so much as
a hint or allusion to the Kievan legacy' (in the Kremlin)[28] curiously misses
the point. The term 'Kievan Rus[sia]' is a modern concept; Muscovites
knew, and promulgated, the glories of their pre-Tatar heritage chiefly
from the Vladimir lands whither the glory of Kiev was earlier seen to have
migrated (actually they were well aware of the role of Kiev itself, since
their canonical account of Russian history began with the *Tale of Bygone
Years*). But both Kiev and Vladimir were only stages in the process of
historical legitimation and thus iconization of the land of Rus: behind
them stood Constantinople, the 'second Rome', and indeed Rome itself;
while prior to, and holier than either was the heavenly city of Jerusalem.
For 150 years – from early in the reign of Ivan IV to that of Peter I – it was
not the fallen and disgraced Constantinople that invited iconic emulation
as the prototype for a 'symbolic landscape', but Jerusalem itself.

The period opens with a great military triumph (probably Russia's
greatest prior to the Northern War): the capture of the Tartar capital of
Kazan on 1–2 October 1552. This was more than a mere campaign: it
had the resonances of a crusade, and gave rise to probably the best-
known, certainly one of the most symbolically rich of Russian
landmarks: the church on Red Square, Moscow, usually known as 'St
Basil's'. Rich in layers of meaning, this building is a whole symbolic
landscape in itself: it 'energized' and gave meaning to a significant part of
the cityscape of Moscow. Let us look at two aspects of the symbolization
of landscape that both lead back to St Basil's.

As was mentioned earlier (p. 117), this building's correct designation is
not St Basil's, but 'Church of the *Pokrov*' (usually translated as

---

[28]  E. L. Keenan 'On Certain Beliefs and Russian Behaviours' in S. F. Starr
(ed.) *The Legacy of History in Russia and the New States of Eurasia* (New York,
1994) p. 22.

Plate 24  The wooden 'Throne of Monomakh' or 'Tsar's Place', made for
Ivan IV (1551) in the Dormition Cathedral (1475) of the Moscow Kremlin:
scenes on its carved side-panels emphasize Ivan's imperial descent from the
Byzantine Monomachos dynasty.

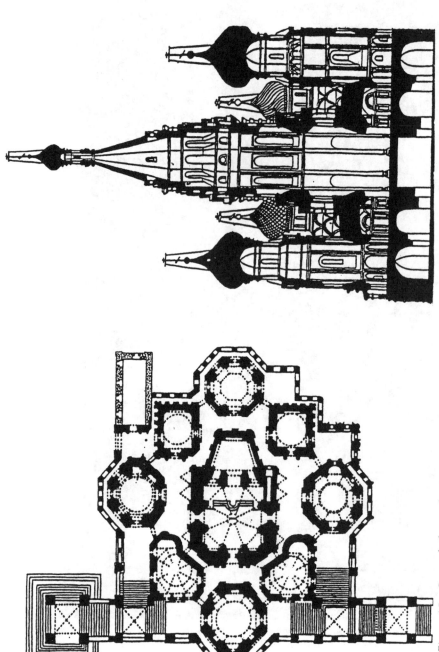

Figure 15 Ground plan and cross-section of 'St Basil's Cathedral' (Church of the Pokrov on the Moat, 1558), Moscow, a radically innovative design, formed from a cluster of nine separate tower or 'tent' churches with interconnecting passageways, and later tenth chapel dedicated to Basil the Blessed

Intercession', or, more properly, 'Veil' or 'Protection'). This is in turn only a partial truth: the Pokrov is more precisely the dedication of the central one of the nine small churches or chapels from which the building is composed, its dedication celebrating the victory of 1 October (the feast-day of Pokrov). Six of the other chapels likewise commemorate the days of events in or associated with the siege of Kazan, turning the whole building into a symbolic map of the action. But the Pokrov dedication simultaneously 'opens out' the semiotics of the building and its location. It is a specifically Russian feast-day (deriving from the vision of the Virgin extending a protective veil over the congregation of one of the great churches of Constantinople, Blachernai) that was enthusiastically taken up by the twelfth-century Grand Princes of Vladimir.[29] The dedication establishes an obvious link with the prestige of both these ancient capitals, and I am sure it is no accident that the early to mid-sixteenth century is precisely the time when the theory of 'Moscow the Third Rome' was propagated, and indeed when the *Tale of the Princes of Vladimir* (which attempted to establish the direct heritage of the Muscovite royal family from both Romes) was particularly popular. Whether or not the Pokrov dedication is here a direct reminiscence of Constantinople and Vladimir, however, there is no doubting that from 1552, if not before, it acquired the most powerful symbolic overtones as a 'protective' dedication, specifically referring to the protection of the Russian land from its enemies extended to it by the Mother of God. At least one other battle was subsequently (1618) fought on I October, and commemorated in the same way.

A ceremonial axis of streets led in the later Muscovite period from Red Square, close to St Basil's, past at least three Pokrov churches to the suburb of Pokrovskoye (Rubtsovo) – part of this route is still called the Pokrovka – and out to the chief late-Muscovite royal preserve at Izmaylovskoye, with its own Cathedral of the Pokrov: thence towards Vladimir, the old capital. (The fact that the 'German Suburb' adjoins this ceremonial route might well be regarded as a sign of the Suburb's high status – it was not a lowly ghetto, as is often assumed.) The semiotics of cityscape in this area of Moscow have been interestingly explored by N. G. Gulyanitskiy.[30] What has not, I think, been pointed out is that if this axis is continued in the opposite direction, westwards, one reaches the most

[29] See L. Ouspensky and V. Lossky, *The Meaning of Icons*, (Olten, 1958) pp. 153–8. M. Ilyin however suggests that a primary impulse for the building's dedication could have been Ivan's visit to the Monastery of the Pokrov at Suzdal after the capture of Kazan, to offer thanks for the birth of his son Dmitriy (in A. Artsikhovsky et al., eds *Ocherki russkoy kul'tury XVI veka*, 11, (Moscow, 1977) p. 302).

[30] N. G. Gulyanitskiy 'Moskva yauzskaya' in *Arkhitekturnoye nasledstvo* XXXIV (Moscow, 1986); see fig. 17, p. 224.

*Figure 16    Church of the Pokrov, Fili, near Moscow, (1690s).*

magnificent of Pokrov churches after St Basil's, at Fili. It duly
commemorates the victory over the Polish forces in 1618, but was
rebuilt as a most unusual two-storeyed structure by Lev Naryshkin (Peter
I's uncle) to celebrate Peter's and his own deliverance from the crises of
1682 and 1689 (thus in a sense the ending of Old Russia).[31] Though on a
suburban estate, it was as much a planned and prominent expression of
royal patronage as St Basil's itself: it stands at a point (the only such point,
indeed) where it can dominate both the road and river approach to
Moscow from the west. It is often nowadays taken as the exemplary
building of the so-called Moscow Baroque (or 'Naryshkin') style, and of
course it features much superficial Baroque, or at least Western European,
detail. Yet its overall forms are not altogether typical of the Moscow
Baroque architecture, and I should suggest that its spectacular

---

[31]    See N. A. Gordeyeva and L. P. Tarasenko, *Tserkov Pokrova v Filyakh*,
(Moscow, n.d.).

pyramidality, the massing of its subsidiary domes, the raising of its main structure on a heavy foundation-storey with an external platform and ceremonial stairways, even its colour contrasts, can plausibly be explained as a reminiscence, in later stylistic terms, of the forms of St Basil's, and before it of an ancient Russian tradition of church architecture.

A second, related but not identical, thread of symbolism unwinds from the great church of St Basil's and stretches through the last century and a half of Muscovite Russia. To follow it we need to go back to the building's dedication. As I have mentioned there is a central axis of chapels that have special status. The easternmost is dedicated to the Trinity, which had a special and not (I think) yet fully investigated significance for Ivan IV: it seems to have represented national unity and cooperation, the resolution of schism, the affirmation of Orthodoxy. Islam was often regarded by Eastern Christians as an anti-Trinitarian heresy: Kazan itself was dedicated to The Trinity when it was 'reborn' as a Russian city. Sometimes (as for Paul of Aleppo) the whole building was simply called 'The Trinity'. [32] But even more often Russians and foreign visitors referred to it by a name that recalled not the easternmost but the westernmost of the central chapels: 'The Jerusalem'.[33] That chapel, dedicated to the Entry into Jerusalem, is located straight ahead of the visitor who approaches up the great flight of steps from ground level. Ivan IV instituted the remarkable procession (see also p. 73) that on Palm Sunday would wind its way out of the Kremlin, across Red Square in zigzags and into the church, with the Patriarch riding on a horse standing in for an ass led by the Tsar. Recent investigators have argued that the individual cells from which the building's interior is composed 'symbolize the buildings, squares and houses of the Holy City'.[34] I should add that the highly unusual adornment of the interconnecting interior passageways with plant-scrolls, flowers and tendrils must represent the gardens of paradise associated with it.

[32]   Paul of Aleppo's mid-seventeenth-century account of a visit to Russia 'The Travels of Macarius', is translated in W. Palmer, *The Patriarch and the Tsar*, vol. II, (London, 1875) – 'It is not indeed a single church, but many churches in one, the whole named after the blessed Trinity' (p. 180); Paul also refers to a procession to the 'Great Church of the Trinity' on the feast day of the Pokrov, 1 October (p. 255).

[33]   A. L. Batalov and T. N. Vyatchanina 'Ob ideynom znachenii i interpretatsii Ierusalimskogo obraza v russkoy arkhitekture XVI–XVII vv' in *Arkhitekturnoye nasledstvo* XXXVI, (Moscow, 1988).

[34]   Faensen and Ivanov *Early Russian Architecture*, p. 443; note Paul of Aleppo's interesting comment 'for the above-mentioned churches are likened to the house of Annas and the palace [*sic!*] of Jerusalem' (Palmer, *The Patriarch and the Tsar*, vol. II, p. 180).

Why was a Jerusalem wanted? I can suggest only a provisional answer, but believe it relates both to the 'crusade' against Kazan and to the desire to fuse a priestly function with the imperial title (of Tsar) adopted by Ivan IV at his coronation; certainly by around 1600, probably much earlier, Russia began to be regarded as specifically a 'holy land',[35] while some regarded old Jerusalem – like Constantinople – as defiled by Saracen occupation.[36] It should be noted that individual buildings symbolizing and sometimes imitating those in Jerusalem – generally the Holy Sepulchre – are known in many locations of the medieval Christian world, though St Basil's seems to be unique in representing the entire Holy City through one iconic structure.[37]

When, with Ivan IV's son Fyodor, the Ryurik dynasty died out in 1598, its ambitious successor Boris Godunov set in motion a large building programme that included a revival and modification of what we may term the Muscovite 'Jerusalem idea'.[38] Clearly he was worried that the symbolic Jerusalem of St Basil's lay outside the citadel-walls: it is recorded in several sources that he planned to build a Holy of Holies inside the Kremlin. His completion of the great Kremlin belfry, known as Ivan Velikiy ('Big John' – nothing to do with either Ivan III or IV), with a solemn inscription celebrating what he hoped would be a new dynasty, is often mentioned as the only completed part of his project (bells, incidentally, have a demonstrable and close symbolic connection with the Holy Land, as Edward V. Williams has recently shown).[39] However, it is probable that he also remodelled or even originated a most important, though often overlooked, item of the Moscow cityscape: the *Lobnoye mesto* ('Place of the skull') in Red Square. A small circular tribune (rebuilt in the late eighteenth century), it is often taken by visitors to be a place of execution, but this interpretation is erroneous. Rather, its sombre name signifies that it is a Golgotha, related to the Jerusalem nearby. Hence it becomes a symbolic *omphalos*, centre of Moscow and Russia as Golgotha itself was taken to be centre of the world.[40]

---

[35]   D. B. Rowland 'Moscow – the Third Rome or the New Israel?', *Russian Review* 55:4 (1996) emphasizes a self-identification with biblical Israel.

[36]   Yu. Lotman and B. Uspensky 'Echoes of the Notion "Moscow as the Third Rome" in Peter the Great's Ideology', in A. Shukman (ed.) *The Semiotics of Russian Culture* (Ann Arbor, 1984).

[37]   See R. Ousterhout, 'Loca Sancta and the Architectural Response to Pilgrimage', in his *The Blessings of Pilgrimage*, (Urbana, 1990).

[38]   See Batalov and Vyatchanina 'Ob ideynom znachenii . . .'.

[39]   E. V. Williams, 'Aural Icons of Orthodoxy', in Brumfield and Velimirović, *Christianity and the Arts in Russia*.

[40]   See M. Eliade *Patterns in Comparative Religion*, (London, 1958) p. 375.

The culmination of the Muscovite Jerusalem idea comes, of course, with the Patriarch Nikon (1605–81). Nikon's dramatic story has already been recounted (pp. 120–2): his swift rise from humble origins, his authoritarian personality, his unpopular church reforms, his initial dominance over the young Tsar Aleksey, their breach (1658), his eventual dethronement (1667) and exile till shortly before his death. In the dozen years of his greatest power Nikon initiated a remarkable number of ambitious building works in whose planning and realization he took an intense personal interest, showing high sensitivity to their symbolic resonances. His culminating project (though he attributed the idea for it to the Tsar) was closest to his heart: the monastery at Voskresensk ('Resurrection') that he called New Jerusalem. The project was a breathtaking one, shifting Jerusalem forty miles away from Moscow and creating an entire landscape-icon of the Holy Land by renaming, and sometimes modifying, local topographical features.[41] At its centre stands a simulacrum of the Holy Sepulchre (or Resurrection) church itself, and we are fortunate that the iconic model from which Nikon partly derived his concept has survived, whereas the great church itself was largely destroyed in the Second World War. His own nearby skete, too, survives – a relic of Old Russian domestic architecture unique in its form and symbolic functions. When he was deposed and exiled one of the charges against him was his presumption in founding a New Jerusalem, no 'mere copy as from a pattern, but the very prototypal Jerusalem itself'.[42] Yet this was only one of his major building projects, several of which to some extent iconized landscape: the Valday monastery has Athonite, the Kiy Island monastery Jerusalemic reminiscences.[43] The strangest example dates from his years in exile at the Ferapontov Monastery, when he built a cross-shaped island of stones in the adjacent Lake Borodava and set up

[41] 'The neighbouring accidents of country he called after various sacred sites in Palestine. The river Istra was converted into the Jordan; a brook, purposely formed, became the Kedron; a neighbouring village was dignified into Nazareth; and on the mound on which the Tsar stood when he bestowed the name of New Jerusalem he built a chapel and called it Eleon' (T. Mitchell, (ed.), *Handbook for Travellers To Russia, Poland and Finland*, 2nd edn, (London, 1868), p. 178). On Nikon as builder: G. Alferova, 'K voprosu stroitelnoy deyatelnosti patriarkha Nikona', *Arkhitekturnoye nasledstvo* XVIII, (Moscow, 1969).

[42] W. Palmer, *The Patriarch and the Tsar*, vol. I (London, 1871) p. 82.

[43] G. Alferova, 'Ansambl Krestnogo monastyrya na Kiy-ostrove', *Arkitekturnoye nasledstvo* XXV (Moscow, 1976), p. 83: 'Nikon considered it essential to restore the image of Old Jerusalem as the holy place of all Christendom, and its artistic traditions, in Russian architecture. This idea . . . can also be seen in the Holy Cross monastery [on Kiy Island].'

*Plate 25   So-called 'skete' (hermitage) of Patriarch Nikon, built for his
own use close to his great monastic church at New Jerusalem (Voskresensk),
and a unique example of mid-seventeenth century domestic architecture
(incorporating chapels).*

crosses with minatory inscriptions at the approach roads – a sort of little
'no-go' territory of his own, a landscape symbolic of his sufferings in a
just cause.[44]

Even in the pre-Petersburg period, Peter the Great already concerned
himself with the creation of symbolic landscape and townscape. In
this he was both following and contradicting his Muscovite predecessors (as Lotman and Uspensky well demonstrate in 'Echoes of the
Notion "Moscow as the Third Rome" in Peter the Great's Ideology').[45]
I shall merely draw attention to two or three examples here. First, there
is Peter's notorious counterfeit capital at a village near Moscow,

[44]   There is an interesting account of these works in the hagiographic *Life* of
Nikon written by a disciple: I. Shusherin, *Izvestiye o rozhdenii i vospitanii i o
zhitii sv. Nikona*, Arkhimandrit Leonid (ed.), (1871), p. 88. See also G. Bocharov
and V. Vygolov *Vologda, Kirillov, Ferapontovo, Belozersk* (Moscow, 1969)
pp. 211–12.
[45]   Lotman and Uspensky 'Echoes of the Notion "Moscow as the Third
Rome"', in A. Shukman (ed.) *The Semiotics of Russian Culture*, (Ann Arbor,
1984).

Preobrazhenskoye (which he and his cronies called Plezpurkh, usually explained as a distortion of Pressburg or Bratislava, coronation-city of the Holy Roman Emperors); here he centred his youthful war-games and, more sinisterly, carried out most of the interrogations and executions of the *streltsy* (defeated at New Jerusalem!); it will be observed that it is close to the Pokrovka axis of the city. Second, his deliberate relocation of the main highway out of the city northwards (i.e. towards Archangel and the sea) was signalled by the construction, where it crossed the city walls, of the vast Sukharev Tower, secular rival to the Kremlin belfry, built like a lighthouse or a ship and subsequently containing a school of navigation.[46] He even planned a 'Petropolis' long before the Northern War, at Azov: it is clear that both in this and at Preobrazhenskoye he was playing with the concept of a counter-capital (even a counter-Jerusalem) – another motif going back to Ivan IV – that was to reach its culmination on the banks of the Neva.[47]

There, though, on ancient Novgorodian territory wrested from the Swedes and reincarnated as his personally founded city by Peter in May 1703, we sense more strongly than anywhere the power of what Sidney Monas has termed 'geopoetics' in the Russian historical experience. Despite Peter's no-nonsense image and secularizing intentions, his city remains a great symbolic landscape with iconic as well, perhaps, as 'anti-iconic' resonances.

From the start Petersburg was defined in terms of places outside itself: it was to be a new Rome (but the fourth such – and traditionalists believed 'a fourth there shall not be'), a new Holland, a new Venice, a new Novgorod, a new Archangel, a new Moscow (from which it inherited not so much the title of 'capital' as of 'reigning city'). It was 'Palmyra of the North' (a dreadful Russian pun on *polmira*, 'half the world'). Dostoyevsky's 'underground man' famously called it 'the most abstract and contrived city in the whole round world'. This 'roundness' was picked up by its greatest celebrator, Andrey Beliy, in his early twentieth century novel *Petersburg*: he saw it as a circle, all 'edge' (unlike limitless Russia itself!), implying among much else the symbol for a capital city on a map, explosiveness and a zero. The metonymy is reinforced when one recollects that for Peter (at least in Pushkin's attribution) it was to be a 'window' (*okno*) or 'eye' (*oko* – both are from the same root, as indeed are the two

---

[46] See I. Grabar 'Sukhareva bashnya', in *O russkoy arkhitekture* (Moscow, 1969).
[47] Apart from Ivan IV's well-known retreat to Aleksandrov and his later installation of a 'counterfeit Tsar', Semyon Bekbulatovich, it seems likely that he considered making Vologda the 'alternative capital' of the *oprichnina*: see Bocharov and Vygolov *Vologda, Kirillov, Ferapontovo, Belozersk*, pp. 17–19.

English words: 'window' = 'wind-eye') onto the outside world, while Moscow remained Russia's heart'. Russian writers in the nineteenth and twentieth centuries have perceived it in terms of a Baroque series of scarcely reconcilable oppositions: stone (unlike traditional Rus, it was to be a stone and brick-built city from the start) and water (the 'energetic' element capable of sweeping all away); a planned city on a trackless bog; a capital, but on the edge of its realm, without hinterland; soulless, but 'alive' (Beliy's 'centipede' of feet passing constantly along Nevsky Prospect); a busy industrial metropolis that is also a carnival site (every year in June, night turns into 'day'); a great stage-set whose 'masked' quality is the personification of power. It was a hell for its builders, but for Peter it was 'paradise' (for which he used a Latin-derived, not Russian, word). In Beliy's words, with its foundation 'Russia was divided into two'.[48] This division can be symbolically expressed in Biblical terms: between the apostle Peter (whose name of course implies 'stone', and who is associated with the 'first' Rome) and his brother Andrew (patron saint of Rus, who supposedly foretold the greatness of Kiev, and whose name was indeed adopted by Boris Bugayev when he renamed himself 'Andrey Beliy'). Peter the Great himself was well aware of the strength of such symbolic-religious resonances in what he and his crony Menshikov thought of as their 'holy land'. Lotman and Uspensky have interestingly investigated the dedications of the five churches that Peter himself founded there: each is symbolically and ideologically motivated. As they point out, the very name 'Sankt-Peterburg' is ambiguous – either 'St Peter's City' or 'The Holy City of Peter'.[49]

The urge towards the creation of symbolically charged, often iconically meaningful landscape features did not end with Peter the Great. Indeed the greatest such feature, the summation of the semiotic aspect of Petersburg, dates from the 1780s: the monument to Peter universally known, after Pushkin, as the 'Bronze Horseman'. Much could be written about its implications: here I want to draw attention not to the statue itself (one of the finest of modern times, by Ètienne-Maurice Falconet and Marie Collot – not in fact bronze but copper), rather to the huge base on which it stands. This is a single block of red granite, shipped with great difficulty from the shores of the Gulf of Finland (where it was an object of folk veneration), most of which is now concealed beneath the ground. This launch-pad for Peter's rearing horse is shaped at the top like a breaking wave, 'frozen' into preternatural immobility as if at the behest of the conquering Emperor (or 'idol', as

---

[48]   A. Bely *Petersburg* trans. R. Maguire and J. Malmstad (London, 1978 etc.) p. 64.

[49]   Lotman and Uspensky 'Echoes of the Notion "Moscow as the Third Rome"'.

*Plate 26    Equestrian statue of Peter the Great, in Senate Square, St Petersburg, known (after Pushkin) as the 'Bronze Horseman', by Étienne-Maurice Falconet and Marie Collot, installed 1782, with a massive red granite rock as pedestal.*

Pushkin calls him). The effect is deeply ambiguous. There is a simple inscription, intended to associate Catherine II's reign with Peter I's – in Latin on one side, in Russian on the other, as if to bring home the dichotomy within the new Rossiya. The oval plan of the monument as a whole suggests it too is a symbolic *omphalos* like the *Lobnoye mesto* in Moscow (see above), intended as centre of the post-Petrine realm.

The urge towards symbolic landscapes took other forms too in the eighteenth and nineteenth centuries: we can do little more than mention them here. In a letter to Diderot, Catherine the Great described a vast

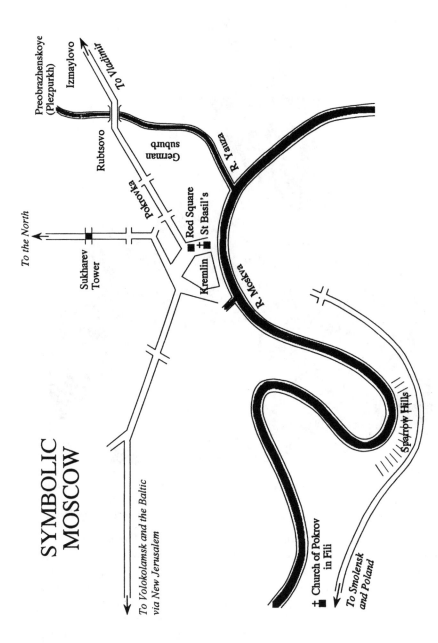

# SYMBOLIC
# MOSCOW

To the North

Sukharev
Tower

Pokrovka

Preobrazhenskoye
(Plezpurkh)

Izmaylovo

To Vladimir

Rubtsovo

German
suburb

R. Yauza

Red Square

St Basil's

Kremlin

R. Moskva

To Volokolamsk and the Baltic
via New Jerusalem

Sparrow Hills

✝ ■ Church of Pokrov
in Fili

To Smolensk
and Poland

*Figure 17  'Symbolic Moscow' (sixteenth to seventeenth centuries), indicating the 'Pokrov axis' of the city.*

temporary re-creation of a campaign against the Turks on the Khodynskoye Field outside Moscow. More permanent – and of great iconic interest – was her creation at Tsarkoye Selo of a village called Sofiya (= Sophia) in a landscape symbolizing the Eastern Mediterranean, complete with a lake for sea and a domed church (that still stands) dedicated to Santa Sophia, representing its prototype in Constantinople. Over the gate was the inscription *Ty v pleskakh vnidesh v khram Sofii* ('Thou shalt enter into the temple of Sophia in applause' – or 'in splashing': the word has both meanings). The whole thing was a symbolic visual embodiment of the 'Greek Project' of the 1780s: a dream, rather than a practical policy goal, of Catherine and Potyomkin to restore Constantinople to Christendom (and which also led to her having a grandson christened 'Constantine' and giving him a Greek nanny). On a humbler, far more widespread if less calculated level, the estates of country landowners from the later eighteenth century begin to take on features of a symbolically charged landscape with its associated way of life, revolving round such age-old pursuits as hunting and church-going; L. Sizintseva, analyzing the 'chronotope' (space-time matrix) of the provincial estate-owners' life, points out that after Peter the whole country was seen as the 'anti-capital', provincialism the repository of real, timeless Russianness.[50] The classic iconic portrayal of such a symbolic world in nineteenth-century literature is 'Oblomovka' in Ivan Goncharov's chapter 'Oblomov's Dream' of *Oblomov*.

The war against Napoleon of 1812, the 'First Fatherland War' (the second was of course against Hitler, 1941–5 – it is often mistranslated as 'Patriotic') gave rise to what would have been a symbolic landscape modification and construction to outstrip even the Patriarch Nikon's, had fate permitted its realization. This was Alexander Vitberg's vast project for a tri-partite commemorative church, excavated into and towering above the Sparrow Hills in Moscow, a place of much historical significance (and personal significance – his 'Holy Place' – to the writer Herzen, who knew Vitberg as an exile later on and left a most memorable account of the visionary architect and of his scheme).[51] Successive storeys were to have been a 'coffin' within the hill, dedicated to the dead; a Greek cross as a 'temple of life'; and a domed Pantheon as 'the home of the spirit': the whole structure would have symbolized the Trinity (also one of the symbolic aspects of the commemorative church of 'St Basil's'). It was to have a curious secular counterpart a century

[50] L. Sizintseva 'Khronotop provintsiala' in *Russkaya provintsiya: kultura XVIII-XX vekov* (Moscow, 1993).

[51] A. Herzen *Childhood, Youth and Exile* trans. J. Duff (Oxford, 1980 edn) p. 242ff.

later in the form of an equally unrealized, perhaps unrealizable, project, Tatlin's Monument to the Third International (see also p. 206; a monument to something in the future, intended to serve as the headquarters of the thing commemorated!), known familiarly as 'Tatlin's Tower'. It was supposed to bestride the Neva in Petrograd – a successor to the 'Bronze Horseman' in what Tatlin called the 'materials of modern classicism'. John Milner has wittily and perceptively called it the command-module of Spaceship Earth: a structure which is cosmically as well as terrestrially symbolic.[52]

Tatlin's Tower was the grandest and most resonant, but by no means the only, Soviet attempt to make use of the iconic connotations of symbolic landscape and construction. The vast 'Stalinist Gothic' skyscraper of Moscow University and its associated park came to occupy the intended site of Vitberg's cathedral on what had been renamed the Lenin Hills. Long before that, the 'mass spectacles' of the early Soviet years utilized 'topographic reality' and 'real objects and actions' to create a 'utopian and mythological' worldview[53] – for a short time creating a truly popular sense of the appropriation and symbolization of townscape. But our last example of Russian symbolic landscape has a farcical, if also pathetic, aspect to its overweening ambition: the creating in Moscow of the huge 'Agricultural Exhibition' which became the all-Union 'Exhibition of Economic Achievements'. This was truly the visible summation and justification of the whole Soviet endeavour, laid out symbolically with pavilions representing the various republics and areas of achievement. When the site began to be neglected, invaded by hucksters, and it ceased to be possible to find a decent meal there, the signs of the Soviet Union's ideological death were plain for all to see.

The large-scale, hastily-confected restoration and construction projects of post-Soviet Moscow under mayor Luzhkov have opened another chapter in the story of Russian symbolic landscapes: one still in progress at the time of writing.

[52]  J. Milner *Vladimir Tatlin and the Russian Avant Garde* (1983); also R. Milner-Gulland 'Tower and Dome' in Slavonic Review 1988:1, pp. 39–49. Note however that the span of the Monument's 'legs' would not nearly have reached across the Neva if it were realized at its intended height (400 metres).
[53]  A. Zakharov 'Mass Celebrations in a Totalitarian System' in A. Efimova and L. Manovich (eds) *Tekstura* (Chicago, 1993) p. 203. See also K. Clark *Petersburg: Crucible of Cultural Revolution* (Harvard, 1995), Chapter 5.

# Conclusion

Our first chapter began with an examination of the land and location of Russia/Rus, and the final section of the last chapter has returned us to its landscape, in particular those aspects of it that were endowed with transformative significance by its inhabitants. When Russians from early times have asked themselves 'who are we?' the even bigger questions *what* are we?' and *where* are we?' have loomed in the background. Inability to answer any of these questions conclusively has been a psycho-historical factor in the restless dynamic of Russian cultural and general history. Russia/Rus was never wholly definable in geographical terms, in political terms, in ethnic terms or even (despite the speedy dominance of the East Slav 'Russian' language) in linguistic terms. Rather it has been a cultural entity: but that involves us in further complexities, since 'culture' will include all the above categories as well as, for example, economic, social and educational structures, and most importantly habits of mind and belief systems. Still, the inhabitants of Russia/Rus have never doubted its existence as a meaningful concept, of no little personal as well as public importance. One of the most remarkable constants of Russian history has been the country's resolute refusal over 1100 years to succumb completely to the centrifugal forces engendered by its large size, thin population, frequent 'ungovernability', and of course foreign interventions of various kinds: thus remaining recognizably itself through a series of historical transformations.

The material examined in the five main chapters of this book leaves us with the realization, I feel, that common generalizations about 'Russianness' or the 'Russian tradition' in mentality, politics, artistic creativity or whatever have little or no validity. Anyone who thinks Russians are by nature passive or submissive should ponder, for example, the religious history dealt with in Chapter 3. Anyone imagining that (as President Reagan asserted on one memorable occasion) 'the Russians have no word for freedom' – and hence presumably lack the concept – may ponder the institutions of medieval Novgorod and Pskov; the freebooters of Vyatka; the Cossack communities; the 'peasant wars' of Razin and Pugachov; the popularly based liberation movement of 1613; the hermit and peasant colonists of the north and subsequently Siberia; the cultural and social ideas of the Decembrists, of Herzen, and their successors – all this before we reach 1905 or 1917. Actually, the Russians have two excellent words for 'freedom': *svoboda*, a general and political term, and *volya*, existential, inner freedom, liberty, licence, the exercise of one's will. (The Russian language has no word for 'efficiency', but that's another story.) Anyone imagining the course of Russian premodern history to have been particularly barbarous or bloodstained should remember the near-absence, in comparison with Western lands, of witch-hunting, crusading, institutionalized capital punishment (abolished under Elizabeth in the mid-eighteenth century). The brutal episodes in the reigns of Ivan the Terrible and Peter the Great were traumatic because uncharacteristic. Anyone thinking that Russian culture has been essentially derivative, or even parasitical on other 'advanced' cultures, should consider the nature of Russian 'iconicity' as explored in Chapter 5, and more generally how the dialectic between a rich folk culture and the 'high' culture that often did battle with it, sometimes blended with it, sometimes tacitly agreed to carve up the cultural territory with it, has determined an overall configuration of the arts in Russia.

This brings us to the characteristic feature of Russian culture: it only makes coherent sense if the ordinary people – the rural population who until the twentieth century have made up the bulk of the population, with their language, proverbs, way of life, historical experience, folklore, structuring of time and living space, their sound-world, visual environment, public and private beliefs, utopian dreams, sense of fairness and so on – are taken into account. This applies as much to ostensibly fully 'Westernized' figures of relatively modern times such as Pushkin, Turgenev, Tchaikovsky or Tolstoy as it does to 'Slavophiles' or, say, to purveyors of orchestrated folksongs. Further back in time the dialectic may be more concealed but is all the more powerful. It scarcely made sense, for example, in Russian circumstances to propound a Marxian contrast between the 'idiocy of rural life' and the progressivism of the city – the archetypal modern city for Russia, St Petersburg, was a place of phantoms, tensions, concealment, unhappiness, unreality. Yet Russian culture was never self-sufficient, cut off from the rest of the world: on the contrary, it has always required interaction with Europe, whether Eastern, Central or Western, and to a lesser extent with Asia (but the idea that it is essentially 'Scythian', barbarous, spontaneous and Asiatic is an early twentieth-century affectation). As a totality it has striven, whether in socio-political life or the arts, for an ideal of integrity (*tselnost*), wholeness, balance, moderation and harmony, therefore all the more bitterly (occasionally triumphantly) aware of disbalance, excess, inconsistency, fragmentation when they have all too often become apparent. The notion that the arts in Russia have cultivated large gestures and extreme effects for their own sake is a sentimental myth.

As for the image of Russia/Rus itself, the object of our preliminary discussion (Chapter 1, Introductory), we can let some twentieth-century poets who were writing in the fraught years on either side of the Revolution have the last word. Alexander Blok's poem of 1910 that begins "My Rus, my life, are we to pine away together?" (*Rus moya, zhizn moya, vmeste li mayatsya?* – called by Blok's best translators, Peter France and Jon Stallworthy, 'Russia and I') finds metaphors in its mere five stanzas that measure up to the vastness and ambiguities of the geography, history and religious experience of Rus, all in a tone that differs little from that of his most anguished love poems (note that *Rus* and *Rossiya* are grammatically feminine nouns): 'Isn't it time now to part and repent?/What use is your darkness to a free (*volnomu*) heart?' Students reading this poem with me recently questioned in amazement whether in twentieth-century English poetry such writing about one's country was conceivable. Doubtless not; yet Blok was no simple-minded chauvinist, but a Petersburg cosmopolitan, a thoroughgoing modernist, an ironist and indeed one of the luminaries of modern European literature, while this is not an isolated poem, but one of many that probe similar themes. A somewhat younger poet, Sergey Yesenin, a déraciné countryman rather than a city intellectual, could evoke Rus in 1917 with no less intimacy, but in terms of his native provincial upbringing:

O ploughlands, ploughlands, ploughlands,
Kolomna sadness;
Yesterday is on my heart,
While within the heart shines Rus
. . . O region of menacing floods
And gentle Spring forces;
Here I had my schooling
From dawn and from the stars.
And I pondered, and I read
The Bible of the winds,
And with me Isaiah tended
My golden cattle.'

After the revolutions and civil war, in 1921 a third poet, Velimir Khlebnikov, could proudly title a poem 'I and Russia' (*Ya i Rossiya*

– most exceptionally using the formal state name rather than Rus). In a single splendid metaphor he finds himself, and all his bodily cells, to be the microcosm of Russia itself:

> 'Russia has given freedom (*svobodu*) to thousands of thousands;
> A fine thing! and long to be remembered,
> While I just took off my shirt
> . . . And the citizens and citizenesses
> Of the state called 'Me'
> Crowded to the windows of my thousand-windowed curls.
> Olgas and Igors,
> Spontaneously
> Taking joy in the sun, looked through my skin.
> The prison of the shirt has fallen!
> And I had simply removed my shirt
> And given sun to the peoples of Me!

These three poets, as different from each other as could easily be imagined (and many other examples could have been taken), show that a new concept of Russia has taken its place beside the threefold image of Rus as people, as land and as political entity that dates back to its beginnings, and that our first chapter discussed. This is the apprehension of Rus/Rossiya/Russia as living organism – more than that, as a human body, perhaps coterminous with (and anyhow inseparable from) the perceiving subject. Russians, poets or non-poets, seem to have found such awareness of their country as their own 'double' both painful and exhilarating.

# Select Bibliography

The bibliography of Russian cultural history is of course immense, and it would not I believe be of practical use here to give a seemingly endless and undifferentiated list of titles, mostly in Russian, that would be needed for even partial coverage of the field. Bearing in mind the probable needs of readers of this volume, I have opted for an annotated and inevitably subjective selection of background works and a few more detailed articles, preferring English language sources and translations into English as far as possible. They are arranged according to the themes of the five main chapters, whose footnotes provide further references on more specialized topics.

## 1 General history, geography, way of life

The foundations of Russian historiography are the multi-volume works (themselves constituting landmarks in cultural history) that appeared from the early nineteenth to the early twentieth centuries from the pens of N. Karamzin, S. Solovyov, V. Klyuchevsky and S. Platonov: all are available – sometimes selectively – in English. The most enduringly useful is probably Vasiliy Klyuchevsky's: V. Kliuchevski (Klyuchevsky), *A History of Russia*, trans. C. J. Hogarth, London, 1911, etc. Only one comparable endeavour has been attempted in English: the multi-volume *A History of Russia* by G. Vernadsky and M. Karpovich. The five volumes completed before his death by Vernadsky go as far as the late Muscovite period and remain indispensable (particularly *Kievan Russia* (volume II of the series), New Haven 1948). There are several serviceable single-volume histories of Russia in English: e.g. by P. Dukes *A History of Russia* 2nd edn; (London, 1990) B. Sumner, *A Survey of Russian History* (London, 1944 – but still an unusual and stimulating treatment); R. Auty and D. Obolensky, eds, *Cambridge Companion to Russian Studies*, vol. I (Cambridge 1976); N. Riasanovsky, *A History of Russia* (3rd edn, New York, 1977), which is probably the fullest and most generally useful. R. R. Milner-Gulland with N. Dejevsky [*Cultural*] *Atlas of Russia* (Oxford/New York, 1989) is, despite its title, basically a single-volume history with many maps and illustrations.

*Primary sources:* There are several anthologies of Russian historical source-materials in English. Note particularly G. Vernadsky et al. (eds), *A Source-book for Russian History*, 3 vols, (New Haven and London, 1972); B. Dmytryshyn, *Medieval Russia, 900–1700* (Hinsdale, 1967 etc.); D. Kaiser and G. Marker, eds, *Reinterpreting Russian History: Readings 860–1860s* (Oxford, 1994), with interpretative articles as well as documents. For the eighteenth century, note P. Dukes (ed.), *Russia under Catherine the Great: Select Documents* 2 vols, (London, 1977–8) which includes Pugachov's proclamations.

*Other general works:* A. Brown et al., eds, *Cambridge Encyclopedia of Russia* (new edn., Cambridge 1994); J. Billington, *The Icon and the Axe* (New York, 1966), an ambitious interpretative cultural history, stronger on the seventeenth and eighteenth centuries than on earlier periods; A. Cross (ed.), *Russia under Western Eyes* (Norwich, 1981) – perhaps the best of several anthologies of travellers' account of Russia: note also that there are modern editions available of the main early European travellers (Sigismund von Herberstein, H. von Staden, Olearius etc.) – those from England are in L. Berry and R. Crummie, eds, *Rude and Barbarous Kingdom* (Madison, 1968).

*Historical geography:* W. H. Parker, *An Historical Geography of Russia* (London, 1968) is probably best. Good geographical chapters begin the *Cambridge Companion to Russian Studies* vol. I (see above; chapter by D. J. Hooson) and R. Pipes, *Russia under the Old Regime* (London, 1974); while several general historians have a strong geographical orientation, e.g. Klyuchevsky and Sumner (see above). Note too R. J. Kerner, *The Urge to the Sea* (New York, 1971, largely on the role of Russian waterways); A. Chew, *An Atlas of Russian History* (New Haven, 1970).

*Way of life:* R. E. F. Smith, *The Origins of Farming in Russia* (Paris, 1959) and *Peasant Farming in Muscovy* (Cambridge, 1977); R. E. F. Smith and D. Christian, *Bread and Salt* (Cambridge 1984 – a pioneering study of food and drink in Russian cultural history); B. D. Grekov, *Kiev Rus* (Moscow, 1959) and M. Tikhomirov, *The Towns of Ancient Rus* (Moscow, 1959), neither unfortunately in fully adequate translation, give much socio-economic information; A. and Y. Opolovnikov, *The Wooden Architecture of Russia* (London, 1989) is an outstanding contribution not just to architectural, but to social history.

## 2 East Slavs: the origins of Rus, the development of state and government in Rus/Russia

M. Gimbutas, *The Slavs* (London, 1971) and P. Dolukhanov, *The Early Slavs* (London, 1996) are both strong on the interpretation of early archaeological evidence; better still in this regard is the substantial first part of S. Franklin and

J. Shepard, *The Emergence of Rus 750–1200* (London, 1996). On language: G. Corbett, *The Slavonic Languages* (London, 1993); G. Vinokur, *The Russian Language – a Brief History* (London, 1971). On the civilizational location of early Rus: F. Dvornik, *The Slavs, their Early History and Civilization* (London, 1959) and *The Making of Central and Eastern Europe* (London, 1949); D. Obolensky, *The Byzantine Commonwealth* (London, 1971) and 'Russia's Byzantine Heritage' in *Oxford Slavonic Papers*, vol. 1 (1950), reprinted in his *Byzantium and the Slavs* (London, 1971).

Outstandingly the most important primary source for the history of early Rus is of course the twelfth-century *Tale of Bygone Years* (or Primary Chronicle), and the lack of an up-to-date English translation is acutely felt (a new one, by H. G. Lunt, is forthcoming from Harvard). The existing version, *The Russian Primary Chronicle*, trans. and ed. by S. H. Cross (Cambridge, Mass., 1955, etc.) nevertheless has informative footnotes. Meanwhile nothing has superseded the two-volume Russian edition with fine commentary and translation into modern Russian by D. S. Likhachov, *Povest vremenykh let* (Moscow/Leningrad, 1950). Note also R. Mitchell and N. Forbes (trans.) *The Chronicle of Novgorod 1016–1471* (London, 1914), and S. Zenkovsky (trans. and ed.) *The Nikonian Chronicle*, 3 vols (Princeton, 1984–6).

On socio-political history up to the nineteenth century, R. Pipes, *Russia under the Old Regime* (London, 1974), pungent and sometimes perverse, is a classic work. Note also M. Cherniavsky, *Tsar and People* (New Haven, 1961); J. Blum, *Lord and Peasant in Russia* (Princeton, 1961); R. Hellie, *Slavery in Russia* (Chicago, 1982); N. S. Kollman, *Kinship and Politics: the Making of the Muscovite Political System* (Stanford, 1987); R. E. F. Smith (ed.), *The Enserfment of the Russian Peasantry* (Cambridge, 1968); E. Levin, *Sex and Society in the World of the Orthodox Slavs, 900–1700*, (Ithaca, 1989); also some good recent survey volumes of general history: Franklin and Shepard *The Emergence of Rus* (see above), J. Martin, *Medieval Russia 980–1584* (Cambridge, 1995), R. H. Crummey, *The Formation of Muscovy 1304–1613* (London, 1987); P. Dukes, *The Making of Russian Absolutism, 1613–1801* (London, 1982). Of course there are numerous valuable studies of narrower topics, individual figures etc., of which only a few will be mentioned here. G. Vernadsky (ed.), *Medieval Russian Laws* (New York, 1947, etc.); H. Birnbaum, *Lord Novgorod the Great* (Columbus, 1981); J. L. I. Fennell, *The Crisis of Medieval Russia 1200–1304* (London, 1983). C. Halperin, *Russia and the Golden Horde* (Bloomington, 1985) and *The Tatar Yoke* (Columbus, 1986) open new and surprising vistas on Russo-Tatar relations. See also A. Presniakov *The Formation of the Great Russian State*, trans. A. E. Moorhouse, (Chicago, 1970); J. L. I. Fennell, *Ivan the Great of Moscow* (London, 1961) and (ed.), *The Correspondence between Prince Kurbsky and Ivan IV of Russia* (Cambridge, 1955); R. G. Skrynnikov *Ivan the Terrible*, trans. H. Graham, (Gulf Breeze, 1951) and *Boris Godunov* (Gulf Breeze, 1978); S. F. Platonov *The Time of Troubles*, trans. J. Alexander, (London, 1970); P. Longworth, *Alexis, Tsar of All the Russias* (London, 1984) and *The Cossacks* (London, 1969); L. A. J. Hughes, *Sophia, Regent of Russia* (New Haven, 1990).

The best study of the Petrine period is L. Hughes *Russia in the Age of Peter the Great* (Yale U.P. 1998); the classic biography of Peter is in German: R. Wittram, *Peter I, Czar und Kaiser*, 2 vols (Göttingen, 1964). Views on the 'Petrine Revolution' are collated in M. Raeff (ed.), *Peter the Great: Reformer or Revolutionary?* (London, 1963). The remarkable brief study by B. Uspensky of Peter's self-image, 'Historia sub Specie Semioticae' has been translated in D. P. Lucid (ed.), *Soviet Semiotics* (Baltimore, 1977); see too Yu. Lotman and B. Uspensky, 'Echoes of the Notion "Moscow as the Third Rome" in Peter the Great's Ideology' in A. Shukman (ed.), *The Semiotics of Russian Culture* (Ann Arbor, 1984). Various contemporary accounts of Petrine and post-Petrine Russia (Foy de Neuville, Peter Bruce, Patrick Gordon, Friedrich Weber, Christian von Manstein) are now available in English. Aspects of cultural and social history are treated in J. Garrard (ed.), *The Eighteenth Century in Russia* (Oxford, 1973). Previous accounts of Catherine II's reign have been superseded by I. de Madariaga's magisterial *Russia in the Age of Catherine the Great* (London, 1981), disposing of several ingrained myths. On the world-view of the eighteenth-century Russian upper class, note H. Rogger, *National Consciousness in 18th Century Russia* (Cambridge, Mass., 1960) and a remarkable 'psycho-historical' study, M. Raeff, *The Origins of the Russian Intelligentsia* (London, 1966). G. Hosking's thought-provoking essay *Empire and Nation in Russian History* (Waco, 1992) is a concise investigation of the problematics associated with these two concepts; so, differently is I. de Madariaga 'Tsar into Emperor', in R. Oresko et al. (eds) *Royal and Republican Sovereignty* (Cambridge, 1996), pp. 351–81, demonstrating Peter's debt to the Byzantine imperial idea. Hosking has expanded his ideas in *Russia: People and Empire 1552–1917* (London 1997).

## 3   Belief Systems

*Paganism, folk religion, 'double belief'*:   M. Gimbutas, 'Ancient Slavic Religion: a Synopsis' in To Honour Roman Jakobson, vol. 1 (The Hague, 1967); R. Jakobson, 'Slavic Folklore and Slavic Mythology' in M. Leach (ed.), *Standard Dictionary of Folklore and Mythology*, vol. 2 (New York, 1950); L. Ivanits, *Russian Folk Belief* (New York, 1989) – a concise account with selected texts; J. Vytkovska, 'Slav Mythology' in *The Feminist Companion to Mythology*, ed. C. Larrington (London, 1992). In Russian, there are two standard works by B. Rybakov: *Yazychestvo drevnykh slavyan* (Moscow, 1981) and *Yazychestvo drevney Rusi* (Moscow, 1987). Most writers on the Russian church have things to say about 'double belief' (e.g. Fedotov, Fennell – see below), but note also articles in W. Brumfield and M. Velimirović, *Christianity and the Arts in Russia* (Cambridge, 1991) that touch on it in, respectively, artistic and musical contexts: A. Hilton, Piety and Pragmatism and M. Mazo, We don t summon spring in the summer . M. Balzer (ed.), *Russian Traditional Culture* (New York, 1992) has translations of several recent (1980s) Russian investigations such as I. Froyanov et al., 'The Introduction of Christianity in Russia and the Pagan Traditions', T. Bernshtam, 'Russian Folk Culture and Folk Religion',

N. Veletskaya 'Forms of Transformation of Pagan Symbolism in the Old Believer Tradition'. Note too N. Andreyev, 'Pagan and Christian Elements in Old Russia', *Slavic Review* 21 (1962) pp. 16–23; D. Obolensky, 'Popular Religion in Medieval Russia' in his *The Byzantine Heritage of Eastern Europe* (London, 1982), and a thought-provoking semiotic study of folk belief and much else, Yu. Lotman and B. Uspensky 'Binary Models in the Dynamics of Russian Culture', in A. D. and A. S. Nakhimovsky (eds.) *The Semiotics of Russian Cultural History* (Ithaca, 1985); on *Skomorokhi*, R. Zguta *Russian Minstrels* (Oxford 1978).

*Christianity in Rus/Russia*: There is as yet no comprehensive history of the Russian church in any language, but valuable substitutes include G. Fedotov, *The Russian Religious Mind*, 2 vols (Cambridge, Mass., 1946 and 1966)– note too his *Treasury of Russian Spirituality* (New York, 1961) – and G. Florovsky, *Ways of Russian Theology* (Nordland, 1979). J. L. I. Fennell, *A History of the Russian Church to 1448* (London, 1995), a posthumous work, is essential reading, if thin in some respects. Two volumes called *Medieval Russian Culture*: (vol. 1 edited by H. Birnbaum and M. Flier, (Berkeley 1984); vol. 2 edited by M. Flier and D. Rowland, (Berkeley, 1994) contain many relevant studies, one of which must be mentioned here: Ya. Luria 'Unresolved Issues in the History of the Ideological Movements of the Late 15th Century' (vol. 1). On other specific topics within the field: V. Lossky, *The Mystical Theology of the Eastern Church* (Clarke, 1957); A. V. Soloviev, *Holy Russia: The History of a Religious-Social Idea* (The Hague, 1954 – see also Cherniavsky, above); W. K. Medlin, *Moscow and East Rome* (London, 1952); D. Stremoukhoff 'Moscow the Third Rome – Sources of the Doctrine' in *Speculum* 1953:1, pp. 84–101; P. Bushkovich *Religion and Society in Russia (16th–17th cc.)* (Oxford, 1992). The two broad surveys in English of Russian religious nonconformity – F. C. Conybeare, *Russian Dissenters* (London, 1921, etc.), S. Bolshakoff, *Russian Non-conformity* (Philadelphia, 1950) – each have serious flaws, but fortunately the scholarly study on the Vyg community by R. O. Crummey, *The Old Believers and the World of Antichrist* (Madison, 1970) helps to fill the gap. A remarkable nineteenth-century work, W. Palmer, *The Patriarch and the Tsar*, 6 vols (London, 1871-6) is a huge ragbag of materials (some still unpublished elsewhere) on the Schism and the Russian church generally.

## 4 The traditions of Russian Literature

*Sources*: S. Zenkovsky (ed.), *Medieval Russia's Epics, Chronicles and Tales* (New York, 1963, etc.) is still the only anthology in English giving an idea of the range of Old Russian writing (also some oral literature). Harvard is beginning to publish a series of pre-Tatar texts with up-to-date translations and commentaries: e.g. S. Franklin (ed.), *Sermons and Rhetoric of Kievan Rus* (Harvard, 1991). The *Igor Tale* has been translated several times, e.g. in D. Obolensky, *The Penguin Book of Russian Verse* (Harmondsworth, 1962 etc. – a most judiciously selected bilingual anthology). There is a classic translation of Avvakum's *Life* by Jane Harrison and Hope Mirrlees (London, 1924, etc.). For those with some Russian, there is a notable recent series of volumes *Pamyatniki literatury drevney Rusi* (Moscow/Leningrad, various dates) arranged by centuries with facing modern Russian translations; also A. Stender-Petersen (ed.), *Anthology of Old Russian Literature* (New York, 1954), well set-out and annotated. For Chronicle translations, see (2) above. Zguta (see 3 above) gives examples of non-Christian folk literature; for folk literature generally, see for example Y. M. Sokolov *Russian Folklore* (Detroit, 1971).

*Language and literacy*: see Corbett, Vinokurov (see 2, above). My approach has been much influenced by that of Boris Uspensky, notably his 'The Language Situation and Linguistic Consciousness in Muscovite Rus', in Birnbaum and Flier (see 3, above). A more traditional view of the relationship between Old Russian and Church Slavonic is put forward in, for example, A. Vlasto, *A Linguistic History of Russia* (Oxford, 1986); yet another approach is that of B. Unbegaun, *Selected Papers on Russian and Slavonic Philology* (Oxford, 1969) and 'The Russian Literary Language: a Comparative View', Presidential Address in *Modern Language Review* 68:4 (1975). On early literacy, including 'birchbark documents': S. Franklin, 'Literacy and Documentation in Early Medieval Russia' in *Speculum* 60:1 (1985) pp. 1–38; G. Marker, 'Literacy and Literary Texts in Muscovy: A Reconsideration' in *Slavic Review* 49 (1990) pp. 74–89.

*Some studies*: the best general account in English is D. Čiževskij, *A History of Russian Literature from the 11th Century to the End of the Baroque* (The Hague, 1960), while J. Fennell and A. Stokes, *Early Russian Literature* (London, 1974) has good chapters but is curiously limited. The doyen of early Russian literary-cultural studies is D. S. Likhachov: his series of essays *The Great Heritage* has been translated (Moscow, 1981) with additional material not in the original edition; note too his 'Byzantium and the Emergence of an Independent Russian Literature' in D. Daiches and A. Thorlby (eds), *Literature and Western Civilization* vol. 2 (London, 1973) and 'The Histrionics of Ivan the Terrible' in *Acta Litteraria Academiae Scientarum Hungaricae* 8 (1976). His indispensible *Poetika drevnerusskoy literatury* (Leningrad, 1967) awaits its translator, as does his unique study that places literature within the whole cultural spectrum of fourteenth- and fifteenth-century Rus, *Kultura Rusi vremeni Andreya Rublyova i Yepifaniya Premudrogo* (Leningrad, 1962) – for a briefer account of this period, see R. R. Milner-Gulland, 'Russia's Lost Renaissance' in Daiches and Thorlby *Literature and Western Civilization*, vol. 3. Much has been written on the *Igor Tale*, including articles by Roman Jakobson such as 'The Puzzles of the *Igor Tale*', *Speculum* 27, 1952 reprinted in *Selected Writings* vol. 4 (The Hague, 1966) and by Likhachov, but one must single out the fresh approach – relating it to oral epic poetry – in R. Mann, *Lances Sing* (Slavica, 1989). There are expert articles on almost all significant early Russian works and literary topics (including within folk literature) in V. Terras (ed.), *Handbook of Russian Literature* (New Haven, 1985); note too several articles in

*Medieval Russian Culture*, vols 1 and 2 (see 3 above). Only Likhachov in *Poetika drevnerusskoy literatury* (see above) has had much to say about the relationship between pre-and post-Petrine Russian literature.

## 5   Art, architecture, music in pre-modern and modern Russia

*General*:   the most detailed history of Russian art before the twentieth century in English is still G. H. Hamilton, *Art and Architecture of Russia* (London, 1954, 1975); the *Cambridge Companion to Russian Studies* vol. 3, *An Introduction to Russian Art and Architecture* (written by R. Milner-Gulland and J. E. Bowlt; Cambridge 1980 – see 1 above) is a concise and more recent account. For architecture see: H. Faensen and V. Ivanov, *Early Russian Architecture* (London, 1975); W. C. Brumfield, *A History of Russian Architecture* (Cambridge, 1993). On iconic art G. Mathew, *Byzantine Aesthetics* (London, 1963) is a good introduction to the conceptual world of Orthodox art; also R. Cormack, *Writing in Gold* (London, 1985); V. Lossky and L. Ouspensky, *The Meaning of Icons* (Olten, 1952) is an essential work of reference.

*On more specific pre-modern topics*:   there are of course many picture-albums, some with excellent texts, and also nowadays scholarly exhibition-catalogues – e.g. *Gates of Mystery: the Art of Holy Russia* (London, 1993). Some works by the dominant scholar of the mid-twentieth century, V. Lazarev, have been translated: *Old Russian Murals and Mosaics* (London, 1966) and *Novgorodian Icon Painting* (Moscow, 1969); also some by Lazarev's rival M. Alpatov, e.g. *Art Treasures of Russia* (London, 1968). But the richest and subtlest investigation into the nature and function of icons is B. Uspensky, *The Semiotics of the Russian Icon*, ed. S. Rudy (Lisse, 1976). Again, there are several articles in *Medieval Russian Culture vols 1 and 2 (see 3 above) that help to place Old Russian art in its semiotic and civilizational context, and more in W. Brumfield and M. Velimirović (eds) Christianity and the Arts in Russia* (Cambridge, 1991), including T. Vladishevskaia 'On the Links Between Music and Icon Painting in Medieval Rus', N. Teteriatnikov, 'The Role of the Devotional Image in the Religious Life of Pre-Mongol Rus' and A. Hilton 'Piety and Pragmatism'. On folk and popular art: A. Hilton 'Piety and Pragmatism' and *Russian Folk Art* (Bloomington, 1996); A. and V. Opolovnikov *The Wooden Architecture of Russia* (see 1 above); A. Sytova (ed.), *The Lubok* (Leningrad, 1984).

*On relevant musical topics*:   A. J. Swan, *Russian Music and its Origins in Chant and Folk Song* (London 1973), G.R. Seaman, *History of Russian Music*, vol. 1 (Oxford, 1967); several articles in *Christianity and the Arts in Russia* (see above), including Vladishevskaia (see above), M. Mazo "We Don't Summon Spring in Summer": Traditional Music and Beliefs' and E.V. Williams, 'Aural Icons of Orthodoxy: The Sonic Typology of Russian Bells'. There are many relevant articles in S. Sadie (ed.) *The New Grove Dictionary of Music and Musicians* (London 1980), 20 vols.

*On traditional Russian art and modernity*: J. Cracraft, *The Petrine Revolution in Russian Architecture* (London, 1988 – a most informative though resolutely unsymbolic treatment); J. E. Bowlt (ed.), *Russian Art of the Avant-Garde: Theory and Criticism 1902–34* (New York, 1976); C. Gray, *The Russian Experiment in Art*, (only 3rd edn, London 1988, is recommended); C. Lodder, *Russian Constructivism* (London, 1985). More focused studies: D. Jackson, 'Icons in the 19th Century' in S. Smythe and S. Kingston (eds), *Icons 88* (Dublin, 1988); M. Betz, 'The Icon and Russian Modernism' in *Art Forum 15*, (1977) pp. 38–44; J. E. Bowlt, 'Neo-Primitivism and Russian Painting' in *Burlington Magazine 116*, (1974) pp. 133–40; also many monographs on individuals, among which we may select W. Simmons, *Kasimir Malevich's Black Square*, New York, 1981); J. Milner, *Vladimir Tatlin and the Russian Avant-Garde* (London, 1983), also his *Kazimir Malevich and the Art of Geometry* (London 1996), J. E. Bowlt and N. Misler, *Pavel Filonov: a Hero and his Fate* (Austin, 1983), and an astonishing recent contribution to the burgeoning industry of Kandinsky studies: P. Weiss, *Kandinsky and Old Russia* (London, 1994) which reads him largely in terms of pagan imagery.

# Chronological Table
# (to 1917)

## Before the ninth century

Migrations of Slavs from central Europe southwards, westwards and eastwards (onto future territory of Rus)
Vikings (= Varangians) explore waterways to the east of the Baltic, establish chief base at Ladoga for trade first along Volga to Arab lands, subsequently southwards

## Ninth century

| | |
|---|---|
| 839 | First mention of the 'Rhos' (who turn out to be Swedes) in Frankish *Bertinian Annals* |
| 860 | 'Russians' (Rhos) raid Constantinople under Askold and Dir; subsequently Patriarch Photius reports their conversion to Christianity |
| 862 | Legendary 'invitation to Varangians' under Ryurik to rule in northern (subsequently Novgorod) area |
| *c.*882 | Oleg, Ryurik's supposed kinsman, unites northern and southern Rus by capturing Kiev |

## Tenth century

*Rulers*:
Oleg (d. 913)
Igor (d. 945), leaves widow Olga (d. 960s) as regent
Svyatoslav (*c.*962–72) – wars of conquest from late 960s
Yaropolk (d. *c.*978)
Vladimir I (*c.*978–1015)

911, 944    Treaties with Byzantine Empire
988–9       Traditional date of Conversion of Rus to Christianity
996         Dormition Cathedral ('Tithe Church') in Kiev completed


## Eleventh century

*Main rulers*:
Yaroslav I (1019–54, diarchy with brother Mstislav 1026–36)
Izyaslav I (1054–73 and 1077–8)
Vsevolod I (1078–93)
Svyatopolk II (1093–1113)
Vseslav of Polotsk takes Kievan throne 1068–9

1015    Martyrdom of Sts Boris and Gleb
1037    Santa Sophia of Kiev begun
1051    Ilarion: first native Russian Metropolitan of Kiev, writer
1097    Conference at Lyubech to settle inter-princely rivalries

Till mid-century Pechenegs, thereafter Polovtsians threaten Kiev's southern flank


## Twelfth century

*Main rulers*:
Vladimir II Monomakh (rules in Kiev 1113–25)
Mstislav I (sometimes called 'The Great') 1125–39
Yuriy Dolgorukiy (Prince of Rostov; of Kiev 1155–7)
Andrey Bogolyubsky (reigns from Vladimir 1157–75)
Vsevolod 'Bolshoye Gnezdo' (='Big Nest', rules in Vladimir 1176–1212)
Svyatoslav II (ruler of Kiev 1177–94)

1136        Novgorodians establish effective control over their princes
1147        First mention of Moscow in chronicles
1169        Andrey Bogolyubsky captures and sacks Kiev
1170        Andrey fails to take Novgorod
1174        Andrey assassinated by his servitors
1158, 1185  Building and enlargement of Dormition cathedral, Vladimir
1185        Unsuccessful attack on Polovtsians, subject of the *Igor Tale*
1194        St Demetrius, Vladimir

Early in century: Tmutorakan passes from Russian to Byzantine control
During century: increased prosperity of north-eastern Rus, also of Galicia

## Thirteenth century

| | |
|---|---|
| 1204 | Constantinople falls to Fourth Crusade (retaken 1261) |
| 1206 | Gengis Khan organizes Mongols (Tatars) for world conquest |
| 1221 | Foundation of Nizhniy Novgorod |
| 1223 | A Tatar expedition defeats Russian forces on River Kalka |
| 1238–40 | Tatars sack Vladimir, Chernigov, Kiev etc. and establish rule |
| 1240 | Alexander, Prince of Novgorod, defeats Swedes on the Neva (acquires surname 'Nevsky') |
| 1242 | Alexander Nevsky becomes Grand Prince of Vladimir |
| 1299 | Metropolitan of Russian Church moves from Kiev to Vladimir |

## Fourteenth century

*Main rulers*:
Danilovich line, established in Moscow, competes for supremacy with princes of Tver.
*Moscow rulers*:
Ivan I Kalita ('Moneybags', 1325–41)
Semyon Gordy ('The Proud'; 1341–53)
Dmitriy Donskoy (1359–89)
Vasiliy I (1389–1425)

| | |
|---|---|
| 1320s | Metropolitan Peter transfers residence to Moscow |
| 1321–91 | St Sergius of Radonezh |
| 1380 | Dmitriy Donskoy defeats Tatar army under Mamai at Kulikovo |
| 1382 | Tatars burn Moscow |
| 1386 | Dynastic union between Poland and Lithuania (which accepts Catholicism) |
| 1390s | Timur (Tamerlane) weakens Tatar 'Golden Horde' |

## Fifteenth century

*Main rulers*:
Vasiliy II (1425–62, with rival claimants)
Ivan III 'The Great' (1462–1505)

| | |
|---|---|
| 1408 | Last major Tatar raid (by Edigei) |
| 1410 | Lithuania defeats Teutonic Knights at Tannenburg |
| 1425–50 | Civil war for throne of Moscow |
| c.1400–30 | Andrey Rublyov active as painter |
| 1438 | Council of Florence agrees union of churches; repudiated by Russians 1441; they elect anti-union Metropolitan 1448 |
| 1453 | Fall of Constantinople to Ottoman Turks |
| 1472 | Ivan III marries Zoe (Sophia) Palaiologina |

| mid-15th c. | Golden Horde disintegrates into separate khanates |
|---|---|
| 1470s | Hostilities between Moscow and Novgorod, leading to latter's annexation in 1478 and deportations of leading citizens |
| 1479 | Dormition Cathedral of Moscow Kremlin rebuilt; remodelling of Kremlin continues into early sixteenth century |
| 1480 | End of Tatar rule in Rus with 'non-battle' on the Ugra |
| 1485 | Annexation of Tver by Moscow |
| 1494 | Closure of Hanseatic depot in Novgorod |
| 1497 | First Muscovite law-code |
| late 15th c. | Spread of 'Judaizer' heresy (condemned 1504) |

## Sixteenth century

*Rulers*:
Vasiliy III (1505–33)
Ivan IV 'the Terrible' (='Awesome', 1533–84)
Fyodor I (1584–98)
Boris Godunov (1598–1605)

| early 16th c. | Dispute of 'possessors'/'non-possesors' (latter condemned 1531) |
|---|---|
| 1510 | Annexation of Pskov by Moscow |
| 1520 | Annexation of Ryazan by Moscow |
| 1547 | Coronation (as Tsar) of 17-year-old Ivan IV |
| 1550 | Law-code issued |
| 1551 | *Stoglav* Church Council convened |
| 1552 | Kazan captured and annexed by Moscow |
| 1553 | Trade with England through White Sea established |
| 1556 | Astrakhan annexed to Moscow, which now held entire Volga |
| 1561 | 'St Basils' in Moscow completed |
| 1564–72 | *Oprichnina* – division of realm and reign of terror |
| 1568 | Metropolitan Filipp deposed, subsequently killed |
| 1569 | Poland and Lithuania united in one Commonwealth |
| 1570 | Sack of Novgorod by Ivan IV |
| 1571 | Crimean Tatars burn Moscow |
| 1575–6 | Ivan IV 'abdicates' briefly in favour of Semyon Bekbulatovich |
| 1582 | Cossack force defeats Khanate of Siberia |
| 1589 | Creation of Russian Patriarchate |
| 1596 | Union of Brest creates 'Uniat' church |
| 1598 | Death of Tsar Fyodor – end of Ryurikid dynasty |

## Seventeenth century

*Main rulers*:
First 'False Dmitriy' (1605–6)
Vasiliy IV Shuysky (1606–10)
Mikhail Romanov (1613–45)
Aleksey (1645–76)
Fyodor III (1676–82)

Sophia (regent, 1682–9)
Ivan V and Peter I (co-tsars, Ivan d. 1696)

| | |
|---|---|
| till 1613 | Time of Troubles', with various claimants to throne, Polish and Swedish intervention, breakdown of government |
| 1606–7 | Bolotnikov's revolt (first major peasant uprising) |
| 1613 | 'Assembly of the Land' elects Tsar Mikhail; his father Filaret is Patriarch |
| 1648 | 'Salt Revolt' in Moscow; Khmelnitsky's uprising against Poland leads to incorporation of much of Ukraine (including Kiev) into Muscovy |
| 1652 | Nikon becomes Patriarch (withdraws 1658, deposed and exiled 1666) |
| 1666–7 | Church council and formalization of Schism |
| 1670–1 | Popular rebellion led by Cossack Stepan Razin |
| 1682 | Archpriest Avvakum executed by burning (after completing his autobiography) |
| 1687 | Higher educational academy founded in Moscow |
| 1687, 1689 | Treaties with Poland and China*c.* |
| 1693 | Church of Fili built (culmination of 'Moscow Baroque') |
| 1697–8 | Peter (with retinue of 200) undertakes 'Great Embassy' |
| 1698 | Embassy curtailed by *streltsy* revolt; subsequent harsh reprisals |

### Eighteenth century

*Main rulers*:
Peter I 'the Great' (effective ruler from 1689; sole ruler from 1696, d. 1725)
Catherine I (Peter's widow, 1725–7)
Peter II (boy-tsar, 1727–30)
Anna (1730–40)
Elizabeth (Peter I's daughter, 1741–62 NS)
Peter III (1762; deposed, subsequently killed)
Catherine II 'the Great' (Peter III's wife; 1762–96)
Paul (1796–1801)

| | |
|---|---|
| 1700 | Patriarchate lapses |
| 1700–21 | 'Northern War' – Russia and Poland vs. Sweden |
| 1703 | St Petersburg founded on land regained from Sweden |
| 1709 | Battle of Poltava |
| 1721 | Peter proclaimed Emperor, titled 'The Great' |
| 1725 | Academy of Sciences founded in St Petersburg |
| 1730 | Anna briefly agrees to be constitutional monarch |
| 1755 | University of Moscow founded |
| 1762 | 'Liberation' of landowning class from state service |
| 1769 | Legislative Commission set up |
| 1773–4 | Major rebellion led by Cossack Yemelyan Pugachov |
| 1782 | Completion of 'Bronze Horseman' monument to Peter the Great |

| 1783 | Annexation of Crimea, followed by war with Turkey |
| 1785 | Charter of the Nobility |
| 1790 | Publication of Alexander Radishchev's *Journey From St Petersburg to Moscow* and his arrest |
| 1795 | Third 'partition' ends independent existence of Poland |

### Nineteenth to early twentieth century

*Rulers*:
Alexander I (1801–25)
Nicholas I (1825–55)
Alexander II (1855–81)
Alexander III (1881–94)
Nicholas II (1894–1917)

*Writers, composers, artists*:
A. Pushkin (1799–1837)
M. Glinka (1804–57)
N. Gogol (1809–52)
I. Goncharov (1812–91)
M. Lermontov (1814–41)
I. Turgenev (1818–83)
F. Dostoyevsky (1821–81)
L. Tolstoy (1828–1910)
M. Musorgsky (1839–81)
P. Tchaikovsky (1840–96)
V. Surikov (1860–1916)
A. Chekhov (1860–1904)
V. Kandinsky (1866–1944)
K. Malevich (1878–1935)
I. Stravinsky (1882–1971)

| 1807 | Peace of Tilsit |
| 1812 | Napoleon's invasion of Russia and defeat (Russians occupy Paris) |
| 1825 | 'Decembrist' revolt |
| 1830 | Polish uprising |
| 1853–6 | Crimean War (at first vs. Turkey, then Britain and France) |
| 1861 | Emancipation of serfs; period of major reforms |
| 1864 | Modernization of legal system; local government introduced |
| 1867 | Alaska sold to USA |
| 1881 | Assassination of Tsar Alexander II leading to harsh police regime |
| 1891 | Trans-Siberian railway begun |
| 1905–6 | Revolutionary activity leads to introduction of constitutional government and other reforms |
| 1914–18 | First World War |
| 1917 | (February, OS) Overthrow of tsarist regime; (October, OS) Bolshevik *coup d'état*. |

# Index

Index compiled by Chris Ovenden and Lucy Milner-Gulland